Inside London's Airports Policy

publishing

Inside London's Airports Policy

Indecision, decision and counter-decision

Paul Le Blond FCILT

Published by ICE Publishing, One Great George Street, Westminster, London SW1P 3AA

Full details of ICE Publishing representatives and distributors can be found at: www.icebookshop.com/bookshop_contact.asp

Other titles by ICE Publishing:
The Railway Metropolis: How Planners, Politicians and Developers Shaped Modern London.
Michael Schabas. ISBN 978-0-7277-6180-4
Planning Major Projects.
Roger J Allport. ISBN: 978-0-7277-4110-3
Jubilee Line Extension: From Concept to Completion.
Robert Mitchell. ISBN: 978-0-7277-3028-2

www.icebookshop.com
A catalogue record for this book is available from the British Library

ISBN 978-0-7277-6365-5
© Thomas Telford Limited 2019

ICE Publishing is a division of Thomas Telford Ltd, a wholly-owned subsidiary of the Institution of Civil Engineers (ICE).

All rights, including translation, reserved. Except as permitted by the Copyright, Designs and Patents Act 1988, no part of this publication may be reproduced, stored in a retrieval system or transmitted in any form or by any means, electronic, mechanical, photocopying or otherwise, without the prior written permission of the Publisher, ICE Publishing, One Great George Street, Westminster, London SW1P 3AA.

This book is published on the understanding that the author is solely responsible for the statements made and opinions expressed in it and that its publication does not necessarily imply that such statements and/or opinions are or reflect the views or opinions of the publisher or the Institution of Civil Engineers. While every effort has been made to ensure that the statements made and the opinions expressed in this publication provide a safe and accurate guide, no liability or responsibility can be accepted in this respect by the author or publisher.

While every reasonable effort has been undertaken by the author and the publisher to acknowledge copyright on material reproduced, if there has been an oversight please contact the publisher and we will endeavour to correct this upon a reprint.

Cover photo: Aerial view (from control tower) of landing 747 jet and showing expanse of airport land at London Heathrow.
RichardBakerRisk/Alamy Stock Photo

Commissioning Editor: Michael Fenton
Production Editor: Madhubanti Bhattacharyya
Marketing Specialist: April Asta Brodie

Typeset by Academic + Technical, Bristol
Index created by Laurence Errington
Printed and bound by in Great Britain by TJ International, Padstow

Contents

	Preface	ix
	List of abbreviations	xi
01	**Introduction**	**1**
	1.1. From John Nott's statement in 1979 to parliamentary approval in 2018	1
	1.2. Objectives	1
	1.3. What's in this book (and what's not)	1
	1.4. Distilling the frenzy	2
	References	2
02	**A brief overview of air-transport history**	**3**
	2.1. Introduction	3
	2.2. The growth of aviation from the earliest years of the twentieth century	3
	2.3. International obligations	5
	2.4. From wood, fabric and wire to carbon composites and electronics	6
	2.5. Airports depend on airlines	7
	2.6. Airport ownership and regulation	9
	Notes	12
	References	13
03	**Airports policy up to the 1974 Maplin Review**	**17**
	3.1. Introduction	17
	3.2. The interwar years	17
	3.3. World War 2 developments	17
	3.4. Post-war expansion of Heathrow and Gatwick and the proposals for Stansted	19
	3.5. The Roskill Commission	20
	3.6. The end of an era	22
	Notes	22
	References	22
04	**Airports in the wider planning-policy context**	**25**
	4.1. Introduction	25
	4.2. Why plan? The evolution of planning	25
	4.3. Airports and their local economies	26
	4.4. Transport planning: vital but low down the pecking order	27
	4.5. The UK planning system	28
	4.6. Policymaking in other sectors: HS2 and nuclear power	30
	4.7. Politics and policy	31
	4.8. Theories of decision-making: muddling through the policy swamp	34
	Notes	37
	References	37
05	**Environmental issues: a fundamental factor**	**39**
	5.1. Introduction	39
	5.2. Aircraft noise: the longest-running complaint	39

	5.3. Local air quality: from smoke to NO_x	43
	5.4. Climate change: a growing concern since the 1990s	44
	5.5. Other impacts: agricultural land, ecology, archaeology, water and drainage, visual impact, green belt and surface access	45
	Notes	47
	References	47
06	**1974–1991: an incremental approach**	**49**
	6.1. Introduction	49
	6.2. Maplin is cancelled and a 'third way' is sought	49
	6.3. Step by step: new terminals for Heathrow, Gatwick and Stansted	54
	6.4. Committees and decisions	56
	6.5. Inquiries and a White Paper	60
	6.6. London City sneaks under the radar	68
	6.7. Railways and airports	69
	6.8. Step by step: the strategy is rebuilt	70
	6.9. Themes for 1974–1991	71
	Notes	71
	References	71
07	**1991–1997: policy vacuum**	**75**
	7.1. Introduction	75
	7.2. The inconclusive search for a strategy for the next decade	76
	7.3. 'A little yellow at the edges': policy at the Terminal 5 Inquiry	79
	7.4. The 1990s: not much happened (apart from the Terminal 5 Inquiry)	84
	7.5. Themes for the 1990s	84
	Notes	84
	References	85
08	**1997–2010: a new deal for air transport**	**87**
	8.1. Introduction	87
	8.2. National consultations on a long-term strategy	87
	8.3. A 30-year national strategy: the 2003 White Paper	90
	8.4. Progress checked by increasing environmental concerns	93
	8.5. The New Deal ended by a perfect storm	99
	8.6. Themes for the 2000s	100
	Notes	100
	References	100
09	**2010 onwards: policies reversed, reviewed and reinstated**	**105**
	9.1. Introduction	105
	9.2. A coalition government implements its manifesto commitments	106
	9.3. Short-term policies established quickly	106
	9.4. The longer term kicked into the long grass	107
	9.5. HS2: a diversion?	109

	9.6. The Airports Commission: a comprehensive review?	110
	9.7. Government decisions and further steps	117
	9.8. What happened to the support and opposition groups?	118
	9.9. It's not over yet	119
	9.10. Themes for the 2010s	119
	Notes	120
	References	120
10	**Themes**	**123**
	10.1. Bringing forward the common issues	123
	10.2. The forecast is always wrong	123
	10.3. Why does the regional issue keep appearing?	127
	10.4. What is the best way to combine analysis and judgement?	128
	10.5. Should we take incremental steps or have a long-term strategy?	130
	10.6. What is the best way to consult and involve stakeholders?	131
	10.7. Should promises be made and how can they be kept?	135
	10.8. Has consideration of environmental impacts changed?	137
	10.9. Can we avoid policy vacuums?	138
	References	139
11	**Is London unique?**	**141**
	11.1. Introduction	141
	11.2. Europe: some centralised planning, some devolved	141
	11.3. North America: most airports are city or state owned	145
	11.4. The Middle East and East and South East Asia: limited democracy and rapid growth	149
	11.5. Australia: some similarities with London	153
	11.6. The UK outside the South East	153
	11.7. Conclusion – do others do it better?	158
	References	159
12	**The future**	**161**
	12.1. What could happen in the next 40 years?	161
	12.2. Learning from the past: how can we repeat successes and avoid mistakes?	166
13	**Conclusions**	**169**
	13.1. Have the book's objectives been achieved?	169
	13.2. A reminder of the book's structure	169
	13.3. What methodologies were used in the research?	170
	13.4. A few final words	170
	References for further reading	171
	Index	**173**

Preface

The story of London's airports goes back to the first days of flying early in the twentieth century, but significant expansion began only after World War 2 and, in particular, after the introduction of jet transport aircraft in the 1960s. I summarise some of the early history in this book, but the detailed study begins in the mid 1970s, when policy changed dramatically with the cancellation of the Maplin project. This was also the time when my own involvement became significant.

For 30 years I worked at the British Airports Authority, which became BAA plc. For a lot of this time I was involved with planning airports, including preparing and managing parts of the case for airport expansion during studies, consultations and public inquiries. I left BAA in 2001, but have continued this involvement as a consultant and as a Fellow of the Chartered Institute of Logistics and Transport. In all this time, I have not seen any attempt to tell the entire story of how airports policy has developed, although there are a number of books and articles about particular episodes.

Since the cancellation of the Maplin project (see Chapters 3 and 6) there have been many studies, consultations, inquiries and decisions, with the pendulum swinging back and forth between various alternatives, including on a number of occasions the delay or deferment of a decision. Views are often polarised, but there is also an element of pragmatism and compromise apparent and this may have helped to move the story forward. I hope this book will be of interest to all those involved in this type of decision-making, and to those with a particular interest in aviation, by pointing to some lessons that could be learned.

The research for this book began as an academic study, but has evolved into a less constrained project. Although it makes no pretence at academic robustness, there are nevertheless some elements of the research methodology that are adopted from academia. In particular, a review of academic literature has helped to provide a background, while the process of examining files at The National Archives and interviewing key individuals has provided an element of triangulation (a process which enables the cross-checking of information so that it is not solely from one source). In addition, the research has looked thoroughly at the published documentation, such as White Papers, inquiry reports and studies, which are available either online or at the British Library. Parliamentary papers, in particular the Hansard record of statements, debates and questions, have also been examined. Each of these sources has its strengths and weaknesses, but overall they can provide a balanced picture.

I would like to thank in particular the people whom I interviewed. They were civil servants, politicians, planners and managers in the aviation industry and community representatives. Some of them have agreed to be quoted, but I take full responsibility for all of the words in this book. I am very grateful to all of them:

Stan Abrahams, Geoff Ambrose, Chris Cain, Tom Carter, Roy Griffins, Alan Haselhurst, Stan Maiden, Michael Maine, Alastair McDermid, John Mulkern, Steve Norris, John Phillips, Laurie Price, Brian Ross, Peter Sanders, John Stewart, Russell Sunderland and Iryna Terlecky. I would like to make special mention of Vernon Murphy, who encouraged me and was my first interviewee, but who sadly died in 2014. I would also like to thank Theo Steel and David Parish, who read through the manuscript.

Having been an employee of BAA, I am clearly open to a charge of bias. To counter this, in part, I suggest, firstly, that my 'inside' knowledge may help to increase understanding of how airports policy has developed and, secondly, that I have sought to present a range of views representative of supporters, opponents and independent commentators. However, I accept, and the reader should acknowledge, that my research is from a particular perspective. One part of that perspective is having direct experience of some of the people and events, and throughout the book I have included personal anecdotes and viewpoints. Where my personal view is expressed, I seek to identify it as such. While this book is published by ICE Publishing, the publisher of the Institution of Civil Engineers, the views and opinions expressed in this book do not necessarily reflect the views or opinions of the publishers, or indeed, the Institution of Civil Engineers.

I was born in 1949 and my father worked for British European Airways. This meant that our family flew on holiday, initially to the Channel Islands and Scotland and later to the Mediterranean. Staff discounts meant very cheap fares, but sometimes we were on standby and did not always get on the flight. I slept in the sick bay of the Queens Building at Heathrow waiting for the next day's flights, and the Channel Islands flights were (and still are) often delayed by fog. We lived in Harrow and the 140 bus took me to the Heathrow Roof Gardens for aircraft spotting (I was also a train spotter). This meant that I spent a lot of time at airports in the 1950s and 1960s, and saw their growth from the early days. At school I naturally joined the RAF section of the Cadet Force and learned the principles of flight as well as experiencing flying and learning to glide. My initial ambition to be a commercial airline pilot was dashed when I failed the eyesight test, but my Reading University degree in geography nicely led me to airport planning, and I should make special mention of Peter Hall, my professor, and David Starkie, one of my tutors, both of whom are quoted in this book.

Finally I would like to acknowledge the support of my family in writing this book, especially my wife, Chris.

Format and references

In this book, references are given using the Harvard referencing system, where in-text citations are given as (author, date). The full list of references is provided at the end of each chapter. Endnotes, which appear before the list of references, are provided where an explanation or definition is appropriate.

Abbreviations

ACAP	Advisory Committee on Airports Policy
ACARE	Advisory Council for Aviation Research in Europe
AdP	Aeroports de Paris
AENA	Aena SA, Spanish airport company, 51% state owned
ANIS	Aircraft Noise Index Study
AOA	Airport Operators Association
AONB	Area of Outstanding Natural Beauty
APD	Air Passenger Duty
APF	Aviation Policy Framework
ASA	Air Services Agreement
ATM	Air Transport Movement
BA	British Airways
BAA	From 1966 to 1987, the British Airports Authority, sometimes referred to as 'the BAA', subsequently BAA plc
BATA	British Air Transport Association
BCal	British Caledonian Airways
BEA	British European Airways
BOAC	British Overseas Airways Corporation
BR	British Rail
BSAA	British South American Airways
CAA	Civil Aviation Authority
CAAC	Civil Aviation Administration of China
CBA	Cost-benefit analysis
CDG	Paris Charles de Gaulle Airport
CGE	Computable General Equilibrium
Cmnd or Cm	Command document
CO	Carbon monoxide
CO_2	Carbon dioxide
CTRL	Channel Tunnel Rail Link
dB	Decibel
DCLG	Department of Communities and Local Government
DCO	Development Consent Order
DETR	Department of the Environment, Transport and the Regions
DfT	Department for Transport
DFW	Dallas Fort Worth Airport
DoE	Department of the Environment
DoT	Department of Trade
DTp	Department of Transport
ETOPS	Extended-range Twin-engine Operational Performance Standards
ETS	Emissions Trading System (also known as Emissions Trading Scheme)
EU	European Union
G1	Stansted Generation 1 – the plan to make greater use of the existing runway
G2	Stansted Generation 2 – the plan for a second runway

GACC	Gatwick Area Conservation Campaign
GDP	Gross domestic product
GIP	Global Infrastructure Partners
GLA	Greater London Authority
GLC	Greater London Council
GMBM	Global Market-Based Measure
GPDO	General Permitted Development Order
H_2O	Water
HACAN	Heathrow Association for the Control of Aircraft Noise
HC	Hydrocarbons
HS1	High Speed 1
HS2	High Speed 2
IAG	International Airlines Group
IATA	International Air Transport Association
ICAO	International Civil Aviation Organisation
ILS	Instrument Landing System
JACOLA	Joint Airport Committee of Local Authorities
LCC	Low-cost carrier
L_{Aeq}	Equivalent Continuous A-weighted Level
L_{Aeq16h}	Equivalent Continuous A-weighted Level between 7am and 11pm for June, July and August
L_{Aeq8h}	Equivalent Continuous A-weighted Level between 11pm and 7am for June, July and August
MAFF	Ministry of Agriculture, Fisheries and Food
MAG	Manchester Airports Group
MHCLG	Ministry of Housing, Communities and Local Government
MoD	Ministry of Defence
mppa	Millions of passengers per annum
MWAA	Metropolitan Washington Airports Authority
NAPAM	National Air Passenger Allocation Model
NAPDM	National Air Passenger Demand Model
NATS	National Air Traffic Services
NFU	National Farmers' Union
Nimby	Not in my backyard
NNI	Noise and Number Index
NOERC	North of England Regional Consortium
NO_x	Nitrous oxides, the collective name for nitrogen oxide and nitrogen dioxide
NPS	National Policy Statement
NPSE	Noise Policy Statement for England
NSIP	Nationally Significant Infrastructure Project
NWEEHPA	North West Essex and East Hertfordshire Preservation Association
ONS	Office for National Statistics
PANYNJ	Port Authority of New York and New Jersey
PM_{10}, $PM_{2.5}$	The fraction of particulate matter (dust) in the air with an average aerodynamic diameter of less than 10 μm and 2.5 μm, respectively
PNdB	Perceived Noise decibels

PPG 24	Planning Policy Guidance Note 24
PPS	Parliamentary private secretary
PSDH	Project for the Sustainable Development of Heathrow
RAF	Royal Air Force
RASCO	Regional Air Services Coordination
RFC	Royal Flying Corps
RPA	New York Regional Plan Association
RPI	Retail Prices Index
RPK	Revenue Passenger Kilometres, a measure which includes the number of passengers and the distance travelled
RSPB	Royal Society for the Protection of Birds
RUCATSE	Runway Capacity to Serve the South East
SARS	Severe acute respiratory syndrome
SCLSERP	Standing Conference on London and South East Regional Planning
SEATF	South East Airports Taskforce
SERAS	South East and East of England Regional Air Services
SERPLAN	South East Regional Planning Conference
SGSEA	Study Group on South East Airports
SO_2	Sulfur dioxide
SPA	Special Protection Area, an EU designation for the conservation of wild birds
SSE	Stop Stansted Expansion
STOL	Short Take-Off and Landing
TEN-T	Trans European Network – Transport
TGV	Train à Grande Vitesse, French high-speed train
TNA	The National Archives
USAF	United States Air Force
VAT	Value Added Tax
VFR	Visiting Friends and Relatives
WSA	Western Sydney Airport
WSCC	West Sussex County Council
WW1	World War 1
WW2	World War 2

Inside London's Airports Policy

Le Blond, P
ISBN 978-0-7277-6365-5
https://doi.org/10.1680/ilap.63655.001
ICE Publishing: All rights reserved

Chapter 1

Introduction

1.1. From John Nott's statement in 1979 to parliamentary approval in 2018

The subtitle of this book is taken from a statement by John Nott, then Secretary of State for Trade, in the House of Commons on 17 December 1979. He was announcing the approval of Heathrow Terminal 4 after a public inquiry and inviting the British Airports Authority (BAA) to bring forward a proposal to expand Stansted. The full quote is, 'Years of indecision, decision and counter-decision reflect no credit on this country's capacity to make difficult but necessary choices' (HC Deb 17 December 1979). In the 40 or so years since the cancellation of the Maplin Airport project (see Chapters 3 and 6), there have been many periods of indecision, a few clear decisions and several counter-decisions, all of which are outlined in this book. On 25 June 2018, the House of Commons approved a National Policy Statement (NPS) that provides policy support for a third runway at Heathrow (HC Deb 25 June 2018). The Heathrow third runway is one of a number of expansion options that have been proposed, rejected and then supported, and the story of this and other projects makes an interesting study of the mechanics of political processes intertwined with community activism, academic study and international business. The Heathrow third runway story is not finished (if approved, it is unlikely to be operational before the mid 2020s) and, if aviation continues to grow, there will be more decisions to make in the future.

1.2. Objectives

The objectives of this book are to describe how policy for the expansion of London's airports has evolved over the last 40 years or so and to see if there are positive or negative lessons to be learned to help in the future evolution of policy. Positive or negative could depend on your perspective, whether you are likely to benefit or be impacted by expansion, but it is clear that one element that seems to be sought by all sides is certainty. So the research tries to focus on the reasons for certainty when it occurred, and on why certainty was interrupted by uncertainty. The events described in this book may provide some lessons for those involved in these future decisions, but will be of interest to anyone concerned about the way major decisions are made.

1.3. What's in this book (and what's not)

Following this introductory chapter, Chapters 2 and 3 describe some key elements of aviation history and a summary of the evolution of airports policy in the period up to 1974. The year 1974 was chosen as this was one of those occasions when policy was completely changed, with the cancellation of the Maplin project and the start of a period of review. This and subsequent events led to the airports that exist today, and the current debate about airports policy can be traced back to this period. Chapters 4 and 5 provide further context, with a review of planning and decision-making and a chapter on environmental issues. The following chapters look at airports policy in detail in a number of periods. Chapter 6 covers the period from 1974 to 1991, which, as noted above, started with a complete change of policy and then led through a series of studies, consultations and inquiries to decisions that resulted in new terminals at Heathrow, Gatwick and Stansted. Chapter 7 then describes a period of uncertainty in the 1990s, which includes studies and the Heathrow Terminal 5 Inquiry, when the policy was far from clear. Chapter 8 covers the years from 1997 to 2010, when the government tried to create long-term certainty but was thwarted at the end by a general election. Chapter 9 then looks at 2010 to the present, beginning with another period of uncertainty that evolved through studies, a commission and parliamentary activity, which has resulted in the plans for a third runway at Heathrow. The present situation is less uncertain, but still not resolved. Chapter 10 seeks to identify some common themes and Chapter 11 makes comparisons with some international case studies, as well as case studies from within the UK but outside the South East of England. Chapter 12 looks to the future and Chapter 13 seeks to summarise where we are now.

This book is not a history of any of the airports or locations considered for development. However, some such histories contain interesting insights and can be useful if the reader wishes to understand the locations in more detail. A Further Reading section at the end of this book gives some recommendations.

1.4. Distilling the frenzy

Finally, in this introduction, I would like to echo the words of Peter Hennessy (2012), who referred to writing the history of one's own times as 'distilling the frenzy'. Hennessy quotes Sir Robin Butler, formerly Cabinet Secretary to three prime ministers, as saying, 'Every department should have a historical adviser.' Although I do not claim in any way to be such an adviser, I hope that my research may contribute a small amount to the records of a number of government departments, and to the organisations involved in the evolution of airports policy, be they airport operators, airlines, local communities or others interested in the subject. Hennessy also suggests that writing the history of one's own times is like 'stay[ing] behind to catch up', remembering how it was and finding evidence of the situation, putting back into the past the same uncertainty we feel about the future.

REFERENCES

HC Deb 17 December 1979, vol. 976, col. 37.
HC Deb 25 June 2018, vol. 643, col. 649.
Hennessy P (2012) *Distilling the Frenzy: Writing the History of One's Own Times*. Biteback Publishing, London, UK.

Chapter 2
A brief overview of air-transport history

2.1. Introduction
This chapter describes some of the background issues relevant to a consideration of London's airports policy. First is a general, but very brief, summary of how air transport has evolved since its beginnings over a century ago. Aviation has always been an international business, so the next section looks at some of the international factors that have had an impact on airports policy. There have, of course, been many technological changes over the years and some of these are described next. The penultimate section of this chapter looks at the evolution of airlines – without which airports would have no reason to exist. The final section deals with how airports themselves have changed ownership and been regulated.

2.2. The growth of aviation from the earliest years of the twentieth century
The growth of aviation since the early years of the twentieth century has been truly remarkable, as any visit to an aviation museum displaying the flimsy first aircraft will demonstrate. With the first heavier-than-air flights in the first decade of the twentieth century, aviation had only just been established at the start of World War 1 (WW1). However, the war stimulated rapid technological and expertise development, some of which was used to establish commercial aviation in Europe after the war using demobbed airfields, aircraft and pilots. Worldwide activity from 1930 is shown in Figure 2.1. Activity in the interwar years was very limited, although this was, in some respects, a 'golden age', with new airlines, some circling the globe, air shows and races and the establishment of Empire routes from the UK (Budd, 2007). In the 1920s and 1930s, Imperial Airways, a private company, had been the 'chosen instrument' of the UK government to develop routes to its empire in Africa, India, the Far East and Australia. There were also some luxury European routes and a few domestic services, in conjunction with the railways (Halford-Macleod, 2006). However, the number of passengers using Imperial Airways for long-haul routes was very small (Pirie, 2004). Other European countries sought to serve their colonies or mandates, mostly by state-owned airlines. The USA developed its domestic traffic primarily through privately owned carriers, with PanAm circling the globe. Although World War 2 (WW2) brought new technology and a changed world order, this pattern of state and private ownership in the UK remained in place. Winston Churchill, then Secretary of State for Air, had rejected government subsidy in 1920, saying, 'Civil aviation must fly by itself' (Fearon, 1985: p. 25) but in 1945, Lord Winster, the UK Minister of Civil Aviation, said, 'Public ownership shall be the overruling principle in air transport' (Halford-Macleod, 2006: p. 9).

The simple graph of activity in Figure 2.1 shows that growth has been interrupted by events on occasions, but the upward trend has continued over the years. There may be arguments about the rate of growth in the future, but few now predict that growth has ended, which means that pressure on existing airport capacity will remain.

3

Figure 2.1 Absolute growth of worldwide aviation (1930–2016) recorded by the International Civil Aviation Organisation (ICAO) in terms of Revenue Passenger Kilometres (RPKs)
(Data from Airlines for America; after Masiol and Harrison, 2014)

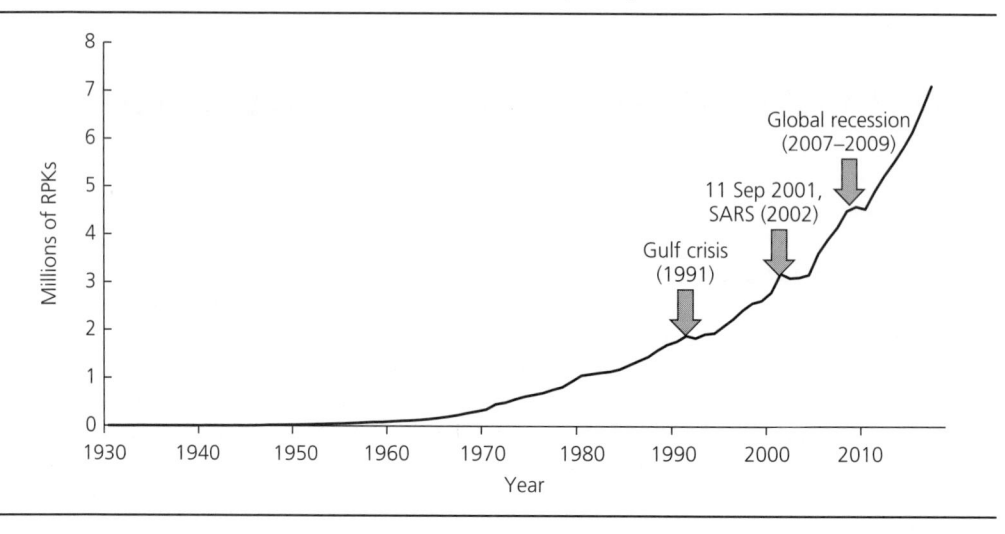

Civil aviation in the UK was effectively suspended during WW2 and a large number of military airfields were built throughout the country. Heathrow, Gatwick and Stansted were developed and used for military purposes during WW2 (Donne, 1991).

After WW2, air travel in the UK took time to become established. Heathrow (which had opened as a civil airport in 1946) was dominant, particularly for international flights. In the 1960s, jet aircraft were introduced and air-passenger growth rates increased, although there were counter trends, such as when the London–Manchester rail route was electrified (Sealy, 1967), demonstrating the importance of journey time in determining demand. Figure 2.2 shows how

Figure 2.2 Passengers at UK airports and GDP, 1960–2016
(After Airports Commission, 2015, redrawn with data from the Office for National Statistics (ONS), Department for Transport (DfT) and Civil Aviation Authority (CAA))

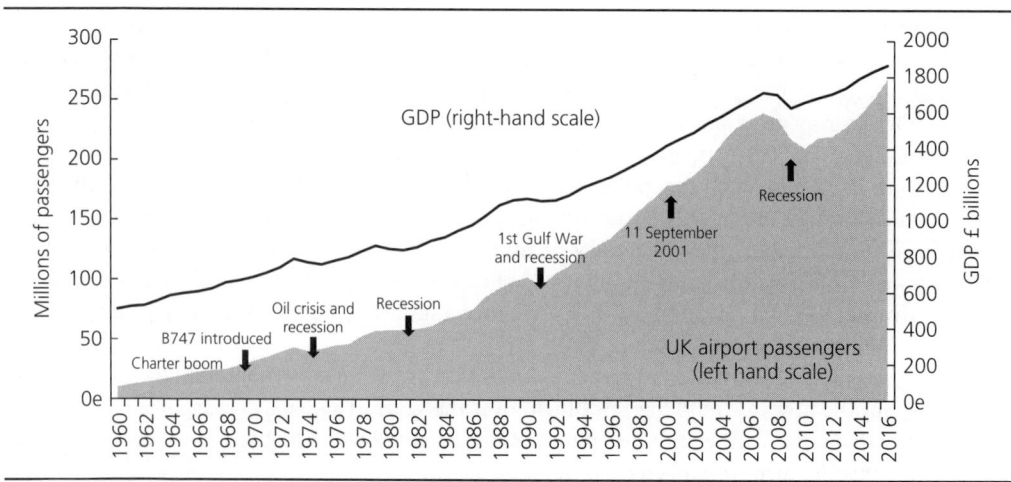

passenger numbers at UK airports have grown since 1960, together with gross domestic product (GDP) and a number of key events along the timeline.

Demand has tended to rise in line with, and at times faster than, economic growth (Airports Commission, 2015). For the purposes of planning, it is important to determine if this relationship between demand and economic growth is likely to continue, or whether there are limits to growth. Such limits to growth have been debated over many years, and there are supply-side limits in terms of the physical and environmental capacity available, but demand limits vary between different segments. For example, the UK international leisure market was described as 'only at the early stages of maturity' (the point at which demand stops growing) by the late 1990s (Graham, 2000: p. 109). However, by 2006, Graham (2006) was asking if low-cost carriers (LCCs) could reverse or postpone any trends towards maturity by enabling sectors of the population who were previously not travelling by air to travel, or by encouraging infrequent travellers to travel more.

There is also a relationship between demand and social factors. As noted earlier, the pre-WW2 UK air-transport industry was based on developing Empire routes and luxury services. In the immediate post-WW2 years, a number of UK aircraft were designed, and some actually built, for the luxury market. The Bristol Brabazon could accommodate 200 passengers, but the British Overseas Airways Corporation (BOAC) specified that it should accommodate only 50 with berths (Phipp, 2007). In 1958, only 0.25 per cent of the population accounted for 90 per cent of passenger movements (Sealy, 1967) because air travel was expensive and therefore used only by the wealthy or when the fare was paid by the employer. However, by 2004, half the UK population had flown (Adey et al., 2007), although Graham, B. (2008) suggests that LCCs have not widened the demographics of the market, even though they encourage leisure travel and immigration. Of particular relevance to this book is the relationship between social factors and opposition to airport expansion. Initially, much of the opposition was based on Nimby (not in my backyard) principles. However, arguments against airport expansion have evolved to deal with the concern that opposing expansion at one airport sometimes means supporting growth elsewhere and thus 'exporting the misery', with many protestors harnessing the rhetoric of social justice (Adey et al., 2007). However, 'aeromobility' has become an 'inverted necessity' (as academics like to call it, meaning that we don't really need to fly so much but it is now perceived as essential) and is embedded in society, and so the possibility of reducing flying is limited.

2.3. International obligations

As part of the general move to establish a new world order after WW2, commercial aviation was considered in the 1944 Chicago Convention, which led to the formation of the International Civil Aviation Organisation (ICAO), which became part of the United Nations, and which established the initial five freedoms of the air (Debbage, 2014).[1] International routes were arranged according to government-to-government bilateral agreements, some of which still exist. Such geopolitics have influenced airports policy, as they include the rules about 'grandfather rights'[2] for airport slots and the requirement not to levy tax on fuel (Anger-Kraavi and Köhler, 2013). ICAO is also involved in setting environmental standards for aviation, including noise levels for aircraft and, more recently, in a worldwide approach to managing greenhouse gas emissions from aviation.

ICAO is an inter-state organisation, but the airlines established a worldwide trade association, the International Air Transport Association (IATA) in 1945 and, through IATA, created a system to enable tickets to be issued for multi-airline journeys (interlining). IATA has always contributed the views of airlines strongly in consultations about airport developments.

At the European level, aviation policy has developed in more recent years through the European Union (EU). Deregulation of air services within the EU was facilitated by a series of packages in the 1980s and 1990s that enabled airlines to fly throughout Europe, with the Nouvelles Frontières case decided at the European Court of Justice in 1986 showing that fares could be set without reference to IATA. In 2001, the EU's airports policy was to support growth and EU governments showed 'no sign of collectively accepting resource or waste limits for aviation' (Upham, 2001: p. 241). However, since then, the EU has introduced air-quality limits (Ellermann et al., 2012; Jacobs, 2014), habitats regulations (Kramer, 2009) and noise action plans (King et al., 2011), all of which have an effect on airport expansion proposals. It has also sought to include aviation in its Emissions Trading System. EU transport policy also covers airline liberalisation, bilateral Air Services Agreements, ground handling at airports, airport capacity and the Single European Sky project.[3] It is also related to other transport policies, such as the Trans European Network – Transport (TEN-T) policy. At the time of writing, the UK was planning to leave the EU, but it is not clear what effect this will have on the various regulations and agreements made under the EU's domain.

One of the few remaining areas where the UK government has a direct involvement in air transport (now that most of the industry is in the private sector) is in Air Services Agreements (ASAs). ASAs have their basis in the Chicago Convention, and are negotiated between states (bilaterals) or between groups of states (multilaterals). One of the best-known of these was the Bermuda Agreement, originally signed in 1946 but since updated. Some ASAs now include 'open skies', where there are few limits on airlines operating between states. Within the EU, the ASA is effectively open skies such that any EU airline can operate anywhere within the EU, subject to safety competency and other EU regulations such as restrictions on state aid. ASAs have had a significant impact on airports policy, as will be seen in Chapter 6 when attempts were made to boost traffic at Gatwick, and they are also very high on states' priority lists. One of the first jobs for Russell Sunderland, who rose through the civil service to become a deputy secretary in the Department of Transport (DTp), was to negotiate an ASA with a North African country in the 1960s. He told me that, innocently, the UK government team offered what they thought was a very good deal which would have provided an excellent service to help the country's newly established tourist industry, but the reciprocal routes by the North African country's airline would be to Gatwick, whereas the British airline would operate from Heathrow. This was completely unacceptable to the country and Russell admitted that this led to a poor deal being agreed, although it did at least get British feet in the door and profitable services from Heathrow did follow eventually.

2.4. From wood, fabric and wire to carbon composites and electronics

There have been many technological changes in aircraft and engine design since the first flights of the early twentieth century, some of which have had a significant impact on the evolution of airports policy.

The most obvious advance in technology has been the growth in the size of aircraft and this has a number of impacts. Clearly larger aircraft require more space on the ground for parking and clearances and this has required airports to adapt their layouts. Early aircraft were able to take off and land on grass but, as weight increased, hard runways were required. The length of runway required also increased, although the last major increase was associated with the introduction of jet aircraft around 50 years ago. Since then, even the largest new aircraft have been designed (by having more powerful engines and more efficient wings) to operate from runways with a length of between 3000 and 3500 metres.

Improvements in range have enabled aircraft to adopt new routes, something that has affected airports policy in general, although London's position has, if anything, been enhanced by this.

The first transatlantic crossings required fuel stops at either Prestwick or Shannon and Gander or Goose Bay and these have now been almost completely eliminated (although a British Airways A318 premium service from London City Airport to New York still requires a fuel stop in Ireland). The use of twin-engine aircraft on long, over-water routes from the 1980s (using Extended-range Twin engine Operational Performance Standards or ETOPS) has enabled more routes to be flown. More recently, new aircraft types, such as the Boeing 787 and Airbus A350, have increased the number of potentially economic routes because of their mid size and lower operating costs. However, although some people have predicted that this will mean major hub location such as London will be bypassed, it appears that airlines are using such aircraft from London routes as well as for new routes.

One of the trends that has had most impact on airports policy is the aircraft size in terms of the number of passengers carried. While there has been a general trend of increasing aircraft size, the rate of growth in size has been difficult to predict and, as this is a key factor in assessing the need for runway capacity, it has been a contentious issue. Reference to this will be made in future chapters.

Technological changes have had a major effect on the environmental impact of aviation, although it is a matter of contention as to whether improvements in aircraft and engine design have balanced the sheer scale of activity. Although piston-engined aircraft were by no means quiet, the introduction of jet aircraft in the early 1960s made noise and emissions 'painfully obvious to those living near airports' (Graham et al., 2014: p. 36). This will be covered in more detail in Chapter 5.

Changes in airframe design, such as the greater use of lightweight material, have also affected the impact in terms of noise and pollution. Changes in airspace management affect where and at what height aircraft fly near airports, which may have a noise impact on people on the ground (Budd and Budd, 2013).

Other technological changes in airports, such as for passenger and baggage processing, have altered the design of terminals but have not had a dramatic effect on the need for new airport capacity. Technological changes in radar and communications have enabled increases in airport capacity to be matched by capacity in the air.

2.5. Airports depend on airlines

Demand for airport capacity arises from passengers and shippers and is met by airlines providing flights, with airports providing services to airlines. Different types of airline ownership, structure and business model result in different requirements for airport expansion; growth at individual airports depends on the airlines operating there. The evolution of airports policy cannot be understood without a knowledge of how the ownership, business models and regulation of airlines has changed. However, according to Humphreys and Francis (2002: p. 253), 'There has been next to no recognition by policy makers that it is the airlines that drive the distribution of air services across the UK's airports.' In more recent years, the role of marketing of airports to airlines has grown (Graham, 2013), but this has mainly been concerned with attracting airlines to underused airports. For London's airports, there have been many occasions when airlines have sought to establish or protect themselves at the more popular airport (Heathrow) and declined the opportunity to move to less congested and cheaper airports (Gatwick and Stansted). The fundamental reason for this is that airlines earn higher yields (revenue per seat) at Heathrow than elsewhere. However, there is a corollary in that new airlines can establish themselves at less popular airports away from the direct competition.

In the UK immediately after WW2, the British Overseas Airways Corporation (BOAC), British South American Airways (BSAA) and British European Airways (BEA) were established to fly most of the regulated scheduled services. BOAC and BSAA were both based at Heathrow and BEA was initially based at Northolt. Independent airlines, based at Gatwick and elsewhere, found niches in charters, trooping contracts, associate agreements (flying on behalf of the state-owned corporations) and the Berlin Airlift. BSAA merged with BOAC in 1949 (Halford-Macleod, 2006). In the 1960s, under a Labour government, the independents grew, serving charters and trooping contracts, while scheduled services were heavily regulated. The Edwards report of 1971 recommended the formation of the Civil Aviation Authority (CAA) for safety and regulation, the merger of BEA and BOAC, and the creation of a 'second force' airline, which was to be British Caledonian (BCal), operating from Gatwick. Laker Airways' Skytrain service began operating low-cost flights from Gatwick to the USA in 1977. Therefore, the development of Heathrow was related primarily to the state-owned corporations, while Gatwick grew through its independent airlines.

Airports grew or declined along with the airlines based there. During the late 1970s, some airlines ceased trading (Court Line, based at Luton) while others grew (Britannia and Dan-Air, at Gatwick) (Halford-Macleod, 2010). Long-haul traffic grew at Gatwick and the government attempted to move Spanish, Portuguese and Canadian traffic from Heathrow to Gatwick, in part to resolve growing congestion at Heathrow. This proposal was predicated on lower numbers of transfer passengers on these routes and would have involved both British airlines and the relevant national airline. However, it failed because of concerns about lower yields, which led to objections by the overseas governments, who used diplomatic pressure as well as court injunctions to prevent it. In 1979, Air Europe began operations at Gatwick and Skytrain was operating successfully. The same year, the Advisory Committee on Airports Policy (ACAP) and the Study Group on South East Airports (SGSEA) reported (see Chapter 6) and the government announced that Stansted had been selected for major development. Over the next few years, British Airways (BA) made huge losses (rising to £544 million in 1981–82) and abandoned many domestic routes. People Express (a US prototype LCC) began a long-haul service from Newark to Gatwick in 1983 and Virgin Atlantic began operations at Gatwick in 1984. Between 1979 and 1983, passenger numbers declined at Heathrow but grew by over 40 per cent at Gatwick. BA was privatised in 1987. Again there was a relationship between the success or otherwise of airlines and the airports where they were based.

Some scheduled airlines operate their services such that a significant proportion of their passengers are transferring between flights (sometimes called connecting or, if using different airlines, interlining). Major global alliances, such as Star, One World and Skyteam, and other forms of partnership and route or code sharing make such transfers easier, especially with terminal co-location, such as with the Star Alliance carriers in Heathrow's Terminal 2. The benefit to passengers of transferring is that a wider range of destinations or frequencies can be offered, albeit that a transfer is usually less convenient than a direct flight (Bowen, 2014). For airports where there is a high proportion of transfer passengers, known as transfer hubs, there is more pressure on infrastructure because operations may be more peaked, and the airline or alliance may control a large number of slots. On the other hand, non-hubs may lose services if an alliance seeks to concentrate at a hub (Caves, 1997; Doganis, 2006). Doganis suggests that in the future there may be only three or four 'network dominators' per region or continent, with other national carriers demoted to niche passenger operators. The significance of hubs to airports policy is that it has proved very difficult to establish a new hub, such as at Gatwick, while the existing hub, Heathrow, retains its attractiveness to airlines looking to establish new services or grow.

The business model of LCCs began with Southwest Airlines in the USA, following deregulation in the late 1970s. The first EU liberalisation package was introduced in 1983, which enabled LCCs to emerge (Graham, 2013) and they now operate in many parts of the world. Many small airports seek to attract LCCs with lower charges, but open themselves up to the risk of dependency on non-aeronautical revenue (e.g. car parking and retail). For example, EasyJet established a base at London Luton Airport in 1995 when Ryanair moved to Stansted to take advantage of lower charges there, but the initial five-year deal adversely affected Luton Airport's financial performance, and it was only a later deal with the airport's new owners that enabled a partnership to succeed (Francis et al., 2004). LCCs are important at Gatwick, as well as at Stansted and Luton, but play only a limited role at Heathrow and London City airports. Graham, B. (2008) suggests that LCC passengers do not take account of environmental issues, but more recent work by Mayer et al. (2012) shows that passengers do differentiate between airlines based on environmental friendliness, although LCCs are not seen as more or less environmentally friendly than full-service carriers, and the authors note that green attitudes do not necessarily translate into a change in behaviour.

LCCs can switch airports easily (Starkie, 2002) and there is pressure on airports from LCCs to reduce costs (Bush and Starkie, 2014). Doganis (2006) considers that competition in the twenty-first century will lead to only one or two major LCCs surviving in each continent. Indeed, there has been a wave of failures in Europe (33 out of 43 start-ups between 2000 and 2012) (Budd et al., 2014).

2.6. Airport ownership and regulation

While airlines have developed, so has the organisational and management structure of the airport sector. Table 2.1 shows the evolution of ownership of the London airports over time. In 1945, a White Paper on British Air Services (Ministry of Civil Aviation, 1945) established a policy of public ownership to ensure that the finance required for development was provided. As a result, 44 airports were transferred to the Ministry of Civil Aviation in 1947 (Humphreys, 1999). A further White Paper in 1961 (Ministry of Civil Aviation, 1961) facilitated the transfer of some airports to local authorities and, in 1966, the British Airports Authority (BAA) was formed as a nationalised corporation, owning Heathrow, Gatwick and Stansted, plus Prestwick in Scotland (at the time still strategically important for long-haul transatlantic flights). This enabled the airports to take a more commercial stance, while still being ultimately responsible to Parliament (Donne, 1991).

Airport privatisation in the UK was part of a wider process of privatising many organisations under a Conservative government in the 1980s, the aim of which was to reduce government involvement and enable investment to be funded by private capital (Doganis, 1992). BAA was privatised in 1987 under the Airports Act of 1986 as a single entity, thus retaining ownership of Heathrow, Gatwick and Stansted. It was sold without restructuring, on the grounds that a unified company would have the financial resources to fund future investment needs (Parker, 1999). Some argued that the overall case for retaining BAA's unity was not very convincing (Starkie and Thompson, 1985) and Bush and Starkie (2014) describe the privatisation as leaving BAA as a monopoly in a sector 'long characterised by monopolies, distorted by State ownership and dominated by sclerotic business models and practices' (p. 46).

I worked for BAA from 1970 to 2001 and my personal recollections of the organisation were mostly positive. It began with a graduate trainee scheme and evolved through good management training programmes, management development and promotion, in a company which evolved and was probably ahead of the curve (for example, every manager was given a BBC computer to take home and get used to). As a nationalised industry, we were continuously profitable and, although some of our airline customers complained, we felt we were efficient and innovative, and we certainly had a high profile in international comparisons. We were confident that privatisation would bring new opportunities (for me it involved moving into railways in the Heathrow Express

Table 2.1 The ownership of the London airports over time (Compiled by the author from Graham, 2013)

Period	Heathrow	Gatwick	Stansted	Luton	London City	Southend
Pre-WW2	Fairey Aviation	From 1933: Airports Ltd. (Morris Jackaman)		Opened 1938		WW1: RFC. 1935: Southend Borough Council
WW2	RAF	RAF	Opened 1943: RAF/USAF	RAF		RAF
1945–1949	Ministry of Civil Aviation (and successors)			Luton Borough Council		Southend Borough Council
1950–1954						
1955–1959						
1960–1964						
1965–1969	1966–1987: British Airports Authority					
1970–1974						
1975–1979						
1980–1984						
1985–1989	1987: privatisation – BAA plc				Opened 1987: Mowlem	
1990–1994						1993: 150-year lease to Regional Airports Ltd
1995–2000					1995: sold to Dermot Desmond	
2000–2004				1997: 30-year concession awarded to Airport Group International. 1999: sold to TBI		
2005–2009	2006: BAA acquired by Ferrovial consortium	2009: sold to Global Infrastructure Partners (GIP)		2005: sold to Abertis and AENA	2006: sold to AIG and GIP. 2008: GIP and Highstar Capital	2008: lease sold to Stobart Air
2010–2016	2012: renamed Heathrow Holdings. Owned by Ferrovial and six others		2013: sold to Manchester Airports Group (10 local authorities and IFM Investors)	2014: Abertis share sold to AENA	2016: sold to AIMCo and others	

☐ Fully private, ☐ Private lessee or concessionaire, ☐ >50% public, ☐ Fully public project) and the change of culture was embraced. We made mistakes, of course, but we always felt that we had good-quality people and other resources and would therefore succeed. In a later chapter, I will review the effect of changing ownership on airports policy but, from my perspective, it seemed that privatisation brought little initial change in BAA's or the government's approach to airports policy.

Luton Airport remained in the ownership of Luton Borough Council, but the owners met the requirements of the 1986 Airports Act by awarding a long-term (30-year) operating concession (Graham, 2013). In separate ownership from BAA, there was clear competition, particularly with Stansted. The concession has changed hands several times, sometimes into groups owning other airports, and is currently with the Spanish airport operator AENA (currently majority state owned, but moving towards full privatisation).

London City Airport opened in 1987 as a private venture, albeit with a very supportive planning regime under the London Docklands Development Corporation. Ownership has changed hands and for some time was common with Gatwick (Graham, 2013). The land of Southend Airport remains in the ownership of Southend Borough Council but is leased to the private-sector operator.

Under the 1986 Airports Act, Heathrow, Gatwick, Stansted and Manchester airports were 'designated', meaning that the prices charged would be capped to a RPI+ or -X formula. The regulatory process involves five-yearly reviews by the Competition and Markets Authority (and its predecessors the Office of Fair Trading and the Competition Commission) and imposition of the formula by the CAA, with no grounds for appeal other than for a judicial review. The formula is set to prevent excessive monopoly pricing while providing an incentive to invest. There are diverse views on whether this is achieved. For example, on the issue of single versus dual till pricing,[4] the CAA has argued that dual till pricing could promote better use of capacity and provide incentives for investment, while the Competition Commission found no evidence of underinvestment with the single till and the airlines favoured this approach (Graham, A., 2008: p. 117). Humphreys et al. (2007) suggest that single till pricing encourages investment in retail and that investment in runways would be delayed in order to increase the return, which would not be in the best interests of the UK economy. Starkie (2005 and 2006) examines both sides of the argument, on the one hand that price-capped firms tend to underinvest and 'sweat' assets, and on the other that they can earn more by 'gold-plating' or deter entrants by 'building large'. The investment at Stansted in the late 1980s could be an example of the latter, while Heathrow Terminal 5 was delayed by the planning process and then required a significant increase in charges.

BAA was acquired by the Ferrovial Group in 2006, with Humphreys et al. (2007) suggesting that this raised national security issues, although it is not clear why this is so, as airports work to government standards. Then the Office of Fair Trading announced an investigation into the airports market, at a time when there was significant criticism of BAA's service quality. Subsequent events (Terminal 5 opening, the need for increased security, bad weather) meant that political, public and airline opinion had an impact on the future of ownership and regulation (Graham, A., 2008) and the outcome of the investigation was that BAA was required to dispose of a number of its airports. Gatwick was sold to Global Infrastructure Partners in 2009, Stansted to the Manchester Airports Group in 2013, and Glasgow, Southampton and Aberdeen were sold to a consortium of Ferrovial and Macquarie in 2014.

More generally, Starkie (2002) had argued that in the airports industry there is a trade-off between imperfect (or monopolistic) competition and economic regulation, with the latter introducing separate economic distortions. Market power is the consequence of the problems of gaining access to competing sites rather than of natural monopoly, although there are opportunities for substitution between airports (and other modes of transport), particularly for charter airlines and LCCs. In recent years the European airport market has changed (Bush and Starkie, 2014; Starkie, 2012). Three factors underlie the changed relationship: the creation of a single European aviation market; the development of pan-European airline business models; and the increasing use of the internet, which has reduced the costs of entry for airlines into local markets. Starkie (2012) argues that it is a false assumption that capacity restraint is deliberate and passengers do not benefit, so price-capping regulation is unnecessary. Since liberalisation of airlines, airports have had to compete for both transfer and point-to-point traffic, with pressures to reduce costs (Bush and Starkie, 2014). The argument against continuing regulation is that 'even where dominance is present, the fundamental economics of airports make it unlikely that abuse through restriction of output will be a profitable strategy' (Bush and Starkie, 2014: p. 48). This viewpoint marks a very significant change in relation to London's airports from that given by the Competition Commission in 2009, following the sale by BAA of Gatwick and Stansted.

A number of cities or regions around the world have multiple airports, some of which are also managed as a system. A total of 59 multi-airport cities or regions have been identified based on their 2006 passenger throughput (Bonnefoy, 2008), defined as where there are airports with more than 0.5 million passengers a year within 120 miles (193 km) of each other. De Neufville and Odoni (2003) suggest there were around 30 multi-airport systems worldwide in 2003, involving around 80 airports, which catered for over half of worldwide passengers, with examples in New York, San Francisco, Washington, Paris and Tokyo. At the time, it appeared that around 14 mppa (millions of passengers per annum) of originating traffic was needed for a city or region to have more than one airport. As an example, Montreal's Mirabel and Dorval airports served only 4 mppa originating traffic, a prime reason for Mirabel's failure to attract traffic (see Chapter 11). Many new airports, including Washington Dulles, took many years for their capacity to be used, while the older, congested airport remained popular. With Heathrow, Gatwick and Stansted being owned by BAA until recently, they could be managed as a system and, in accordance with de Neufville and Odoni's advice, land for future expansion could be safeguarded or 'banked' and facilities could be developed incrementally and flexibly, working with the airlines. Now that these airports are separately owned, airports policy has to take account of the fact that they compete with each other.

There are many other types of regulation with which airports are required to comply. Some types are specific to the aviation industry, such as the safety and security rules imposed either directly by the government or through the CAA. While these rules are fundamental to the operation of an airport (for example, an airport cannot operate without the appropriate certification), they are taken as a given and do not, as a rule, tend to influence airports policy. Like any other business, airports have to operate within the wide range of business legislation. A particular area of relevance is the UK planning regime, which is discussed in Chapter 4, while the effect of privatisation and the break-up of BAA on the evolution of airports policy is discussed in later chapters.

Notes

1. The first five freedoms of the air are: (1) the right to fly over a country (2) the right to land for refuelling or maintenance (3) the right to fly from a home country to another (4) the right to fly from another country to a home country (5) the right to fly between two foreign countries.
2. Effectively, 'grandfather rights' are that if an airline uses a time slot at an airport for a service in one year, it has the right to use the same time slot in the next year.
3. The Single European Sky project is a long-running project to provide for the growth of aviation in the European air traffic management system.

4. The single till assumes that all revenue is accounted for when deciding on a regulatory formula. The dual till approach would separate aeronautical revenues (such as landing fees) from commercial revenue (such as retail and car parks), with the regulatory formula applying only to the aeronautical revenues.

REFERENCES

Adey P, Budd L and Hubbard P (2007) Flying lessons: exploring the social and cultural geographies of global air travel. *Progress in Human Geography* **31(6)**: 773–791.

Airports Commission (2015) *Final Report*. Airports Commission, London, UK.

Anger-Kraavi A and Köhler J (2013) Aviation and the EU Emissions Trading System. In *Sustainable Aviation Futures* (Budd L, Griggs S and Howarth D (eds)). Emerald Group Publishing, Bingley, UK, pp. 109–130.

Bonnefoy P (2008) *Scalability of the Air Transportation System and Development of Multi-Airport Systems: A Worldwide Perspective*. PhD thesis, MIT, Cambridge, MA, USA.

Bowen J (2014) The economic geography of air transport. In *The Geographies of Air Transport* (Budd L and Goetz AR (eds)). Ashgate, Farnham, UK and Burlington, VT, USA.

Budd L (2007) Producing airspace: the contested geographies of Nottingham East Midlands Airport. PhD thesis, Loughborough University, Loughborough, UK.

Budd L and Budd T (2013) Environmental technology and the future of flight. In *Sustainable Aviation Futures* (Budd L, Griggs S and Howarth D (eds)). Emerald Group Publishing, Bingley, UK, pp. 87–107.

Budd L, Francis G, Humphreys I and Ison S (2014) Grounded: characterising the market exit of European low cost airlines. *Journal of Air Transport Management* **34(1)**: 78–85.

Bush H and Starkie D (2014) Competitive drivers towards improved airport/airline relationships. *Journal of Air Transport Management* **4**: 45–49.

Caves R (1997) European airline networks and their implications for airport planning. *Transport Reviews* **17(2)**: 121–144.

de Neufville R and Odoni A (2003) *Airport Systems Planning, Design and Management*, 2nd edition. McGraw-Hill, London, UK and New York, USA.

Debbage K (2014) The geopolitics of air transport. In *The Geographies of Air Transport* (Budd L and Goetz A (eds)). Ashgate, Farnham, UK and Burlington, VT, USA.

Doganis R (1992) *The Airport Business*. Routledge, London, UK.

Doganis R (2006) *The Airline Business*, 2nd edition. Routledge, London, UK.

Donne M (1991) *Above Us The Skies: The Story of BAA*. Good Books, Whitley, UK.

Edwards R (1971) British Air Transport in the Seventies: Report of the Committee of Inquiry into Civil Air Transport. HMSO, London, UK.

Ellermann T, Massling A, Løfstrøm P, Winther M, Nøjgaard J and Ketzel, M (2012) Assessment of the air quality at the apron of Copenhagen Airport Kastrup in relation to the working environment. *Technical Report from DCE–Danish Centre for Environment and Energy* **15**.

Fearon P (1985) The growth of aviation in Britain. *Journal of Contemporary History* **20(1)**: 21–40.

Francis G, Humphreys I and Ison S (2004) Airports' perspectives on the growth of low-cost airlines and the remodelling of the airport–airline relationship. *Tourism Management* **25**: 507–514.

Graham A (2000) Demand for leisure air travel and limits to growth. *Journal of Air Transport Management* **6(2)**: 109–118.

Graham A (2006) Have the major forces driving leisure airline traffic changed? *Journal of Air Transport Management* **12**: 14–20.

Graham A (2008) Airport planning and regulation in the United Kingdom. In *Aviation Infrastructure Performance: A Study in Comparative Political Economy* (Winston C and Rus G de (eds)). Brookings Institution Press, Washington, DC, USA, pp 100–135.

Graham A (2013) *Managing Airports: An International Perspective*, 4th edition. Routledge, London, UK and New York, USA.

Graham B (2008) UK air travel: taking off for growth? In *Traffic Jam: Ten Years of Sustainable Transport in the UK* (Docherty I and Shaw J (eds)). Policy Press, Bristol, UK, pp. 139–159.

Graham W, Hall C and Morales V (2014) The potential of future aircraft technology for noise and pollutant emissions reduction. *Transport Policy* **34**: 36–51.

Halford-Macleod G (2006) *Britain's Airlines: Volume One: 1946–1951*. Tempus Publishing, Stroud, UK.

Halford-Macleod G (2010) *Britain's Airlines Volume Three: 1964 to Deregulation*. The History Press, Stroud, UK.

HMG (Her Majesty's Government) (1986) *Airports Act 1986*. Chapter 31. HMSO, London, UK.

Humphreys I (1999) Privatisation and commercialisation: changes in UK airport ownership patterns. *Journal of Transport Geography* **7(2)**: 121–144.

Humphreys I and Francis G (2002) Policy issues and planning of UK regional airports. *Journal of Transport Geography* **10**: 249–258.

Humphreys I, Ison S and Francis G (2007) UK airport policy: does the government have any influence? *Public Money & Management* **27(5)**: 339–344.

Jacobs (2014) 6. Air Quality Baseline, prepared for the Airports Commission.

King E, Murphy E and Rice H (2011) Implementation of the EU environmental noise directive: lessons from the first phase of strategic noise mapping and action planning in Ireland. *Journal of Environmental Management* **92**: 756–764.

Kramer L (2009) The European Commission's opinions under Article 6(4) of the Habitats Directive. *Journal of Environmental Law* **21(1)**: 59–85.

Masiol M and Harrison R (2014) Aircraft engine exhaust emissions and other airport-related contributions to ambient air pollution: a review. *Atmospheric Environment* **95**: 409–455.

Mayer R, Ryley T and Gillingwater D (2012) Passenger perceptions of the green image associated with airlines. *Journal of Transport Geography* **22**: 179–186.

Ministry of Civil Aviation (1945) *British Air Services*. Cmnd 6712, HMSO, London, UK.

Ministry of Civil Aviation (1961) *Civil Aerodromes and Air Navigation Services*. Cmnd 1457, HMSO, London, UK.

Parker D (1999) The performance of BAA before and after privatisation. *Journal of Transport Economics and Policy* **33(2)**: 133–146.

Phipp M (2007) *The Brabazon Committee and British Airliners 1945–1960*. Tempus Publishing, Stroud, UK.

Pirie G (2004) Passenger traffic in the 1930s on British imperial air routes: refinement and revision. *Journal of Transport History* **25(1)**: 63–83.

Sealy KR (1967) The siting and development of British airports. *The Geographical Journal* **133(2)** (June): 148–171.

Starkie D (2002) Airport regulation and competition. *Journal of Air Transport Management* **8(1)**: 63–72.

Starkie D (2005) Making airport regulation less imperfect. *Journal of Air Transport Management* **11**: 3–8.

Starkie D (2006) Investment incentives and airport regulation. *Utilities Policy* **14**: 262–265.

Starkie D (2012) European airports and airlines: evolving relationships and the regulatory implications. *Journal of Air Transport Management* **21**: 40–49.

Starkie DNM and Thompson DJ (1985) The Airports Policy White Paper: privatisation and regulation. *Fiscal Studies* **6(4)**: 30–41.

Upham P (2001) A comparison of sustainability theory with UK and European airports policy and practice. *Journal of Environmental Management* **63**: 237–248.

Chapter 3
Airports policy up to the 1974 Maplin Review

3.1. Introduction
The previous chapter described some of the developments in air transport of particular relevance to airports, such as the historic growth of air travel and its relationship to economic, social and political factors, the creation of international regulatory bodies, some particular technological developments and the close relationship between airports and airlines. The chapter ended with a description of how the ownership of London's airports has moved from the public to predominantly the private sector and the consequent regulatory regimes that have been established.

This and subsequent chapters note how many of these issues have had a significant effect on the evolution of policy specifically related to airports. This chapter summarises the way airports policy evolved up until the mid 1970s. Later chapters then include a detailed analysis from this date forward.

3.2. The interwar years
From the first airfields in 1919 there were a number of attempts to rationalise and plan civil airport capacity up to and during World War 2 (WW2). Civil aviation and land-use planning developed as separate activities throughout the 1920s, neither recognising the significance of the other (Meyrick, 1983). Croydon was selected (from a list which included Hounslow Heath, Northolt and Wormwood Scrubs) in 1919 as the 'London terminal'. Although most aerodromes were privately owned and operated, there were a number of committees which sought to advise the government on how to accommodate the growth of air transport, and many other sites were considered, including Hendon and King's Cross/St Pancras. Donne (1991) describes and illustrates this early history, noting that Heathrow was 'where highwaymen once rode' (p. 30) and was also the site of the Great West Aerodrome, developed in 1930 by Richard Fairey as a manufacturing base. Gatwick went 'from racetrack to runway' (p. 44), also opening in 1930, and saw the building of the 'Beehive' terminal in 1936.

The development of air transport and airports in these interwar years was, of course, closely linked to the events of the time. Economic recession was probably a factor in holding back the commercial growth of aviation (although it did not stop the pioneers who broke various records, entrepreneurs who set up businesses, and some far-sighted planners). The attempt to maintain the British Empire was clearly a factor in the establishment of Imperial Airways and the specification of types of aircraft to serve Empire routes.

3.3. World War 2 developments
There had been pre-WW2 attempts to plan further airports and post-WW2 plans were drawn up as early as 1940 (Meyrick, 1983). However, the rapid changes in technology that occurred during

Figure 3.1 Abercrombie's plan for London's airports, satellites (new towns) and road and rail links

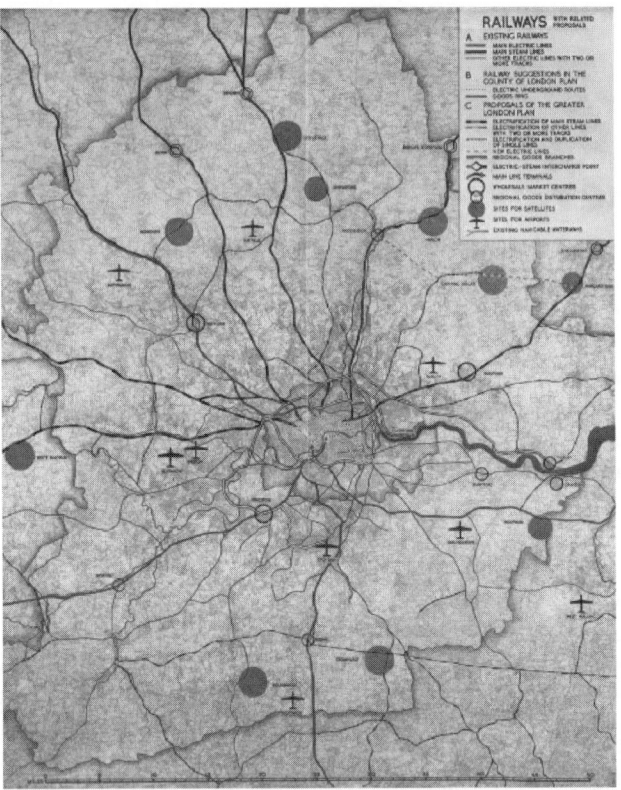

WW2, plus the growth in air transport that was expected post-WW2, meant that these plans had to be urgently revised. Having been planned initially as a military airfield, Heathrow was selected as the main London airport in 1943. Land was acquired under wartime emergency powers and it opened for civil operations in 1946. The story of Heathrow, including the wartime acquisition, is described in detail in *Heathrow: 2000 Years of History* (Sherwood, 2009). Aviation was completely dominated by WW2 from 1939 to 1945, but, remarkably, thought was given to the post-war period and Abercrombie's *Greater London Plan* of 1944 included proposals for a ring of airports around London (see Figure 3.1). The plan, described as 'the most successful regional plan of modern times' (Self, 2002: p. 145), was prepared by a small staff and was only advisory, but it included ambitious road and rail proposals. Its objectives were primarily about housing, minimising journeys to work and preventing the spread of London and the loss of countryside and agricultural land. The plan included airports at Heathrow and Gatwick, as well as a number of locations that subsequently closed or were not developed (Croydon, Heston, Bovingdon, Hatfield, Fairlop, Roding, Lullingstone and West Malling). There would be a hierarchy of airports, with some being developed early and others later, in effect creating a multi-airport region. Abercrombie also claimed that the location of aerodromes had been carefully considered in relation to railway connections, stating, 'Here is an opportunity from the start to plan a system of new communications adequately related to older forms of road and rail transport' (Abercrombie, 1945: p. 10).

3.4. Post-war expansion of Heathrow and Gatwick and the proposals for Stansted

Air travel in the UK took time to become established after WW2. London and Heathrow were dominant, particularly for international flights.

A White Paper on London's Airports in 1953 sought to rationalise the then seven airports where there were air-traffic conflicts. Heathrow (then just called London Airport) was the main airport, and Gatwick was selected as the main alternative to handle summer peak traffic and diversions. Blackbushe, in Hampshire, was to be retained as a supplementary alternative for diversions. Although it had long been assumed that Stansted was the second London airport as it possessed one of the finest runways in Europe, built by the US Air Force in WW2, the intensification of the Cold War meant more military air activity over East Anglia, so Stansted was to be held in reserve and Gatwick was an unexpected choice (Needham, 2014). Northolt, Croydon and Bovingdon would cease civil operations. Heathrow and Gatwick were developed through the 1950s, with the new Central Terminal Area at Heathrow opening in 1955 (Ares *et al.*, 2009) and the new runway and terminal opening at Gatwick in 1958.

An Interdepartmental Committee considered the question of a third London airport and in 1963 recommended that Stansted be developed (Helsey and Codd, 2014). Peter Hall, in his seminal book *Great Planning Disasters* (Hall, 1982), notes that the committee's main conclusion was based on a 'hopeless underestimate of both Heathrow's and Gatwick's capacity' (p. 24). The first Annual Report of the British Airports Authority (BAA, 1967) looked at Heathrow's capacity in some detail and, noting that the runways were likely to be the constraint, compared the capacity with a number of American airports, where many more aircraft movements were handled. Such analyses may have contributed to the debate about the need for more capacity which occurred in the next inquiry. This report also included a map showing the location of a proposed second runway at Gatwick.

The Stansted recommendation was considered at a public inquiry in Chelmsford in 1965–1966, described by Cashinella and Thompson (1971) as a 'scandal' (p. 18). The North West Essex and East Hertfordshire Preservation Association (NWEEHPA) was founded in 1964 to coordinate resistance to the proposed airport expansion. At the inquiry, the performance of civil servants was heavily criticised and the independent technical advisor (JWS Brancker) subsequently published what became known as the 'black book' criticising the outcome. The inspector at the Chelmsford Inquiry was clear in his report that a major airport development at Stansted could be justified only by national necessity and his criticism was noted in the bare phrase, 'Necessity was not proved by evidence at this inquiry' (Sanders, 2016: p. 313). Despite the negative recommendation, the government persisted and a White Paper in 1967 (Board of Trade, 1967) considered alternative sites but concluded that Stansted was the best option. There were then impassioned debates in both Houses of Parliament, with 285 MPs (including 91 Labour MPs, who were then in power) signing an Early Day Motion condemning the choice of Stansted (Needham, 2014). The Lords' debate concluded that 'the House in general was not in sympathy with the Government's case' (HL Deb 11 December 1967). There was then a technical and constitutional challenge to the White Paper, as the little-known Council on Tribunals ruled that, since the White Paper proposed a new runway alignment, there must also be a new planning inquiry (Needham, 2014). The Stansted proposals were subsequently abandoned in 1968, when the Roskill Commission was set up (see later in this chapter).

John Mulkern, who rose to be BAA's managing director in the 1980s, provided me with copies of the minutes of the first meetings of the British Airports Authority in 1965, before it took over operations in 1966. The notes show that, from the start, the Authority 'should seek to utilise the existing developed airports at Heathrow and Gatwick to the fullest, in order to maximise the return upon the heavy investments there before becoming too heavily involved in any large-scale development of a third London Airport'. At subsequent meetings, the board debated what the Authority's position should be at the forthcoming Chelmsford Inquiry. One strange aspect of these meetings was that one of the board members, Sir John Elliot, declared that he was vice chairman of NWEEHPA, one of the main objectors, and a local resident. Having declared his position, he took no part in the discussion or the decision, but remained at the meetings.

The historic context of this period covers many events, beginning with the election of a Labour government that nationalised many industries, introduced the National Health Service and had to deal with post-war housing requirements alongside continued rationing. The 1950s were politically mixed, with Winston Churchill returning to power, the Suez Crisis and the Korean War. The 1960s saw rapid technological and social change and airports became involved, for example, in the media reports of The Beatles at Heathrow.

3.5. The Roskill Commission

In 1968, following the abandonment of the Stansted proposals, the government set up the Roskill Commission, which was tasked with examining the whole matter objectively, and considered a wide range of evidence and undertook its own research. It considered 78 sites in its long list, which were reduced to four in the shortlist (Cublington in Buckinghamshire, Nuthampstead in Hertfordshire, Thurleigh in Bedfordshire and Foulness in Essex; see Figure 3.2). In the Commission's cost–benefit analysis, Foulness had ranked 13th, but it had been included in the shortlist to provide a comparison. Stansted was ranked ninth. The cost–benefit analysis had been dominated by passenger user costs and the Commission accepted that planning items were not covered by

Figure 3.2 Existing major airports at the time of the Roskill Commission (shown by circles) and sites shortlisted by the Commission for a new airport (shown by rectangles)
(Commission on the Third London Airport, 1971)

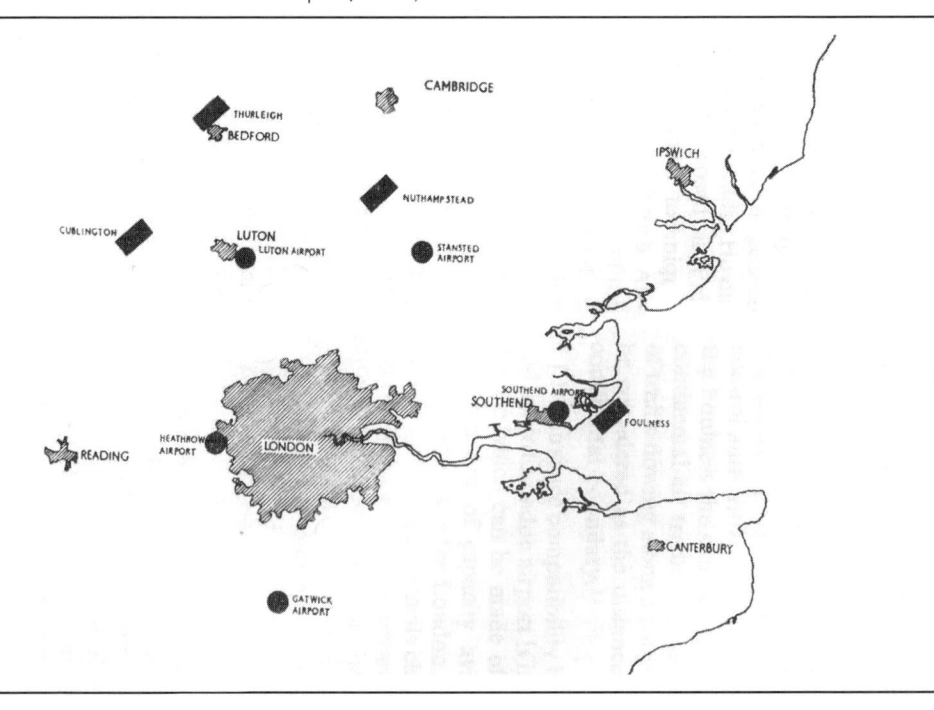

this analysis (Hall, 1982). In 1971 the Commission unanimously recommended that there was a need for additional airport capacity and all but one of the Commissioners recommended that it should be provided at Cublington. One of the Commissioners, Colin Buchanan, recommended Foulness. The government accepted the minority recommendation for the Foulness site and the project, renamed Maplin, began.

A number of views were expressed in retrospect about the process. The Roskill Commission had been set up as a reaction to the previous failure of decision-making (the Chelmsford Inquiry of 1965–1966 and subsequent events). The Commission's method of working – with a research team, use of cost–benefit analysis, plus public hearings – was intended as a rational way to make decisions (Hogwood and Gunn, 1984). For its time, it used some very advanced techniques, in particular cost–benefit analysis.[1] Economist Christopher Foster described the important contributions to the development of the technique made by Michael Beesley, one of the Commissioners (Foster, 2001) and Needham (2014) notes that the Treasury had admired the use of CBA in the Commission's work. On the other hand, there was criticism from planner Nathaniel Lichfield (1971) for the analysis's treatment of regional planning and for its comparisons of different groups, and from geographer Peter Self (1970), who described it as 'nonsense on stilts'. Self's criticism was partly rebuffed by Alan Walters, a member of the Commission, who noted that, in effect, the financial totals of costs and benefits were less important than the differences in these amounts between the sites, as decisions need only be concerned with the differential costs. Walters used the analogy of 'the height of the wave' (the relative differences) being more important than 'the depth of the sea' (the financial totals) (Walters, 1978: p 143). In terms of numbers, the passenger user costs (essentially, the value of passengers' time taken to access the airport) were £207 million more at Foulness than at Cublington, whereas the noise costs were only £13 million more at Cublington than Foulness, and no other cost differences were as great as the passenger user costs (Commission on the Third London Airport, 1971). While the costs can be properly calculated based on evidence, this major difference caused disquiet.

As mentioned above, the Commission's majority recommendation for Cublington was overturned by the government, who preferred Buchanan's minority recommendation for the Foulness site (later renamed Maplin). Needham (2014) notes that Prime Minister Edward Heath was of the opinion that the pressures on the environment that would be created by an inland site, such as the one at Cublington, would be so outrageous that they must be allowed to outweigh any small financial advantage of a more central site. Foster (2001) was critical of this minority recommendation, saying that Buchanan 'was able to overthrow his colleagues' unanimous decision to recommend Cublington' (p. 16), and that the minority report, which 'had passages of purple prose but no quantification', had 'triumphed' (p. 16). Furthermore, Foster stated, 'The effect on administrators of the Roskill debacle would be hard to overstate, as they saw the most important weapon in the battle for rationality and decisions about transport investment and subsidy lose credibility among politicians and the public' (p. 17). As will be discussed in Chapter 6, the Maplin project was later cancelled, causing considerable dismay among some parties, particularly local authorities and groups representing residents around existing airports and potential new inland sites, who feared their locations would now be reconsidered for expansion. However, Needham (2014) asserts that the Treasury, which had been 'playing it long', was content that a public expenditure commitment had been curtailed. There is therefore little agreement on why the Roskill Commission process did not lead to a long-term policy solution for increasing London's airport capacity.

Geoff Ambrose, who managed many of BAA's inquiry teams over many years, told me that BAA's limited input to the Roskill Commission exposed a difference of opinion between the then chairman, Peter Masefield, and the director of planning, Norman Payne. Masefield continued to press for Stansted to be considered, despite it not making the shortlist, while Payne accepted that the decision had been made and was content to debate the merits of the shortlisted sites. Ambrose also reminded me that after the government had decided on Maplin, the precise airport site was moved, which added to the expense of the project, and that the costs and risks of clearing and relocating the Ministry of Defence (MoD) firing ranges became unacceptable.

3.6. The end of an era

The cancellation of the Maplin project in 1974 marked a clear turning point in the way in which airports policy evolved in the UK. It is for this reason that events prior to 1974 have been described only briefly in the early chapters of this book, whereas events after 1974 will be examined in greater detail from Chapter 6 onwards. The years before and during WW2, and for 20 years after the end of the war, saw governments taking the lead in trying to establish an airports policy, with some success until the mid 1960s, when the Stansted plans were rejected. The Roskill Commission was an attempt not necessarily to regain control of policy, but to see it based on rational evidence. But that also failed when the government of the day ignored the Commission's (majority) conclusions, and then had to abandon the policy when circumstances changed. The next 25 years would witness a much more pragmatic process emerge, as we shall see in the remaining chapters.

Notes

1. Cost–benefit analysis (CBA) is a systematic approach employed to estimate the strengths and weaknesses of alternatives (for example in transactions, activities, functional business requirements or projects investments); it is used to determine options that provide the best approach to achieve benefits while preserving savings. The CBA is also defined as a systematic process for calculating and comparing benefits and costs of a decision, policy (with particular regard to government policy) or project (David et al., 2013).

REFERENCES

Abercrombie P (1945) *The Greater London Plan 1944*. HMSO, London, UK.
Ares E, Barclay C, Butcher L and Mellows-Facer A (2009) *Expansion of Heathrow Airport*. Research paper RP09/11, House of Commons Library, London, UK.
BAA (1967) *Report and Accounts, 1965–67*. HMSO, London, UK.
Board of Trade (1967) *The Third London Airport*. Cmnd 3259, HMSO, London, UK.
Cashinella B and Thompson K (1971) *Permission to Land*. Arlington Books, London, UK.
Commission on the Third London Airport (1971) *Report*. HMSO, London, UK.
David R, Ngulube P and Dube A (2013) A cost–benefit analysis of document management strategies used at a financial institution in Zimbabwe: a case study. *SA Journal of Information Management* **15(2)**: 2.
Donne M (1991) *Above Us The Skies: The Story of BAA*. Good Books, Whitley, UK.
Foster CD (2001) Michael Beesley and cost benefit analysis. *Journal of Transport Economics and Policy* **35(1)**: 3–30.
Hall P (1982) *Great Planning Disasters*. University of California Press, Berkeley, CA, USA.
Helsey M and Codd F (2014) *Aviation: Proposals for an Airport in the Thames Estuary 1945–2014*. Standard Note: SN/BT/4920, House of Commons Library, London, UK.
HL Deb 11 December 1967, vol. 287, col. 1002.
Hogwood BW and Gunn LA (1984) *Policy Analysis for the Real World*. Oxford University Press, Oxford, UK.
Lichfield N (1971) Cost–benefit analysis in planning: a critique of the Roskill Commission. *Regional Studies* **5**: 157–183.

Meyrick D (1983) *Civil Aviation and Land Use Planning: The Case of London's Terminal Airports, 1919–1946*. PhD thesis, Birkbeck College, University of London, London, UK.

Needham DJ (2014) Maplin, the Treasury and London's third airport in the 1970s. Submitted to: *Twentieth Century British History*.

Sanders P (2016) *On the Beaten Track – A History of Stansted Mountfitchet*. Stansted Mountfitchet Local History Society, Stansted Mountfitchet, UK.

Self P (1970) Nonsense on stilts: cost–benefit analysis and the Roskill Commission. *Political Quarterly* **41(3)**: 249–260.

Self P (2002) The evolution of the Greater London Plan, 1944–1970. *Progress in Planning* **57(3-4)**: 145–175.

Sherwood P (2009) *Heathrow: 2000 Years of History*. The History Press, Stroud, UK.

Walters A (1978) Airports: an economic survey. *Journal of Transport Economics and Policy* **12(2)**: 125–160.

Chapter 4
Airports in the wider planning-policy context

4.1. Introduction

Chapters 2 and 3 summarised the history of aviation and the evolution of airports policy up to the Maplin project. This chapter considers the context in which airports policy is developed by describing the evolution of planning, the relationship between airports and their local economies, and the particular issues in transport planning, with a brief comparison with some other sectors. It then describes the current planning regime in the UK, and how planning and politics are intertwined. Finally in this chapter is a short foray into some of the theories of political decision-making, to hypothesise how airports policy relates to other areas of policymaking.

4.2. Why plan? The evolution of planning

Sager (1992) provided the traditional rationale for planning as the correction of the deficiencies of the market mechanism, stating also that planning is the preparation for collective decisions and for their implementation. Another definition, from Hall and Tewdwr-Jones (2011), is that planning, as a general activity, is the making of an orderly sequence of actions that will lead to the achievement of stated goals, often involving the reconciliation of competing objectives. Cities have been planned for millennia, but modern urban and regional planning in the UK arose in response to specific social and economic problems in the nineteenth century, initially related to public health (ibid). The history of urban planning includes the work of pioneers such as Ebenezer Howard, Raymond Unwin, Barry Parker and many others who were looking for the 'city beautiful' or a 'new Jerusalem' (Hall, 2002). The first true planning legislation, The Housing, Town Planning etc. Act of 1909, included the word 'amenity' and, in subsequent legal judgments, it became clear that the landowner's economic interests could be overridden by community rights, and the 1947 Town and Country Planning Act limited compensation to landowners (Millichap, 1995). As planning has evolved in the UK, it has moved from the production of blueprints for a desired future state towards a continuous series of controls over development, and from a process of survey–analysis–plan to a continuous cycle (Hall and Tewdwr-Jones, 2011). Government guidance on planning is that it is 'designed to regulate the development and use of land in the public interest', but public interest is difficult to define (Millichap, 1995).

Businesses plan to ensure they can be profitable and survive, in particular when making an investment decision. In the public sector, the goals are likely to be wider than profitability, and may include broader economic and social benefits, or seek to allocate scarce resources between different sectors. Cost–benefit analysis, as used in the Roskill Commission (see Chapter 3), is one of the methodologies used to assist in this.

4.3. Airports and their local economies

There is no doubt that airports are a vital ingredient in the economies of the countries or regions they serve. However, the benefits were not quantified in earlier studies, such as those of the Roskill Commission, but rather were considered as part of the regional planning implications. Thus, for example, it was recognised that jobs would be created which would require urban development to provide housing for employees, and that firms would be attracted to a new airport, but the main concern was that these pressures should be aligned with the regional plans then being developed and would not overheat the local economies (Commission on the Third London Airport, 1971). It was not until the 1990s that the value of employment and other economic benefits from airports were brought into the equation. The economic impact can be measured in various ways, starting with the basic number of jobs at the airport for the airport operator, airlines, control agencies and the myriad of service providers. There are also related jobs in hotels, freight companies and others who directly provide services, and then jobs which follow from those directly employed, such as shops, local trades and even public sector employees providing services to the local population. The multiplier can sometimes be two or three times the directly related number of jobs. Beyond these, there are companies that locate near to an airport to make use of its connectivity. With major airports this can include offices of worldwide companies who need to connect to the rest of the world, and even small airports can attract international organisations if they have links with a hub. Similarly, exporters and importers can benefit from being close to the air-freight services. It has also been argued that London's status as a world city in terms of its key activities – such as financial services, creative industries and culture – is partly due to the worldwide connectivity provided through its airports. The impact of these effects is more difficult to measure and has been the subject of some controversy in a number of studies. One issue that has been questioned by those opposing airport expansion is the balance of tourism benefits, because UK outbound tourists have sometimes spent more money abroad than foreign inbound tourists have in the UK. Some have also questioned the morality of cheap flights that enable short breaks for UK tourists, but this is probably a social rather than an economic issue.

In general terms, the economic impact of an airport is usually seen as beneficial. There have been occasions when new jobs have been seen as a problem in a tight labour market, perhaps leading to extra house-building for the new employees. This was a contentious issue at the Airports Inquiries of 1981–1983 (see Chapter 6) because Stansted's growth would be from a low base and there were few large towns in the area. However, it has not been so much of an issue at Heathrow, because the labour-supply catchment area contains a much higher population. It is undoubtedly the case that the groups that support airport expansion are usually associated with the economic impact, such as business organisations, chambers of commerce and trade unions.

The final measure of all the economic impacts is usually given as a monetary sum in terms of Gross Value Added. This is a difficult concept for non-economists to fully understand, especially as it is often quoted as a present value over many years, and as a net amount after deducting disbenefits. For some studies, it has then been compared with other monetary measures, such as the time savings for passengers in accessing the airport (another concept not always understood) and even monetary values for environmental impacts. In most studies, the monetary comparison is given alongside measures in the 'original' units, such as the number of people affected by a particular level of noise, and the judgement of the balance is left to the political decision-makers.

Regional planning seeks to identify particular parts of a region where growth is encouraged, and other areas of restraint. In Chapter 3, Abercrombie's Greater London Plan was noted as an early example of regional planning, and London has had a number of regional plans, in particular since the establishment of a mayor and the Greater London Authority. Regional planning in other parts of the country has had only limited success, although the more recent establishment of city regions and mayors may see a revival. Regional plans seek to align growth zones with transport facilities, and various attempts at South East regional planning outside London have noted the Thames Valley (west of London) and the London–Cambridge and London–Brighton corridors, each linked in part with the airports. The Thames Gateway concept has also been linked from time to time with a Thames Estuary airport plan, most recently when Boris Johnson was Mayor of London. However, despite the championing of regional planning by such eminent academics as Peter Hall, it has often been the case that the regional plan has followed airport expansion rather than determined it and, in the case of London, drafts of the regional plan have been in conflict with airport expansion, the final versions then having to be amended to align with national policy.

4.4. Transport planning: vital but low down the pecking order

Planning transport infrastructure, including airports, draws on aspects of urban and regional planning, as well as business planning. Transport infrastructure is a vital social and economic asset which influences trade flows as well as the locations of industry and residential development. Significant public funding is required for construction and maintenance and it has significant environmental effects, with decisions having impacts that last for decades, even centuries. Transport infrastructure is highly visible to the public and its planning and financing are often controversial locally, nationally and even internationally (Short and Kopp, 2005).

Planning for infrastructure often requires a long time horizon, given that the assets have a lengthy physical and financial life. For example, airport runways have a financial life of maybe 50 years and cannot be moved. This can be compared with airline planning, where the key assets (aircraft) are very mobile and can be used at many different locations and may also be available on short-term financial leases.

Planning for airports allows for orderly development, ensures safety and efficiency, and safeguards land for future development. Airport master plans have been produced over many years but were a particular requirement of the 2003 White Paper (see Chapter 8). Master plans are for individual airports and were regarded as the centrepiece of airport planning, charting the proposed evolution of the airport through the provision of guidelines for future development that will satisfy aviation demand and will be compatible with the environment, community development and other modes of transportation. However, an airport master plan is not the same as an application for planning permission, which is described in section 4.5 of this chapter.

Glaister *et al.* (2006), in a review of transport planning in Britain, remind us that the Department for Transport (DfT) and its predecessors are certainly not the only policymakers and may not even be the most important, and much of their role is coordinating the views of other departments. We will see in later chapters the influence of the Treasury, although this has been far from absolute, in particular since the privatisations, which mean that most expenditure is by the private sector. The roles of departments covering environmental issues have been significant, in part because these at one time covered local government. The Home Office also plays a role related to its policing and border-control activities. At one time, aviation was covered by the Department of Trade (DoT), separate from other transport responsibilities, but the current business and trade departments are concerned with aviation manufacturing. In addition, transport policy is subject to international regulation, particularly so for aviation because of its international nature. Transport is sometimes seen as a location for ministers on the rise or on their way down, but rarely one for longevity, although there have been exceptions, such as Alistair Darling (2002–2006) and Patrick McLoughlin (2012–2016). Glaister *et al.* (2006) note, 'It remains rare for a prime minister to take much interest in transport policy' (p. 67).

4.5. The UK planning system

Airport planning in the UK is part of a wider process of spatial planning but, as ownership has moved from public towards the private sector, airport planning is no longer the responsibility of central government. Instead the government sets a policy framework within which the industry can operate, with a significant degree of local and community involvement.

The UK planning system is plan-led, meaning that decisions should be made in the context of a wider development plan (Rhodes, 2008). Requests for planning consent for a particular development should be tested for conformity with the wider plan. However, in many sectors, not least in airports, the wider plan has been difficult to create and sustain, as will become clear in the chronology of the decisions and events described in later chapters. Various attempts have been made over many years to create regional plans to give this wider context. In England, the regions are very diverse and it has not proved possible to produce a consistent mechanism. London, which has traditionally had a strong regional tradition, has been able to produce regional plans since the Abercrombie plans produced during World War 2 up to the London Plan of today. However, even here there have been challenges, such as the degree of influence of the capital over the surrounding 'home counties', which has persisted from the time when the London County Council outgrew its boundaries. Heathrow is within the current Greater London Authority (GLA) boundary, but Gatwick, Stansted and Luton airports are not. This influence of the capital has in turn meant that a South East regional plan has always been a challenge. Currently, regional planning outside London is very limited and is within the remit of the Local Development Agencies, which are amalgams of local authority and business interests and are not at all consistent in many respects.

Although regional planning has not been consistent, there are some elements of the planning regime that have been long-standing, such as National Parks, Areas of Outstanding Natural Beauty (AONB), green belt and other designations. National Parks were established by a White Paper in 1945 and an Act of Parliament in 1949 and the Peak District was the first to be designated. There are currently 15 National Parks in the UK and the aims include conservation of the landscape and public access. The planning regime strictly controls development in National Parks and although there have been controversies relating to some activities, such as mineral extraction, there have been no major conflicts between airport development and National Parks. An AONB is an area designated for conservation for its landscape value, and there are 46 in England and Wales. Development is also strictly controlled but there have been examples of transport and other developments being permitted. There are AONBs close to some of the major London airports, such as the Chilterns near Heathrow, the High Weald near Gatwick and the Surrey Hills near both Heathrow and Gatwick. There have been no proposals for major airport development in the South East AONBs, but transport routes and residential development that in part serve the major airports may impact on AONBs, and many AONBs are overflown by aircraft from the airports. Green belt designation is a long-running, and in many ways highly successful, designation, but its purpose is sometimes misunderstood. As the name partly implies, these are areas around cities in which development is restricted to prevent urban sprawl, maintain openness, prevent towns merging, preserve the siting of historic towns and assist in urban regeneration. The use of 'green' in the title is sometimes misinterpreted because landscape appearance is not a prime objective. Land around all of London's major airports is designated as green belt and this is often raised as grounds for an objection to airport development. The site for Terminal 5 at Heathrow, between the two runways and occupied by the Perry Oaks sludge disposal works, was designated as green belt, despite its appearance and use. Development can be permitted in green belt areas only if there are 'very special circumstances'. For Terminal 5, these very special circumstances, as accepted by the government decision to grant approval, were the overriding economic benefits and the lack of an alternative site.

There are many other planning designations, some related to nature conservation, others to employment or other types of use, and these are shown in Local Plans produced by local authorities after consultation and examination. Many of these designations are relevant considerations in deciding applications for airport development.

There are four options for obtaining permission for developments in the UK: a private or hybrid parliamentary bill, a Development Consent Order (DCO) for a Nationally Significant Infrastructure Project (NSIP), a Transport and Works Act Order, or planning permission under the Town and Country Planning Act (Bassford, 2015). Each is appropriate for different types of development and has different requirements in terms of timescales, evidence, consultation and policy background. Parliamentary bills have been used for many railway developments, while the DCO/NSIP process is relatively new but is being used for a wide range of developments, including wind farms and transport schemes, and for the proposed Heathrow third runway. For most of the period covered by this research, the most commonly used option for airports was the Town and Country Planning Act. Under this regime, the applicant, usually the airport operator, applies to the local planning authority for planning permission. The local planning authority can either grant the permission (often with conditions) or refuse it. The applicant may appeal against a refusal, in which case the appeal is referred to the Planning Inspectorate, an executive agency of the Ministry of Housing, Communities and Local Government (MHCLG). An inspector is appointed and a public inquiry may be held, after which the inspector makes a recommendation to the MHCLG. The MHCLG will then decide whether to allow the appeal and grant permission, or refuse it. For airport developments, the decision is usually made jointly by the MHCLG and the DfT (Cullingworth and Nadin, 2002). Glaister *et al.* (2006) noted the unsatisfactory nature of the planning application process for major transport infrastructure projects, and subsequently it has been superseded by the NSIP/DCO process.

While some may argue to the contrary, in particular in relation to the way it deals with major developments such as airports, the UK system is generally considered to be one of the best in the world, being able to preserve historic value while enabling growth, free of corruption, democratic and fair.

Although airports have to get approval for major developments such as a new runway or terminal, they are able to implement some developments without specific permission, under powers known as GPDO (General Permitted Development Order). These powers apply across a wide range of developers, from a householder who can build an extension within certain limits, to the construction of transport facilities. There are limits to the type and size of permitted development and, for airports, a terminal of more than 500 square metres would not be permitted and a runway cannot be constructed or extended. In addition, although a development may be permitted, there are requirements for consultation and notification. In practice, GPDO rights are used only for smaller development of operational facilities, although there are sometimes disputes about the scope. In the mid 1970s, BAA argued that the proposed Terminal 4 should be permitted under GPDO powers (in order to limit the time before the start of construction). However, the legislation includes an appeal process and the London Borough of Hounslow sought, and was granted, an Article 4 Direction (named after the relevant article in the legislation), which required a full planning application to be made.

The length of some airport (and other major infrastructure project) inquiries was part of the reason for introducing a new process for NSIPs in the 2008 Planning Act, which has been modified by the 2011 Localism Act and refined through a number of regulations. For airport proposals that lead to an increase of more than 10 million passengers per annum, the first stage is for Parliament to approve a National Policy Statement (NPS). Once the NPS is approved, the developer can then apply for a DCO, which is then considered by a time-limited consultation and inquiry process. The third runway at Heathrow may be the first airport scheme to be considered under this process, although a number of other transport schemes have been dealt with this way (motorways, rail-freight interchanges, rail improvements).

The appropriateness of the UK planning process for dealing with airport developments, particularly major expansions, is a matter of contention. Walters (1978: p. 142), discussing the Roskill Commission, discounts the statements of 'eminent town planners' as *ex cathedra*. Walters is scathing about planners in general, claiming that 'with understandable professional chauvinism, planners have often proclaimed that decisions about airport investment are first and foremost issues that should be determined by planning criteria'; however, 'in practice, planning has no methodological discipline and no way of organising evidence in a coherent form beyond the form that appears in cost–benefit analysis' (p. 142). At a more local level, Humphreys *et al.* (2007) note that the planning system can block developments but does not plan strategically and there is a dichotomy between government policy and a private operator's objectives. The question of whether the inquiry system is the right kind of mechanism for this type of decision is considered by Farrington (1984), who suggests that terms of reference should be 'determined by common agreement' (p. 179).

4.6. Policymaking in other sectors: HS2 and nuclear power

This is a very wide field, which I do not attempt to cover comprehensively, but I do suggest two current sectors that provide interesting comparisons. Perhaps the most obvious and closest policy decisions are in relation to large infrastructure projects. Particular examples in the UK at present are High Speed 2 (HS2) and nuclear power stations.

HS2 is a transport project that is a step change for the railway network, the last of which took place more than 100 years ago with the building of the last of the main railway lines, the Great Central. Like major airport development, it is subject to local opposition from people along the route, and from some national concern that money spent on it will mean less money elsewhere for vital transport projects. However, there is also UK-wide, cross-party support and the third reading of the bill was approved in the House of Commons by 399 votes to 42 (HC Deb 23 March 2016) and then by the House of Lords. The bill received royal assent in February 2017, and the first phase should be completed by 2026. It is primarily a public sector and publicly financed project and probably the greatest threat to its completion will be the ability to finance the project from the public purse. Although there have been proposals for high-speed rail lines over many years, none ever got as far as a parliamentary bill, except for the Channel Tunnel Rail Link (CTRL), which became HS1 and opened in stages between 2003 and 2007. The CTRL project was linked to the Channel Tunnel project, which opened in 1994. Planning for the CTRL was subject to a number of decisions and counter-decisions, in particular relating to the route, and then later to financial challenges, which are described in detail by Schabas (2017). However, the period between the opening of the Channel Tunnel and the completion of HS1 was 13 years, a far shorter timescale than for development projects at South East airports.

Nuclear power stations have also received parliamentary support in principle from a National Policy Statement on Energy. There is some opposition from anti-nuclear groups, but only limited local opposition at the individual sites. Although the power stations will be financed and delivered by the private sector, there is public finance involved by way of guaranteed prices for electricity, so the greatest risk to non-completion is the ability of the government to afford the guarantee. Previous planning inquiries into particular sites were, like some airport inquiries, very drawn out. The Sizewell B Inquiry took three years, at around the same time as the 1981–1983 Airports Inquiries, and held the record for the longest inquiry until Heathrow Terminal 5. The length of the inquiry, along with Terminal 5 and others, was part of the reason for the new process established in the 2008 Planning Act for National Policy Statements.

Other public policy decision-making in the UK includes areas such as social welfare policies, health provision and education, all of which involve much higher public spending than transport. Airports involve relatively small amounts of public spending, as do some other sectors, such as water, telecommunications and energy, where public policy decision-making is therefore similar.

Wherever parallels are sought, there are usually special factors making it difficult to transfer lessons. Perhaps the key lesson is that long-term certainty, which is sought by all parties in the aviation debate, is best achieved by the balance of national views, essentially agreed by Parliament, and the reconciliation of local concerns by mitigation measures and legally binding agreements.

4.7. Politics and policy

The distinction between politics and policy is that the former tends to be thought of as the actions of politicians and their political parties, whereas the latter is a plan of action or a set of rules. In this section, I try to distinguish between politics and policy and show how, for airports, policy is sometimes, but not always, influenced by politics. I do this by considering a range of interactions: the quasi-judicial role of the Secretary of State, the geography of constituencies, elections, the views of political parties and the activities of Parliament.

The UK planning system, as described above, mostly relies on non-political individuals (council officers and inquiry inspectors) to determine the outcome of applications and inquiries. However, for major developments, the final decision, under the relevant Act of Parliament, is made by the appropriate Secretary of State. For some airport cases the decision is made jointly by the Secretaries of State for Transport and for Local Government. The Secretary of State is, of course, an elected MP appointed to the post by the prime minister. It is open to the Secretary of State to accept or reject the recommendation of an inquiry inspector, although decisions are always open to challenge on legal grounds. There are many examples of Secretaries of State not accepting recommendations, but the last major airport case where this occurred was in 1967, when Douglas Jay, president of the Board of Trade (aviation at that time came under the Board of Trade), overruled an inspector's recommendation and announced the go-ahead for Stansted (see Chapter 3). However, this caused such a furore that the government reversed the decision within a few months. Since then, none of the major decisions on airports in the South East have gone against the key recommendation, although there have been plenty of occasions when a subsidiary recommendation (for example, about a condition) has not been followed. However, as noted above, such decisions are open to legal challenge and ministers are increasingly wary of not following a recommendation lest the decision is challenged.

Undoubtedly a Secretary of State will be influenced by politics and, legal challenges notwithstanding, the system is deliberately designed to include political considerations in the final decision. The Roskill Commission sought a technocratic answer to the question by seeking to put a cost on each element, but it was clear that judgement would be required to balance the different aspects and this judgement should properly come only from an elected person. Having said that, it will become clear from the evidence of briefing papers and interviews that many Secretaries of State were prepared to accept the recommendations of their officials and did not seek to influence the decisions by political considerations. There are exceptions to this, one of which was described to me by Steven Norris, who was a Minister of Transport in the 1990s. The Conservatives had won the 1992 election, perhaps somewhat to their surprise, and were concerned about the ability of the government to serve a full term. When the RUCATSE study (see Chapter 7) produced a rather inconclusive report, it suited the government not to raise any controversial issues and so 'masterly inactivity' was the result. This stance was also apparent in wider transport policy, with a 1996 response to the Houghton Report on transport and the environment being described in the press as 'transport paper opts for easy route' (Glaister et al., 2006).

The next interaction between politics and policy comes from the geography of constituencies. One former civil servant characterised this to me as 'the map of red and blue'. For general elections to Parliament, outside London most of the South East is blue (Conservative) and the constituencies around the major airports have mostly been served by Conservative MPs. Within London, some seats have swung back and forth over the years, and the Liberal Democrats have also had some successes. Airport development is often an issue in some constituencies at elections, but it is difficult to know how significant it is when compared with national issues such as the economy, the NHS or immigration. Results have not particularly demonstrated how candidates who opposed or supported airport developments have fared. One of the 2017 election campaigns where airports had a high profile was in Richmond Park, where Zac Goldsmith, a prominent anti-Heathrow-expansion MP, won with a very small majority, but his opponent was a sitting Liberal Democrat MP, who also opposed Heathrow expansion. The location of constituencies in relation to the airports also has a significant effect on the views of its electorate. If you live under a flight path, you may well object to the noise and overflying, as do many of the residents in Richmond or Hammersmith. However, other constituencies which are the same distance from Heathrow but do not have overflying aircraft, such as Ruislip or Spelthorne, do not take such a strong anti-airport stance. The benefits of airport employment are also a key factor, with many residents of Spelthorne (near Heathrow) or Crawley (near Gatwick) supporting the airports. Steven Norris was the MP for Oxford East from 1983 until 1987 and then for Epping Forest from 1988 until 1997. Neither of these constituencies included a major airport, although they were not far away, and Epping Forest District Council was an objector to the Stansted proposals at the 1981–1983 Airports Inquiries. Airport issues were rarely raised by constituents in Norris's postbag, although he believes that aviation has intensified in recent years, and is now an issue for people living in a wider area, not just in the immediate vicinity of an airport.

Alan Haselhurst (now Sir Alan) was the MP for Saffron Walden, the constituency that includes Stansted, from 1977 to 2017, and had previously represented Middleton and Prestwich in Greater Manchester. He consistently opposed proposals for the expansion of Stansted, reflecting his postbag, but he also recognised the benefits of the airport and, once permissions were granted, his lobbying activity moved towards making the airport work better, in particular by improving rail access. He was Deputy Speaker from 1997 to 2010, which meant that he was unable to speak in debates in the House of Commons, but this position provided him with much greater access to ministers, and he was not prevented from stating his views in the constituency.

The primary role of an MP is to represent his or her constituents, and many MPs express their views in parliamentary debates, at public inquiries and in supporting or opposing expansion proposals. Opposition is more likely, for the simple reason that people are more likely to seek action if they oppose something than if they support it. Nevertheless, there are examples of support for airport expansion from MPs – for example, the MP for Crawley has generally supported growth at Gatwick even though the constituency has elected both Labour and Conservative MPs. In parliamentary debates, MPs tend to follow their constituency line but, with 650 MPs in total, the number opposing expansion at any particular site is often quite small. For the various London airport expansion proposals, many MPs have supported expansion because it enhances the connectivity of their region with London (this is particularly the case with Scottish and Northern Irish MPs). Others are either neutral or at least have no objections and thus, in a free vote, such proposals are often supported with a large majority, as with HS2. Parliamentary debates may be on a statement, a published policy, a bill, or by various other devices such as an adjournment debate or a ten-minute-rule bill, or in the smaller Westminster Hall.[1] In this book, parliamentary debates on airports policy are mentioned in each of the chapters covering the main periods and also in Chapter 10 on the themes.

As well as parliamentary debates, MPs can get involved in select committees whose role is to scrutinise government activity and suggest changes to policies. The Transport Committee has held inquiries into airports policy from time to time, and pushed particularly hard for the break-up of BAA in the 2000s. The Transport Committee has generally been supportive of the proposals for a third runway at Heathrow. Other committees have also inquired into airports issues, and the Environmental Audit Committee has been particularly critical of government airports policy because of its relationship to climate change policy. The most recent Transport Committee Inquiry into the draft National Policy Statement is covered in Chapter 9.

Local authorities also have elected members and naturally take a more local view of issues, with party politics taking perhaps a slightly lesser priority. Planning applications are made first to local authorities and, even though major airport proposals usually end up at public inquiries with decisions made by the Secretary of State, it is local authority planning departments which have the major input into those inquiries, with the local authority's stance being endorsed by their planning committee, or sometimes the full council. Some local authorities complain that they are not sufficiently resourced to fight major inquiries, although they often join with neighbouring authorities or the second tier (county or GLA) to pool resources. Local authorities also have to deal with managing the conditions attached to a permission, and to the myriad of smaller applications that are made by an airport, and so have to have a reasonable degree of expertise.

Over the period covered by this book there have been two main political parties, Conservative and Labour, with the Liberals as a third party, merging into the Liberal Democrats in 1988. Since 1974, the party of government has been as follows

- 1974–1979 Labour (with some time as a minority party)
- 1979–1997 Conservative
- 1997–2010 Labour
- 2010–2015 Conservative–Liberal Democrat coalition
- 2015–2017 Conservative
- 2017– Conservative (minority, with Democratic Unionist Party support).

As will be shown in later chapters, airports policy sometimes changed when the party changed at an election (in particular in 2010), but this was not always the case. Traditionally, Labour was the party that sought employment and social welfare and was strong in urban areas, while the Conservatives were more aligned with business and were strong in the shires. However, for airports policy, this simple distinction has often not applied, although some elements are apparent in the Conservatives' general opposition to airport developments that affect rural areas, or Labour's support for the growth of employment. But the Labour governments of 1997 to 2010 were very supportive of business and Steven Norris told me that, in his view, their persistence with the Heathrow third runway proposals in the late 2000s (see Chapter 8) was part of Gordon Brown's (and Tony Blair's) efforts to show the business community that they were 'on their side'.

The two main political parties' stances on environmental issues have also wavered, although the Liberal Democrats have consistently opposed expansion on both local and global environmental grounds. Labour embraced the green agenda in the 1990s – the decade of the Rio Earth Summit, the Kyoto Protocol and other international actions – but did not respond to the growing concerns about the relationship to airports policy in the 2000s. While in opposition, the Conservatives established a Quality of Life Policy Group, led by John Gummer and Zac Goldsmith, with Steven

Norris leading a transport working group. The 500-page report produced by the Quality of Life Policy Group was highly critical of a policy of aviation growth and led to the Conservatives' 2010 election manifesto commitment to cancel the then proposals for additional runways at Stansted and Heathrow. Subsequently, as members of the coalition government with the Liberal Democrats, the Conservatives had no difficulty in implementing this policy. However, within two years, they had established the Airports Commission to look again at the issue and Steven Norris is very critical of Cameron for later turning his back on his 'no ifs, no buts' statement (Wickham, 2009), with Cameron allegedly referring to 'green crap' (Mason, 2013) and then taking what Norris describes as the 'cynical' step of deferring the Airports Commission's report until after the 2015 election.

While the main political parties' stances on airport expansion were not markedly different, they did differ on ownership. Some transport industries had been denationalised in the 1950s (such as road haulage), but it was the Conservative governments of 1979 to 1997 that privatised British Airways, BAA, the National Bus Company and, eventually, the railways. However, the Labour governments of 1997 to 2010 did not re-nationalise any of these, and in fact continued privatisation of the National Air Traffic Services (NATS).

Finally, in seeking to understand the impact of politics on airport planning policy, it is worth looking at the conclusions of Glaister *et al.* (2006: p. 40) about transport policy generally:

> British transport policy may have been nudged over the years by politicians from either end of the political spectrum, now towards more competition, now towards a stronger emphasis on coordination and integration, but the ever-changing, kaleidoscopic pattern has always been influenced by a powerful streak of British pragmatism.

In terms of airports policy, pragmatism may be seen in some of the decisions that seek compromise and short-term solutions but which are not radical and do not provide long-term certainty.

4.8. Theories of decision-making: muddling through the policy swamp

This section is a very brief summary of some of the theories of decision-making and their relationship to the decisions made about airports policy for London over the last 40 years.

Collis and Hussey (2009) provide a guide to business research and suggest that one of the steps is to identify the research paradigm (the pattern or model of the research). The spectrum is from positivism, which is generally associated with quantitative methods, to interpretivism, in which results are generally induced from the evidence. The research for this book has been towards the interpretivist end of the spectrum and, in terms of theoretical underpinning, the search has therefore been to understand if the various theories of decision-making fit or explain the events described in this book.

Ison (2004), in a book about road user charging, provides a basic review of the theories of decision-making, referring to the work of Parsons, Howlett and Ramesh, Lindblom and Woodhouse, Hogwood and Gunn, Hill, Simon and Dror. Parsons (1995) notes that the dominant framework of policy analysis is to consider the stages and these can be matched to the phases of applied problem-solving (Howlett and Ramesh, 1995). However, this staged approach is criticised by Lindblom and Woodhouse (1993), Hill (2013) and Parsons (1995) as it is continuous rather than a discrete process, in a 'primeval soup' (Lindblom and Woodhouse, 1993).

The two main approaches to decision-making theory are the rational approach described by Simon and the incremental approach of Lindblom (Ison, 2004). The rational decision-making approach involves choosing from options to meet objectives, limiting the aspects considered, intelligence gathering, identifying all options, assessing the consequences, relating them to values, and then choosing. Criticism of the rational approach includes the question of whose objectives and values are set and noting that there is no rational way of resolving conflicts, and that rationality is bounded. The incremental approach works from the branches as opposed to the roots, deals with incremental rather than absolute comparisons and involves agreement between groups and trial and error. The incremental approach is criticised as being anti-innovation and pro-inertia.

Lindblom and Woodhouse (1993), in describing the policymaking process, make a number of key observations, including: 'There are sharp constraints on what can be achieved through policy analysis and other rational methods for understanding social problems... Disagreements... cannot be washed away by even the most rigorous analysis' (p. vii) and 'Political interactions and flawed human judgements play a primary role in making policy, and these necessarily involve partisan disagreements that are settled by voting or other manifestations of power' (p. vii). They also observe the roles of certain groups in policymaking. Many low-income groups are not well represented and have little influence. Interest groups are seen to get more from government and can obstruct change, but not control such change when they want the government to act. According to Lindblom and Woodhouse, the business sector introduces problems through technological and entrepreneurial ingenuity, enjoys extraordinary tax favour and is listened to by governments with care reserved for no other group. Voters vote for who, not what, and many issues are not raised at elections. However, Lindblom and Woodhouse do not mention that businesses have no vote and, in my opinion, this partly balances the influence of business groups. It should also be noted that passengers from outside the UK, who are a significant minority of London airports' customers, do not vote in UK elections and therefore can exert no influence through this channel.

Lindblom had first identified the idea of 'muddling through' in 1959 (Hogwood and Gunn, 1984). By 1979, policymaking was 'still muddling, not yet through' (Lindblom, 1979) and in 2002, it had moved from 'muddling through to muddling up' (Parsons, 2002). Parsons noted that an early hope of the political science movement was that policymaking should be informed by knowledge but, in fact, it has for the most part been more about muddling through. There has been an inability to completely analyse complex problems in what has been described as the policy 'swamp', while uncertainty and change in human affairs mean there is little 'firm ground' on which to base evidence. Lindblom suggested that 'disjointed incrementalism' was better than 'formal completeness which degenerates into superficiality if not fraud' (1979: p. 519). On the other hand, the Plowden Report of 1961 into the control of government expenditure led to a 'planning mood' and concern over weaknesses in expenditure control in projects such as Concorde, the Channel Tunnel and the third London airport (Hogwood and Gunn, 1984). Parsons (2002) describes how, in 1997, the New Labour government sought a new relationship between social science and government, based on 'what works' and evidence, although he argues that this might not be democratic, and has resulted in more muddle.

Ham and Hill (1993) undertake a review of policymaking, considering the ideas of a wide range of theorists, adopting a definition of the subject and examining the causes and consequences of government action. They note the rise of pluralism in the way in which people engage with the state – a political marketplace where what a group achieves depends on its resources and its decibel rating and parties compete for power by responding to the demands of pressure groups. The authors suggest that, in testing decision-making, non-decisions (such as referring matters to a committee) should be noted alongside positive or negative decisions. The roles of civil servants are analysed, noting how they adjust to different political masters and advise how to make policies work, in the UK providing the real second chamber. The authors also discuss incrementalism, comparing it with the rational model of decision-making.

Hill (2013) describes the public policy process, noting first that 'Any discussion of the public policy process needs to be grounded in an extensive consideration of the nature of power in a state' (p. 8). There is a range of approaches, from pluralism to networks, and it is important to consider the role of institutions. Discussing the roles of groups, Hill suggests there is a triangle of actors: authorities, winners and losers. He also suggests that the power of the media is less than might be expected, and that few countries put as much faith in their civil servants as the UK.

Hogwood and Gunn (1984) also note that policy failure may come at the implementation stage, either because of bad execution, bad policy or bad luck, and suggest that this means there is no sharp divide between decision and implementation. They note a number of preconditions for implementation, several of which involve perfect conditions and are thus unlikely to be achieved.

Griggs and Howarth (2017), whose work is considered in more detail in Chapters 8 and 9, relate three particular statements of government airports policy to the theories of political discourse, drawing on the work of Laclau and Mouffe and Foucault. The three statements – 'a balanced approach', 'a genuinely sustainable policy' and 'deliver the maximum connectivity bang for each of our carbon bucks' – are analysed and the authors are able to show how they are related to elements of the theories.

In this brief excursion into the murky world of the theorists, it is possible to see that some of the events in the development of airports policy fit with or can be explained by these different approaches. Examples of the rational approach with evidence-based policymaking include the Roskill Commission of the late 1960s, the 2003 Future of Air Transport White Paper and the 2012–2015 Airports Commission. It is interesting to note that the first two of these did not lead to the implementation of the recommended strategy. The approach during the 1974–1991 and 1991–1999 periods was much more incremental, and included decisions to proceed with and the implementation of a number of airport projects. From the perspective of the aviation industry, therefore, muddling through is much more successful. So far, evidence-based policymaking, although initially leading to decisions to expand airport capacity, eventually led to policy reversals (in 1974 and 2010). However, it could also be argued that it was the steady growth of the evidence base of the impact of aviation on climate change that was a key factor in the reversal of the policy for additional runways in 2010. Ham and Hill's (1993) identification of non-decisions can certainly be seen in the numerous study groups, consultations and commissions that have taken place, such as ACAP/SGSEA in the late 1970s (see Chapter 6), RUCATSE in the 1990s (see Chapter 7) and the Airports Commission from 2012 to 2015. Hill (2013) uses pollution and airports policy as an example. He notes that pollution and climate-change policy owes a great deal to scientific advances, even though curbing the use of things that pollute may be unpopular (for example, if such a policy leads to the loss of jobs). Finally, one detail of the process shows how incrementalism has been used in a number of studies and inquiries. When considering the impact of an airport expansion proposal, for example in terms of noise, a comparison is made between the current conditions, the future without the expansion, and the future with the expansion. The impact is then assessed as the difference between the latter two situations, rather than the future compared with the current.

When considering whether the theoretical approach is of any assistance in understanding the airports policymaking process, it could be concluded that the most recognisable concepts are the 'policy swamp' and 'muddling through', phrases which do not give a lot of confidence to the idea of logical decision-making.

Notes
1. An adjournment debate is a way of enabling a debate to take place in the House of Commons but without a question that the House must then decide. The ten-minute rule allows a backbench MP to make his or her case for a new bill in a speech lasting up to ten minutes. An opposing speech may also be made before the House decides whether or not the bill should be introduced. If the MP is successful, the bill is taken to have had its first reading.

REFERENCES
Bassford H (2015) Getting approval. *Presentation at the UK Air–Rail Update 2015 conference.* Waterfront Conference Company, London, UK.

Collis J and Hussey R (2009) *Business Research: A Practical Guide for Undergraduate and Postgraduate Students,* 3rd edition. Palgrave Macmillan, Basingstoke, UK.

Commission on the Third London Airport (1971) *Report.* HMSO, London, UK.

Cullingworth B and Nadin V (2002) *Town and Country Planning in the UK,* 13th edition. Routledge, London, UK.

Farrington JH (1984) A third London Airport: options and decision-making. *Built Environment* **10(3)**: 168–180.

Glaister S, Burnham J, Stevens H and Travers T (2006) *Transport Policy in Britain,* 2nd edition. Palgrave Macmillan, Basingstoke, UK.

Griggs S and Howarth D (2017) Discourse, policy and the environment: hegemony, statements and the analysis of UK airport expansion. *Journal of Environmental Policy & Planning,* January 2017 (online): 1–15.

Hall P (2002) *Cities of Tomorrow,* 3rd edition. Blackwell, Oxford, UK.

Hall P and Tewdwr-Jones M (2011) *Urban and Regional Planning,* 5th edition. Routledge, Abingdon, UK.

Ham C and Hill M (1993) *The Policy Process in the Modern Capitalist State,* 2nd edition. Harvester Wheatsheaf, London, UK.

HC Deb 23 March 2016, vol. 607, col. 1675.

Hill M (2013) *The Public Policy Process,* 6th edition. Pearson, Harlow, UK.

Hogwood BW and Gunn LA (1984) *Policy Analysis for the Real World.* Oxford University Press, Oxford, UK.

Howlett M and Ramesh M (1995) *Studying Public Policy: Policy Cycles and Policy Subsystems.* Oxford University Press, Oxford, UK.

Humphreys I, Ison S and Francis G (2007) UK Airport Policy: does the government have any influence? *Public Money & Management* **27(5)**: 339–344.

Ison S (2004) *Road User Charging: Issues and Policies.* Ashgate, Aldershot, UK.

Lindblom CE (1979) Still muddling, not yet through. *Public Administration Review* **39(6)**: 517–526.

Lindblom C and Woodhouse E (1993) *The Policy-Making Process,* 3rd edition. Prentice-Hall, Englewood Cliffs, NJ, USA.

Mason R (2013) David Cameron at centre of 'get rid of all the green crap' storm. *The Guardian,* 21 November 2013. www.theguardian.com/environment/2013/nov/21/david-cameron-green-crap-comments-storm (accessed 23 July 2018).

Millichap D (1995) Law, myth and community: a reinterpretation of planning's justification and rationale. *Planning Perspectives* **10(3)**: 279–293.

O'Doherty D (2015) Missing connexions: the politics of airport expansion in the United Kingdom. *Organization* **22(3)**: 418–431.

Parsons W (1995) *Public Policy: An Introduction to the Theory and Practice of Policy Analysis.* Edward Elgar, Cheltenham.

Parsons W (2002) From muddling through to muddling up: evidence-based policymaking and the modernisation of British government. *Public Policy and Administration* **17(3)**: 43–60.

Rhodes J (2008) *The Planning System and Airports Policy*. Report to the Competition Commission on behalf of BAA, RPS.

Sager T (1992) Why Plan? A multi-rationality foundation for planning. *Scandinavian Housing & Planning Research* **9**: 129–147.

Schabas M (2017) *The Railway Metropolis: How Planners, Politicians and Developers Shaped Modern London*. ICE Publishing, London, UK.

Short J and Kopp A (2005) Transport infrastructure: investment and planning. Policy and research aspects. *Transport Policy* **12(4)**: 360–367.

Walters A (1978) Airports: an economic survey. *Journal of Transport Economics and Policy* **12(2)**: 125–160.

Wickham C (2009) David Cameron: 'No third runway – no ifs, no buts'. Bucks Free Press. www.bucksfreepress.co.uk/news/4694685.David_Cameron___No_third_runway_-_no_ifs__no_buts_ (accessed 13 August 2018).

Chapter 5
Environmental issues: a fundamental factor

5.1. Introduction

I devote a chapter to environmental issues because they have been a fundamental element in airports policy over the last 40 years. There are, of course, other key issues, such as the way forecasts of airport activity are used, the economic benefits and the technological changes, but there is no doubt that, were it not for the environmental impact of airports, there would not have been the indecision and counter-decision noted in the subtitle of this book.

The three main environmental impacts discussed in this chapter are noise, local air quality and climate change. Noise has always been important and is generally the environmental issue about which most concern is expressed, especially locally. Local air quality has also been considered for many years, although the nature of pollution has changed over time, from the soot and carbon produced by piston engines and the earlier jet engines to the less visible nitrous oxides of today. Climate change was virtually unheard of in the 1970s, but from the 1990s onwards it has become a significant issue. In addition to noise, local air quality and climate change, there are a number of other environmental issues whose importance has varied in relation to the location of the airport, as well as over time, such as agriculture, heritage, ecology, water quality and health, and these are considered later in this chapter. Environmental issues may occur as a direct result of the airport development, or perhaps as a secondary impact, for example as a result of more people travelling to or from the airport, or the building of more houses for airport employees.

In many studies, inquiries and policies, attempts have been made to weigh or balance environmental impacts against the benefits of airport expansion, the latter mostly economic. However, it was apparent from one of the earliest inquiries noted in this book, the Roskill Commission (see Chapter 3), that such attempts, especially if they involved trying to monetise environmental issues, were always going to be challenging. Today, it is generally accepted that impacts should be measured in the units most appropriate for that impact, and the judgement about balance should be left to politicians, advised by experts. Of course that does not mean that everyone agrees with the judgement.

5.2. Aircraft noise: the longest-running complaint

Noise is unwanted sound. There is a vast body of work on noise and this section will hardly even scratch the surface of that knowledge. Later chapters of this book will describe how noise was dealt with during each study, inquiry or decision, so this section merely seeks to introduce the subject in the context of how it has impacted on the development of policy for London's airports. It begins with a consideration of the development of aircraft engines and moves on to discuss how noise is measured and how these measures have been used in various studies and inquiries.

The first jet-powered air transport aircraft, the Comet and the Boeing 707, appeared in the 1950s, followed by further types such as the Trident, Caravelle, Boeing 727 and 737 (the latter still in production, although dramatically different from the earliest versions) and Russian types.

The jet engines they used channelled all the air through the compressor and turbine and were very noisy and inefficient. In the 1970s, new larger engines were produced which powered the new wide-bodied aircraft such as the Boeing 747, TriStar, DC10 and Airbus A300. As well as being more powerful, these new engines were also less noisy and were then developed for smaller aircraft (such as the Boeing 757 and Airbus A320), which replaced the first-generation jets. These newer high-bypass-ratio engines have lower-speed air from the fan at the front of the engine surrounding the higher-speed exhaust from combustion, which has the effect of encircling the noisy high-speed exhaust with quieter lower-speed air. Improvements have been driven in part by the International Civil Aviation Organisation (ICAO) and equivalent national regulations requiring reductions in noise and emissions, but also by the need to reduce fuel and maintenance costs, so modern engines are more efficient and more reliable. Improved efficiency means that less fuel is needed for the same level of thrust, which reduces emissions per unit of thrust (Masiol and Harrison, 2014).

Compared with earlier technology, modern engines are less noisy (by a factor of four) and less polluting. Reductions in noise on the ground have also come from more powerful engines, which allow steeper departures, which in turn reduces the noise footprint[1] (Girvin, 2009), as shown in Figure 5.1. However, although individual aircraft may be less noisy, this noise reduction has been offset by the growth in numbers of aircraft movements (Graham et al., 2014). The prospects for further reduction in aircraft noise are limited, in part because engine noise may now be less than airframe noise (from flaps and undercarriage), and some of the targets are ambitious. In terms of

Figure 5.1 Noise footprints, showing the area within which noise levels exceed 90 dB for a first-generation jet compared with more modern types
(Source: Boeing data quoted in Australian government, National Aviation Policy Green Paper, 2008. (Airports Commission, 2013))

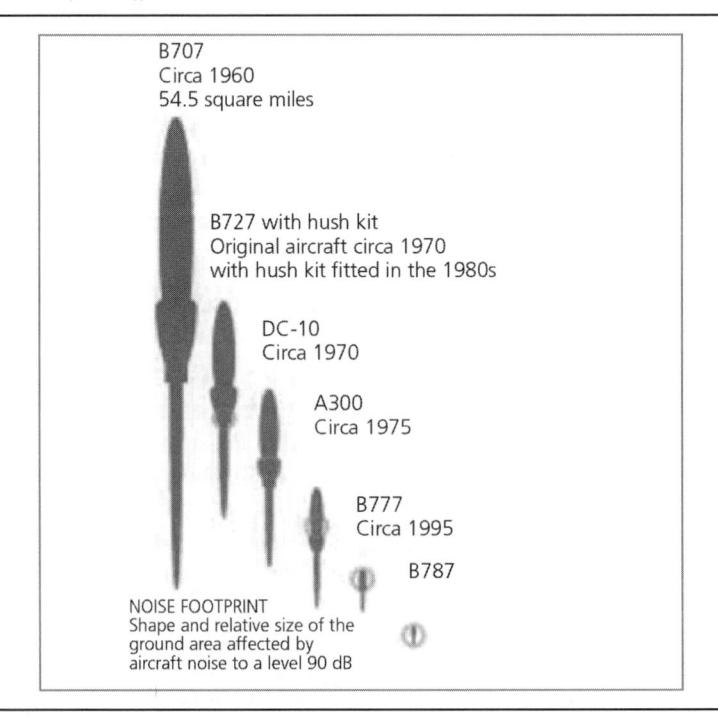

B707
Circa 1960
54.5 square miles

B727 with hush kit
Original aircraft circa 1970
with hush kit fitted in the 1980s

DC-10
Circa 1970

A300
Circa 1975

B777
Circa 1995

B787

NOISE FOOTPRINT
Shape and relative size of the
ground area affected by
aircraft noise to a level 90 dB

emissions, there are targets to continue the improvements, but there are doubts that they can be achieved (Bows-Larkin and Anderson, 2013).

In the UK, the Wilson Committee of 1963 (Wilson, 1963) proposed that noise annoyance around airports be measured by the Noise and Number Index, or NNI (Brooker, 2004). As its name implies, this was an attempt to combine in one unit a measure of the loudness of each aircraft and the number of them. Sound attenuates with distance, so an aircraft flying overhead produces a sound level on the ground dependent in part on its height. Places of equal NNI on the ground can be joined with a line that is known as a contour and the Wilson Committee suggested that the 35 NNI contour should be used as the key measure of 'low annoyance'. This was the main unit used by the Roskill Commission and, at that time, with very noisy first-generation jets operating, as many as two million people lived within the Heathrow 35 NNI contour. NNI continued to be used through the 1970s but was criticised as not reflecting annoyance, so the government commissioned a study from the Civil Aviation Authority (CAA), the Aircraft Noise Index Study (ANIS). Although the NNI had used results from social surveys, it was not statistically sound and so ANIS suggested an improved measure that was also related to the directly measured level of sound in decibels (dB). The sound level was adjusted to reflect better the way aircraft noise is heard by the human ear, so the measure is weighted (known as 'A-weighted') and expressed as Perceived Noise (PNdB). However, the most controversial part of the measure was that it averaged noise over a period, known as the Equivalent Continuous A-weighted Level or L_{Aeq}, and the suggested key measure is for a period encompassing the 16 hours between 7am and 11pm over June, July and August, written as L_{Aeq16h}. Thus the same average noise level could either be a few very noisy aircraft movements or many less noisy ones. Nevertheless, the correlation between this measure and the social survey results was statistically robust, and the 57 dB L_{Aeq16h} was equated with the 'onset of community annoyance', while other levels were used in rules about when soundproofing would be required in homes, or when building new homes would be prohibited, as set out in Planning Policy Guidance note PPG 24, now subsumed into the National Planning Policy Framework (Ministry of Housing, Communities and Local Government, 2018) and the Noise Policy Statement for England (Department for Environment, Food and Rural Affairs, 2010).

One of the key criticisms of any measure is that, while it may properly reflect average perceptions of noise, by definition there will be people who perceive noise differently. One person may well find a certain level intolerable while their neighbour is not at all bothered. While very high levels of aircraft noise (for example, above 63 dB L_{Aeq16h}) are clearly disturbing, interrupting conversation and preventing teaching etc., there are variations in perception at lower levels. Much of the argument, therefore, is about whether it is the 200 000 people within the 57 dB L_{Aeq16h} contour or 750 000 within the 54 dB L_{Aeq16h} contour who suffer from aircraft noise from Heathrow. Perception and disturbance are also related to background noise, so aircraft noise may be more disturbing in rural areas than in cities.

One of the counterarguments is, 'If you don't like the noise, why do you choose to live there?' This goes along with the argument that there are few people who have lived in the area long enough for the noise measure to have ever been lower. Two answers to this are that an airport should not be permitted to cause nuisance to otherwise perfectly acceptable locations for homes, and that we should expect to be experiencing improvements in our quality of life as technology advances. Some people, in particular some from airlines that have invested in quieter aircraft, regard those who object to airports on the grounds of noise as hypocrites, given that many of them accept the benefits of aviation in terms of travel, and choose to live in areas affected by noise. Needless to say, that view is not shared by all, including many others in the aviation industry.

Apart from averaging noise over a 16-hour day, another criticism of the L_{Aeq16h} measure was that it did not measure noise at night. Many studies of sleep disturbance have been undertaken, but there is no consistent agreement about the impact of aircraft noise, and the L_{Aeq8h} measure, which looks at noise between 11pm and 7am, does not have the same level of statistical robustness as the daytime measure. No one measure seems to be acceptable, so more recent studies, such as by the Airports Commission, have examined a range of measures. These have included averages for different times of the day and night, and 24-hour averages with night-time noise given a weighting, as well as measures of exceedences over certain levels, and the noise levels from individual aircraft. However, despite its imperfections, the L_{Aeq16h} measure has been used consistently over many years, and it is therefore able to show how the noise climate has changed and the differences between airports, and between current and future situations.

Noise from individual aircraft has undoubtedly reduced as the older types of aircraft have been replaced, and the most modern Boeing 787s and Airbus A350s are remarkably quiet at a distance. However, this reduction in the noise from individual aircraft has been countered by the increasing number of aircraft movements, and therefore the average noise level has not declined to such an extent. For the future, noise targets have been set by the Advisory Council for Aviation Research in Europe (ACARE) but they are not achievable without a radical shift away from conventional aircraft configurations (Graham et al., 2014) and some argue that the longer-term growth of the air-transport industry will depend to a very significant degree on continuing and credible reductions in aircraft noise at source (Thomas and Lever, 2003). However, forecasts can be made on the basis of the replacement of older aircraft by newer types. Table 5.1 shows some average

Table 5.1 Populations within various noise contours at Heathrow, Gatwick and Stansted (note that the 1974 and 1990 figures are for the 35 NNI contour, the measure which preceded L_{Aeq16h})
(Data from Department of Trade (1975), Department for Transport (2003), CAA (2011a, 2011b and 2011c) and Airports Commission (2015))

Airport	Date/scenario	Population within 57 dB L_{Aeq16h} noise level
Heathrow	1974 2 runways, 3 terminals actual	2 000 000
	1990 2 runways, 5 terminals forecast	289 000
	2000 2 runways actual	275 000
	2010 2 runways actual	228 700
	2030 2 runways forecast	260 000
	2030 3 runways forecast	240 000
Gatwick	1974 1 runway, 1 terminal actual	50 000
	1990 1 runway, 2 terminals forecast	2000
	2000 1 runway actual	8700
	2010 1 runway actual	2850
	2030 1 runway forecast	9000
	2030 2 runways forecast	14 000
Stansted	1974 1 runway actual	4000
	1990 1 runway forecast	2000
	2000 1 runway actual	5700
	2010 1 runway actual	1400
	2030 2 runways forecast	14 000

noise levels at different airports at different times or under different expansion scenarios. Not all of the figures in the table are comparable, but two general conclusions can be drawn. First, for comparable scenarios, the numbers at Heathrow are roughly 100 times more than Gatwick and even more compared with Stansted. Second, the numbers at Heathrow have dramatically reduced over time, despite very significant increases in the number of movements, but the reduction had slowed in more recent years. The addition of a third runway at Heathrow would marginally increase the population within the 57 dB L_{Aeq16h} contour, compared with the 2010 figures, although, ironically, the numbers would increase more if Heathrow remained with two runways (this is because with three runways, new flight paths would overfly fewer people). At Gatwick, there would be a significant increase in the numbers with a second runway, although the numbers are small compared with Heathrow. There would be a similar story at Stansted, but the 2030 two-runway forecast is from the 2003 White Paper and takes no account of improvements that have actually taken place, as is shown in the 2010 actual number.

What can we conclude about the way noise has affected airports policy? Although a complex technical subject, it can be reduced to some fairly basic points. Heathrow has always, and will always, have a much greater noise impact than any other location, but is probably not going to get any worse. The simple question is therefore whether it is acceptable to impose such a level of noise at all. Given that very few people are proposing that Heathrow should be closed, this would seem to lend weight to the argument that it is acceptable as it is what happens now. Gatwick and Stansted clearly have a much better noise case (and incidentally are much better than a number of other UK airports) but still have the challenge of justifying the noise increases. In virtually every study, inquiry and decision, this has been the choice.

5.3. Local air quality: from smoke to NO_x

Early piston and jet engines often produced clouds of exhaust smoke (see Figure 5.2), so 'pollution', as it was named, was obvious. Driven mainly by the need to reduce the costs of fuel,

Figure 5.2 Early jet aircraft were both noisy and smoky
(Photograph: Wikimedia Commons)

engine technology has improved dramatically in terms of efficiency such that this pollution, which was largely unburnt fuel, is no longer an issue. However the products of combustion remain pollutants that can affect human health and the weather, damage buildings and contribute to climate change. The combustion products which affect the first three of these are carbon monoxide (CO), water (H_2O), nitrous oxides (NO_x), hydrocarbons (HC), sulfur dioxide (SO_2) and particulate matter (PM_{10} and $PM_{2.5}$) (for a full review of emissions from aviation see Masiol and Harrison, 2014). Again there have been reductions in many of these as engine technology has improved, but these improvements have been outweighed by the increase in the number of aircraft movements.

There is a trade-off between noise and emissions when designing aircraft engines. The A380 was designed specifically to meet a noise measure at Heathrow Airport (Girvin, 2009), but 'while aircraft can be made to be significantly quieter *or* less polluting, achieving both at the same time is a much harder prospect' (Budd and Budd, 2013: p. 106).

Local air quality is affected by the products of aircraft engine combustion at and close to the airport, either during taxiing or in the take-off and landing stages. Aircraft engines operate most efficiently, and therefore with lowest emissions, at cruise throttle settings. At low settings, for example during taxiing, or at maximum thrust for take-off, emissions may not be as low as for the cruise phase. Local air quality at airports is also affected by other activity, in particular road vehicles.

Local air quality was hardly mentioned in airports policy studies, inquiries or White Papers through the 1970s and 1980s but was a key issue at the 1995–1999 Heathrow Terminal 5 Inquiry (see Chapter 7), by which time EU regulations were being formulated. The pollutants that have caused the most concern in terms of local air quality are NO_x, PM_{10} and $PM_{2.5}$. The EU has set standards for the concentration of these pollutants at locations where they might be received (as opposed to where they are emitted) – that is, at homes, workplaces, schools and open spaces where people can walk (including roadsides). Levels of these pollutants exceed the EU limit at many locations in city centres in the UK, primarily because of road traffic, and the government is required to put in place plans to ensure that levels are reduced, otherwise they would face large fines. Depending on the final agreement reached, leaving the EU could remove this sanction, but would not remove the pollution, and it would be right for the government to continue to take action. However, the levels at many airports do not exceed the EU limits, because they are located outside urban areas. The one airport where the limits are currently exceeded is Heathrow, and there has been much study of this area for many years, with little overall agreement (Carslaw et al., 2006; Ellermann et al., 2012; Graham et al., 2014; Jacobs, 2014; Peace et al., 2006). The 2003 White Paper's support for a third runway at Heathrow (see Chapter 8) was conditional upon the EU limits not being exceeded and therefore air quality was potentially a 'showstopper'. However, by 2009 the government said that studies had shown that the addition of a third runway would not result in such exceedences. Air quality was also a showstopper for the Airports Commission (see Chapter 9) because, although their studies showed that it would be within limits, their recommendation was conditional upon this being demonstrated. Subsequently the government delayed a decision from late 2015 until mid 2016 so that this proof could be demonstrated. The issue remains highly controversial, in part because much of the cause of pollution in the area around Heathrow is road traffic that is not related to the airport, but nevertheless, airport activity is partly the cause.

5.4. Climate change: a growing concern since the 1990s

In global terms, estimates of the proportion of total transport climate-change emissions that comes from aviation show that aviation is the fastest-growing sector, and that radiative forcing effects[2] are not yet fully quantified (Dessens *et al.*, 2014; Lee *et al.*, 2009). There is a government target to reduce the UK's carbon dioxide (CO_2) emissions by 60 per cent by 2050 to avoid dangerous climate change.[3] By this time aviation would account for between 25 and 51 per cent of the total UK emissions budget and therefore other sectors would have to reduce their contribution dramatically, and potentially all be decarbonised (Bows and Anderson, 2007). This leads some scientists to conclude, 'Therefore, until technological and operational solutions can decarbonise air travel at rates well beyond the pace of expansion in the industry, policy measures must place a constraint on growth, for example, through delaying plans for increased airport capacity' (Bows-Larkin and Anderson, 2013: p. 81). However, forecasts of air passengers take account of both the costs of carbon and the attitudes of passengers flying on holiday (Hares *et al.*, 2010) and the Committee on Climate Change has concluded that a rise of 60 per cent in aircraft movements from 2005 to 2050 would be compatible with the UK's targets (Committee on Climate Change, 2009).

Emissions trading was introduced by the EU in 2005, with aviation supposed to be added from 2012. The effect on growth was forecast to be negligible (Anger, 2010; Anger-Kraavi and Köhler, 2013), so it is not clear if there would be any impact on airport expansion. Because of opposition from non-EU countries, implementation was suspended pending ICAO action. But on 6 October 2016, ICAO adopted a Global Market-Based Measure (GMBM) to control carbon dioxide (CO_2) emissions from international aviation. This remains controversial because it includes the option to offset aviation emissions rather than reduce them in absolute terms, but it has been agreed by most major countries.

Climate-change arguments are used by many objectors to individual airport developments, but the response from the government has been that reducing aviation's impact is a matter to be dealt with at national and international levels. Studies of the attitudes of individual travellers have found that most travellers do not change their behaviour, despite knowledge of the climate-change effects of air travel. However, they do rate different airlines according to their green image, although in general airlines are perceived negatively compared to products in other sectors (Mayer *et al.*, 2012).

5.5. Other impacts: agricultural land, ecology, archaeology, water and drainage, visual impact, green belt and surface access

While noise has been a continual concern at virtually every airport, other environmental issues have arisen only at certain locations or at certain times. The impact on agricultural land was an important issue at many of the inquiries involving new or expanded airports, in particular at Stansted. However, it is of less relevance at Heathrow and Gatwick, where less agricultural land would be lost as a result of airport expansion (although it was an issue when Heathrow was originally built, mainly taking Grade 1 agricultural land – see Figure 5.3). Ecological impacts arise from most developments, including airports, but a particular issue has arisen over many years relating to estuarial or offshore sites. Conservationist Sir Peter Scott gave evidence about the impact of airport development on brent geese at Foulness during the Roskill Commission (Commission on the Third London Airport, 1971) and more recently consideration has been given by the Davies Commission to the impact on wildlife of an option for a new airport in the Thames Estuary (Airports Commission, 2014).

Heritage issues arise in particular in relation to historic buildings and sites. Archaeological investigations often follow the approval of a development (for example, the investigations of the Heathrow Terminal 5 site were well funded and shed light on more than 8000 years of human history (Sherwood, 2009)). Sometimes buildings can be dismantled and re-erected, thus mitigating the effects of destroying the site.

Figure 5.3 Heathrow was once the site of extensive market gardening and orchards, as shown on this pre-WW2 Ordnance Survey map
(Map: Ordnance Survey map scanned by Andrew Rowbottom, Wikimedia Commons)

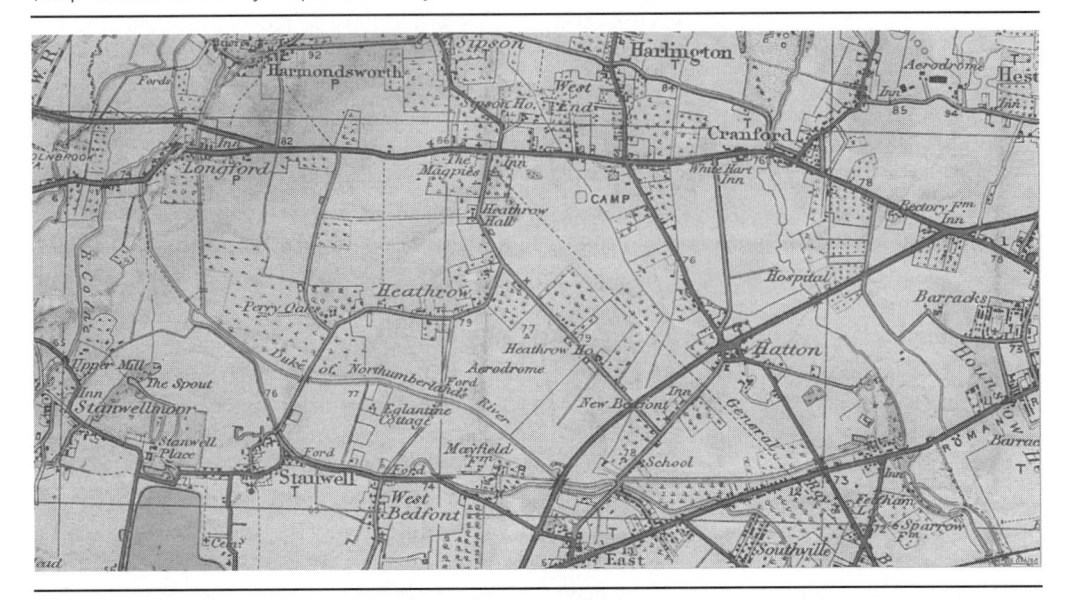

Concerns about water and drainage can include quality, where a watercourse or aquifer is at risk from pollution, and also flooding, given the large amount of impermeable surface at an airport. However, balancing ponds, pollution traps and other measures are usually sufficient to avoid any serious consequences.

Health impacts are related to noise and emissions, and have become a more significant issue in recent studies and inquiries. The visual impact of airports is related to the large buildings, such as hangars and terminals, which, in an open, flat landscape, may be seen as obtrusive. There have been examples at Heathrow, Gatwick and Stansted where the impacts of particular buildings have been discussed at inquiries and have been an element in the overall balance, but it would probably be fair to say that visual impact has never been a showstopper.

In the earlier studies and inquiries looked at in this book, 'planning' was considered under the environmental impact heading, primarily relating to what might be termed 'strategic planning' or 'spatial planning'. Strategic planning at a regional level was considered to be the first stage of a 'plan-led' system for many years, and airports were an element in the strategy. However, the South East has always struggled to produce a regional strategy, in part because of the roles played by London and its hinterland. Regional planning has somewhat fallen out of favour in recent years, although London retains a regional plan that, ironically, is often in conflict with the UK government's airports policy for the region.

Finally, in this section, we should note the environmental issues associated with surface access. The provision and use of road and rail access to the major London airports has always been a significant issue in the evolution of policies, not least because of the environmental impact of the road and rail infrastructure and operations. While some elements can be seen as directly related to the airports (such as the M4 spur to Heathrow or the rail spur from the West Anglia Main Line to Stansted), much transport infrastructure is used by non-airport traffic (for example the Brighton Main Line through Gatwick Airport) and this shared use makes it difficult to ascribe responsibility for the impact. Nevertheless, the adequacy of surface access infrastructure and the need for additional capacity are key factors in the acceptability of airport expansion proposals.

Notes

1. The aircraft noise footprint is the area within a line connecting points of equal noise levels on the ground from a particular aircraft.
2. Radiative forcing is defined by the Intergovernmental Panel on Climate Change as a measure of the influence a factor has in altering the balance of incoming and outgoing energy in the Earth–atmosphere system and is an index of the importance of the factor as a potential climate-change mechanism.
3. Dangerous climate change is defined in the Copenhagen Accord as global temperatures rising more than 2°C.

REFERENCES

Airports Commission (2013) *Discussion Paper 05: Aviation Noise*. Airports Commission, London, UK.

Airports Commission (2014) *Inner Thames Estuary Airport: Summary and Decision Paper*. Airports Commission, London, UK.

Airports Commission (2015) *Final Report*. HMSO, London, UK.

Anger A (2010) Including aviation in the European emissions trading scheme: impacts on the industry, CO_2 emissions and macroeconomic activity in the EU. *Journal of Air Transport Management* **16(2)**: 100–105.

Anger-Kraavi A and Köhler J (2013) Aviation and the EU Emissions Trading System. In *Sustainable Aviation Futures* (Budd L, Griggs S and Howarth D (eds)). Emerald Group Publishing, Bingley, UK, pp. 109–130.

Bows A and Anderson K (2007) Policy clash: can projected aviation growth be reconciled with the UK government's 60% carbon-reduction target? *Transport Policy* **14(2)**: 103–110.

Bows-Larkin A and Anderson K (2013) Carbon budgets for aviation or gamble with our future. In *Sustainable Aviation Futures* (Budd L, Griggs S and Howarth D (eds)). Emerald Group Publishing, Bingley, UK, pp. 65–84.

Brooker P (2004) The UK Aircraft Noise Index Study: 20 years on. *Proceedings of the Institute of Accoustics* **26(2)**: 20–30.

Budd L and Budd T (2013) Environmental technology and the future of flight. In *Sustainable Aviation Futures* (Budd L, Griggs S and Howarth D (eds)). Emerald Group Publishing, Bingley, UK, pp. 87–107.

CAA (2011a) *ERCD Report 1101: Noise Exposure Contours for Heathrow Airport 2010*. Environmental Research and Consultancy Department, Directorate of Airspace Policy, Civil Aviation Authority, London, UK.

CAA (2011b) *ERCD Report 1102: Noise Exposure Contours for Gatwick Airport 2010*. Environmental Research and Consultancy Department, Directorate of Airspace Policy, Civil Aviation Authority, London, UK.

CAA (2011c) *ERCD Report 1103: Noise Exposure Contours for Stansted Airport 2010*. Environmental Research and Consultancy Department, Directorate of Airspace Policy, Civil Aviation Authority, London, UK.

Carslaw D, Beevers S, Ropkins K and Bee M (2006) Detecting and quantifying aircraft and other on-airport contributions to ambient nitrogen oxides in the vicinity of a large international airport. *Atmospheric Environment* **40(28)**: 5424–5434.

Commission on the Third London Airport (1971) *Report*. HMSO, London, UK.

Committee on Climate Change (2009) *Meeting the UK Aviation Target – Options for Reducing Emissions to 2050*. Committee on Climate Change, London, UK.

Department for Environment, Food and Rural Affairs (2010) *Noise Policy Statement for England (NPSE)*. DEFRA, London, UK.

Department for Transport (2003) *The Future of Air Transport*. Cmnd 6046, HMSO, London, UK.

Department of Trade (1975) *Airport Strategy for Great Britain: Part 1 The London Area*. HMSO, London, UK.

Dessens O, Köhler O, Rogers H, Jones R and Pyle J (2014) Aviation and climate change. *Transport Policy* **34**: 14–20.

Ellermann T, Massling A, Løfstrøm P, Winther M, Nøjgaard J and Ketzel M (2012) Assessment of the air quality at the apron of Copenhagen Airport Kastrup in relation to the working environment. *Technical Report from DCE – Danish Centre for Environment and Energy* **15**.

Girvin R (2009) Aircraft noise-abatement and mitigation strategies. *Journal of Air Transport Management* **15(1)**: 14–22.

Graham W, Hall C and Morales V (2014) The potential of future aircraft technology for noise and pollutant emissions reduction. *Transport Policy* **34**: 36–51.

Hares A, Dickinson J and Wilkes K (2010) Climate change and the air travel decisions of UK tourists. *Journal of Transport Geography* **19**: 466–473.

Jacobs (2014) *6. Air Quality Baseline*. Prepared for the Airports Commission.

Lee D, Fahey D, Forster P, Newton P, Wit R, Lim L, Owen B and Sausen R (2009) Aviation and global climate change in the 21st century. *Atmospheric Environment* **43(22–23)**: 3520–3537.

Masiol M and Harrison R (2014) Aircraft engine exhaust emissions and other airport-related contributions to ambient air pollution: a review. *Atmospheric Environment* **95**: 409–455.

Mayer R, Ryley T and Gillingwater D (2012) Passenger perceptions of the green image associated with airlines. *Journal of Transport Geography* **22**: 179–186.

Ministry of Housing, Communities and Local Government (2018) *National Planning Policy Framework*. MHCLG, London, UK.

Peace H, Maughan J, Owen B and Raper D (2006) Identifying the contribution of different airport related sources to local urban air quality. *Environmental Modelling & Software* **21(4)**: 532–538.

Sherwood P (2009) *Heathrow: 2000 Years of History*. The History Press, Stroud, UK.

Thomas C and Lever M (2003) Aircraft noise, community relations and stakeholder involvement. In *Towards Sustainable Aviation* (Upham P (ed)). Earthscan, London, UK.

Wilson A (1963) *Noise: Final Report*. Cmnd 2056, HMSO, London, UK.

Chapter 6
1974–1991: an incremental approach

6.1. Introduction

In the earlier chapters I summarised some of the key events in airports policy before 1974. I now begin a more detailed investigation of the story at the point when the Maplin project was cancelled. This chapter also considers some other events taking place in the UK at the time to provide a context for the evolution of airports policy. At the end of this and subsequent chapters I seek to draw out some themes that appear.

6.2. Maplin is cancelled and a 'third way' is sought

The defeat of Conservative Prime Minister Edward Heath and the change of government at the February 1974 general election enabled a new Labour government to review the Maplin project (the scheme to develop an airport at Foulness in Essex; see Chapter 3). At a time of high inflation (in part caused by the quadrupling of oil prices), rising public spending and economic downturn, the review quickly led to cancellation.

One of the key factors in the decision to cancel was that passenger numbers at the London airports, which had risen continuously in the 1960s and until 1973, dropped in 1974, and this led to the forecasts on which the Maplin project was based being questioned. The Roskill Commission had forecast around 50 million passengers for the London airports in 1975, whereas the actual number was 28.7 million. An even greater shortfall was seen in the number of aircraft movements, which, instead of growing and leading to the need for more runway capacity, fell by 7 per cent between 1973 and 1977. This was the time when the first wide-bodied aircraft – the Boeing 747 jumbo jet, Douglas DC10, Lockheed TriStar (see Figure 6.1) and Airbus A300 – first entered service, replacing aircraft types with half as many seats, and it became clear that this increase in average aircraft size would reduce the need for extra runway capacity and instead put the pressure on the terminals.

Average aircraft size would become an issue on a number of future occasions (because it is the factor that converts the basic passenger demand into forecasts of aircraft movements, which then determines the need for runways) but there is some dispute about how this trend was forecast by the Roskill Commission in 1971. Alan Walters, one of the Commissioners, writing in 1978, said, 'Errors in aircraft size forecast accounted for the largest part of the gap between prediction and outcome in the Roskill forecasts of air transport movements' (Walters, 1978: p. 131). However, Stan Abrahams, a member of the Roskill Research Team, told me that, while their aircraft size predictions were overestimates, a larger difference compared with the actuals for 1981 was in the passenger forecast. Roskill's forecasts of aircraft movements were undoubtedly higher than the actuals, but the reason seems to be mainly because the passenger forecast was much higher than turned out to be the case.

Another change that reduced the need for the Maplin project was that pressure had eased on the groundside access arrangements. This was particularly true at Heathrow, where the heavily

Figure 6.1 Wide-bodied aircraft like this Lockheed TriStar replaced much smaller aircraft in the 1970s (Photo by Steve Fitzgerald, via Wikimedia Commons)

congested roads leading to the Central Terminal Area had been largely relieved by the extension of the London Underground Piccadilly line in 1977.

There were big changes in the airline sector as well. British European Airways (BEA) and British Overseas Airways Corporation (BOAC) had merged to form British Airways (BA) in 1972 and in later years BA and British Caledonian Airways (BCal) swapped a number of routes after government policy established 'spheres of influence' in terms of the regions of the world they would each serve. As well as introducing wide-bodied aircraft, BA launched its first Concorde service in 1976. Britannia and Dan-Air grew at Gatwick and Laker Airways began operating the Skytrain service from Gatwick in 1977. Court Line began operating large TriStars on holiday routes from Luton in 1973 but collapsed a year later. Court Line's TriStars carried 479 passengers and were undoubtedly cheap per seat mile compared to smaller aircraft, but the recession of the early 1970s and other factors resulted in the airline not being able to fill the aircraft. It is interesting to note that no short-haul leisure airlines have subsequently used wide-bodied aircraft in any substantial way, and that low-cost carriers (LCCs) use the Boeing 737 and Airbus A320, with 150 to 200 seats.

New aircraft also had an impact on the major environmental issue of the time – aircraft noise. The new wide-bodied jets were significantly less noisy than the types they replaced, but Concorde was more noisy and was treated as a special case. Concerns about aircraft noise around airports had been raised in many of the debates about expansion, and featured heavily in the Roskill Commission's work. Noise was the reason the government chose the Maplin option over the inland sites, which had better cost–benefit ratios. Other environmental concerns, primarily related to air pollution, were beginning to be recognised as part of a worldwide nascent environmental movement (as an example, in 1978 the opening of the new Tokyo Airport at Narita was delayed by the occupation of buildings by protestors; see Chapter 11).

It is also worthwhile looking at other issues in wider society to provide a context for the way airports policy evolved. Labour took over as a minority government in February 1974, and then secured a majority of three in October of that year. Harold Wilson was prime minister until he resigned in 1976 to hand over to James Callaghan. Key ministers involved in airports policy at this time included Anthony Crosland (Environment) and Peter Shore, then Edmund Dell (Trade). The economic difficulties and inflation have already been noted, and this was related to high levels of unemployment, large pay claims, strikes and, in 1978/79, the 'winter of discontent'. The UK joined the European Economic Community in 1973 and three years later, in transport, the InterCity 125 train was introduced. The general election of May 1979 saw the replacement of Labour by a Conservative government led by Margaret Thatcher. In technology, it is worth noting that Microsoft was first registered in the USA in 1976 and Apple was formed in 1976.

The National Archives files reveal some interesting activity within the civil service after the Maplin cancellation. Working parties were formed for the next steps and the options of inter-departmental committees or independent advisory panels were considered, both of which had not succeeded previously. This led to a search for a third way, with accountable ministers in charge but civil servants and agencies doing the analysis. The need to consult with local authorities and to consider the whole of the UK were high priorities, and on 15 August 1974 the Department of the Environment (DoE) wrote to local authorities and amenity groups to ask for views (Wilks, 1974), having published the Maplin Review report a month earlier. The DoE received 125 responses, with many of the comments complaining that too much account was taken of aviation interests, that more consideration should be given to regional diversion and that there would be widespread local opposition to Heathrow expanding beyond four terminals, to a second terminal at Gatwick and to major expansions at Stansted and Luton. There were tensions between government departments and agencies, with the Civil Aviation Authority (CAA) and the Department of Trade (DoT) arguing about who should prepare forecasts. Perhaps the most significant decision was that the future work should be led by the DoE, which included planning and local authority oversight, rather than the DoT, responsible for aviation.

The next step was the publication of two consultation documents under the heading 'Airport Strategy for Great Britain'. Part 1 (Department of Trade, 1975) covered the London area and was published in November 1975, and Part 2 (Department of Trade, 1976), for the remainder of the country, followed a few months later. The London document had been prepared by a group chaired by the DoE but including other government departments, the CAA and BAA. The options were a fifth terminal at Heathrow (the fourth being assumed), a second at Gatwick, development at Stansted to either 4 mppa (millions of passengers per annum) or 16 mppa and at Luton to either 5 mppa or 10 mppa. The documents also reviewed the noise issue and predicted very significant reductions in noise exposure over the next 15 years at Heathrow, and relatively small populations exposed for the other options. The capability of regional airports for expansion was canvassed in Part 2. While the government had been keen to promote regional diversion, BAA was not in favour, as a file note of a dinner attended by Peter Shore (Trade Secretary) and Nigel Foulkes (BAA chairman) on 9 December 1974 makes clear, the careful language saying that the BAA's description of the situation 'did not conform with the government's view' (Hutton, 1974).

Responses to the consultation documents, of which there were more than 1000, were much as expected, with local authorities and representative groups around the option sites noting opposition. British Airways noted the national significance of Heathrow and pressed for both a fourth and a fifth terminal, and also pointed out that Gatwick was more suited to holiday flights and there would be considerable costs if flights were moved from Heathrow to Gatwick

(Finlay, 1976). Tom Carter, who was BA's airport planning manager for many years, told me that BA was somewhat ambivalent about the site for Terminal 4, but the background was that, since the merger of BEA and BOAC, the focus had been on a single terminal, but neither Terminal 1 (used by BA's short-haul routes) or Terminal 3 (long haul) would be able to accommodate all BA's flights. BA had considered the Terminal 4 site for a Shuttle terminal (Shuttle was an operation of turn-up-and-go domestic flights that started in 1975) but transfers to their remaining operations in Terminals 1 and 3 would be difficult. BA's preference was for the Perry Oaks sludge works site, where a new terminal could be built sufficient for all of BA's services. In its response to the consultation, BCal also expressed concerns about transfers to Gatwick, related to the capacity of the single runway (Ritchie, 1976). The CAA and BAA disagreed about the capacity of the single runway at Gatwick, with the former calling for a second runway and the latter rebutting the arguments.

Armed with these consultation responses, the government then set about preparing a White Paper. First drafts of a synopsis appeared in October 1976, but the final version was not published until February 1978 (Department of Trade, 1978). The delay may in part be due to some interesting differences of opinion revealed in the files. There was continuing tension between the DoE and the DoT about leadership, harking back to concerns about the influence of the aviation sector on the DoT, with a DoE official suggesting that an early draft would be 'greeted by cynicism by many readers' (Webber, 1977a). In a remark that echoes probably the only relevant theoretical approach to political decision-making (see Chapter 4), he goes on to suggest that the process could be seen as 'muddling through'. The same official also suggested that there could be an argument for limiting Heathrow to three terminals, albeit with expansion at Gatwick and Stansted (Webber, 1977b). It is also interesting to note the sequence of the proposed developments. A fourth terminal at Heathrow was always assumed as the first step but, in early drafts of the White Paper, Stansted appears as the second step, followed by Luton, with a second terminal at Gatwick fourth. In the published White Paper, Gatwick had been elevated to second place, and the major developments of Stansted and Luton deleted from the list of short-term options, but it is not clear why.

One example of the workings of the civil service from The National Archives files is a letter from Sir Ronald Melville in June 1977 to Sir Ian Bancroft. Melville was a former Permanent Secretary in the Ministry of Aviation and Bancroft was the Permanent Secretary at the DoE. The letter, signed 'Yours ever, Ronnie', was from his home address in Bengeo, Hertfordshire (about halfway between Luton and Stansted Airports) and is confirming a lunch and, referring to airports policy, says, 'I fear that a disastrous mistake is about to be made which would destroy a large section of the most beautiful part of Hertfordshire and Essex. May I talk with you about this?' (Melville, 1977).

A major feature of the 1978 White Paper was the categorisation of all UK airports. This was proposed in response to calls for a national airports plan and the categories would be used by government when considering licensing applications and for planning and transport infrastructure. Table 6.1 shows the categories given to some of the airports.

Prestwick was given Category A status because, at the time, it was a key refuelling point for transatlantic flights. Birmingham and East Midlands were noted as possibly achieving Category A status in the longer term. Other Scottish airports were left to a new Scottish Assembly to decide. In the event, the categorisation meant little (although an attempt was made to revive the idea in the 2003 White Paper) and some airports fared better than others, irrespective of their category (Liverpool and Bristol grew significantly, Bournemouth took on much more than general aviation, while Cardiff struggled and Blackpool has effectively closed).

For the London area, there was a clear rejection of forced regional diversion, noting that the measures required would be impractical and costly. The policy until 1990 would be for a fourth

Table 6.1 1978 White Paper airport categories (Department of Trade, 1978)

Category	Description	Examples
A	Gateway international	The London system, Manchester, Prestwick
B	Regional	Birmingham, East Midlands, Leeds Bradford, Newcastle, Cardiff
C	Local	Liverpool, Norwich, Blackpool, Humberside, Teesside, Bristol, Exeter, Southampton
D	General aviation	Coventry, Carlisle, Bournemouth, Dundee

terminal at Heathrow, a second terminal at Gatwick and limited expansion at Stansted (4 mppa) and Luton (5 mppa). This would provide terminal capacity of 72 mppa compared with the forecast demand of between 66 mppa (low) and 89 mppa (high). For the longer term, the options were a major expansion of Stansted, development of a military airfield, or at a new site, to be considered by a new, inclusive body, the Advisory Committee on Airports Policy (ACAP). Ruled out, even for the longer term, were a fifth terminal and a third runway at Heathrow, a second runway at Gatwick and a second terminal at Luton. A Heathrow fifth terminal had been supported by British Airways and, as a long-term option, by BAA, but the opposition to it has already been noted. It seems that this opposition swayed the arguments as, by October 1976, the first drafts of the White Paper suggested that a fifth terminal would not be contemplated, even as a long-term option for planning, employment and environmental reasons. The published White Paper noted the difficulty of providing road and rail access and the level of noise disturbance and concluded that Heathrow's ultimate development should not go beyond that of a four-terminal airport. BAA's argument that a second runway would not be needed for a second terminal at Gatwick prevailed in the White Paper, although the White Paper did not rule it out for all time.

The Treasury, whose attitude during the Roskill Commission was noted in section 3.5 of this book, played a more active role in the White Paper preparation period, not always getting its own way. Bearing in mind that British Airways was then in the public sector, the Treasury noted that the airline's fleet plans, on which the forecasts had been based, included the early replacement of much of the Trident and VC10 fleet, which had not been allowed for in the public expenditure projections, and it asked for the offending paragraphs to be removed. Tom Carter told me that there had been a long history of BEA and BOAC attempting to buy American aircraft, whose seat–mile costs were lower than their British equivalents. The Treasury's concerns were partly related to the balance of payments, while the Department of Industry was responsible for the manufacturing sector. However, when Rolls-Royce Ltd went into voluntary liquidation and was nationalised in 1971, it became acceptable to purchase the Lockheed TriStar and Boeing 747, which were powered by the Rolls-Royce RB211 engine, the production of which had been financed by the UK government. In the final version of the White Paper, references to the Trident replacement remained in the section on aircraft noise, showing that the issue of noise reduction trumped the concerns about industrial strategy and public expenditure.

The draft White Paper went to a Ministerial Committee on Economic and Industrial Policy on 14 December 1977 and to the Cabinet on 19 January 1978 (Cabinet Office, 1978). Prime Minister James Callaghan chaired the meeting, and other matters considered on that day included a bill to extend the powers of the European Assembly, Russian and Cuban activity in the Horn of Africa, Rhodesia, the prime minister's visit to South Africa and his concern about the situation in India, the European Common Fisheries policy, food imports and exports and exchange controls. After all these complex foreign and technical issues, the last item on the agenda was the paper on airports policy, presented by the Secretary of State for Trade, Edmund Dell. There was particular debate about regional diversion, the possible need for a second runway at Gatwick, the lack of a need for a decision on Stansted, the relative status of airports in Yorkshire and the North East and in South Wales and South West England (the latter being a matter of disagreement between Edmund Dell and Tony Benn, the MP for Bristol South East) and the possible transfer of the Highlands and Islands airports to BAA. No discussion of Heathrow is noted. In the careful way these meetings are recorded, the minutes conclude that the prime minister, summing up the discussion, said that the Cabinet endorsed the proposals contained in the draft White Paper, with some exceptions and presentational points. The decision was that the Cabinet took note, with approval, of the prime minister's summing up of their discussion, and invited the Secretary of State to be guided accordingly.

Immediately after publication of the White Paper, there was a debate in the House of Commons on 1 February 1978 (HC Deb 1 February 1978), which gave opportunities for MPs to speak about their local airport or to reiterate their concerns. A few days later, Professor Peter Hall, at a conference at the Institution of Civil Engineers, claimed that Stansted would become London's third airport by a process of incremental creep and that it was difficult to conclude that we had not come full circle, back to 1966 or 1967, with an interdepartmental committee, dominated by air operational interests (Hall, 1978). BAA welcomed the White Paper, but noted that the proposals to use all the capacity available in the South East were unrealistic because of an uneven distribution of demand (BAA, 1978).

6.3. Step by step: new terminals for Heathrow, Gatwick and Stansted

In parallel with the preparation of the White Paper, progress was being made on implementing some elements of the policy that had been set out in earlier documents. Although the Perry Oaks site had been suggested as the logical place to expand Heathrow, it would clearly have taken many years to re-provide the sludge works and make the site available. In the Maplin Review, it was suggested that a fourth terminal at Heathrow could be developed quickly within the existing airport boundary (to the south of the southern runway in an area then known as Maintenance Area 2), under BAA's General Permitted Development Order (GPDO) powers (see Chapter 4). However, the London Borough of Hounslow sought an Article 4 Direction under the Town and Country Planning Act, which was granted and which meant that a public inquiry would take place. The Terminal 4 Inquiry took place in 1978 and lasted 93 days. Geoff Ambrose, who managed many of BAA's inquiry teams over many years, told me that the inquiry would have been much shorter but for the Greater London Council (GLC) who, although they were neutral, took a long time explaining their position. In contrast, the local community representatives were not particularly strong (with the notable exception of Evelyn Attlee of the Heathrow Association for the Control of Aircraft Noise/HACAN), but BAA took their arguments seriously and treated them with respect. Noise was clearly the most significant issue and the inspector, Ian Glidewell, listened carefully to both the existing noisy types of aircraft like the Trident and VC10 and to the new wide-bodied aircraft. Evidence from supporters was not always helpful. Roy Watts, chief executive of BA, volunteered that BA had no intention of using Terminal 4 because it was on the wrong side of the airport. Ironically, when Terminal 4 was built, BA did occupy it, but a similar stance on airlines using the proposed development reappeared in BCal's evidence at the Stansted Inquiry in 1981–1983. The inspector's report recommended approval with a number of conditions, including a 260 000 annual limit on the number of Air Transport Movements (ATMs)[1] specifically in response to the noise evidence.

Earlier in the 1970s, as well as supporting the growth of airlines at Gatwick through licensing and bilateral agreements, the government made several attempts to transfer flights from Heathrow to Gatwick. The plan, announced in 1977, was for UK and foreign airlines operating to Canada, Spain and Portugal to transfer flights from Heathrow to Gatwick, on the basis that most passengers on these flights were not connecting. However, the plan was opposed by the foreign airlines, who threatened reprisals such as moving UK airlines to secondary airports in their own countries. Although the USA was not involved in these proposals, a later attempt to move Boston flights to Gatwick resulted in the matter being discussed between Prime Minister James Callaghan and US President Jimmy Carter, a sign of how such issues can rise up the diplomatic agenda very quickly (Dell, 1978). BA did move a number of its flights to Gatwick unilaterally, although it later moved some back to Heathrow. John Mulkern, who was director of Gatwick from 1973 to 1977, told me that the Gatwick airlines – BCal, Dan-Air, Laker and a number of charter operators – were very enthusiastic about the airport and the obvious signs of growth in terms of new buildings and facilities. Delta Airlines, then primarily a US domestic airline, began services to Gatwick under the bilateral agreement from its Atlanta and New York hubs and operated from Gatwick until 2012.

BAA's application for a second terminal at Gatwick was considered at an inquiry in 1980. However, BAA had signed a legal agreement with West Sussex County Council (WSCC) in 1979 not to build a second runway for a period of 40 years. In turn, the council agreed not to argue that a second terminal would lead to a second runway, and also not to object to the creation of an emergency runway. Laurie Price, who was BCal's airport expert at the time, and went on to hold positions in consultancy and as a parliamentary adviser, told me that BCal was not consulted by BAA before this agreement was signed, that it led to Gatwick having to spend '40 years in the wilderness' and was probably the 'death knell' for BCal. A second runway would have provided enough peak-hour runway capacity to enable Gatwick to operate as a hub, with BCal providing passenger and freight services to compete with Heathrow. Geoff Ambrose had a slightly different perspective and suggested that BCal's main concern was about a blockage of the single runway, which could be mitigated by the creation of an emergency runway on the parallel taxiway and, in any event, a second runway at Gatwick could not be supported by the airspace technology which was used for the South East of England at that time. John Mulkern also suggested that the newly built M23 and associated A23 link road conflicted with the safeguarded surfaces for the second runway, which was also constrained by high ground to the west, so BAA lost nothing by agreeing not to build it. The agreement suited WSCC because it provided them with the certainty to plan for the expansion of towns and the retention of strategic gaps between the towns in the county. The Second Terminal Inquiry itself was relatively straightforward, in part because of the agreement with WSCC but also because no additional land was required, although ground noise (for example, from aircraft taxiing) did cause some concerns.

Sir Alan Haselhurst, formerly MP for Saffron Walden, the constituency including Stansted, told me that there has been a 'swathe of opposition from Tory grandees' to Gatwick expansion over many years. Some of the views of the local MPs are well documented, for example in Parliament, but their influence may well have been stronger than just their constituency interests. Haselhurst has consistently supported the notion of multi-runway hub airports (but not at Stansted) and believes that the BAA/WSCC no-second-runway agreement was like the Molotov/Ribbentrop pact, enabling the battle to be fought over Stansted.

Laurie Price also told me the story of the Gatwick–Heathrow Airlink, which operated from 1979 to 1986, some of which is also told by Hugh Ashpole, the operations manager and chief pilot (Ashpole, undated). Because BCal was not permitted to operate from Heathrow and because Gatwick did not have enough runway capacity to operate a hub, a link was required to

Heathrow's much larger range of services to enable transfer passengers between Heathrow and Gatwick to use BCal's connections. A helicopter was purchased by BAA (who also benefited from being able to operate the two-airport system), operated by British Airways Helicopters (who had experience of the type) and managed by BCal (who took the revenue risk). Ten return trips per day took 18 minutes for the airside transfer. It added £9 million to BCal's bottom line from connecting passengers. There were environmental objections from people on the route and the government withdrew the licence in 1986, after the M25 was completed. However, the road journey was longer and less reliable and has never been good enough for a realistic transfer operation.

The 1978 White Paper had assumed that Stansted would grow to 4 mppa within its existing boundaries in any event, but the option for major expansion was to be the subject of further study.

6.4. Committees and decisions

For the longer-term options, it took some time to set up ACAP, which first met on 20 September 1978, and its sub-group the Study Group on South East Airports (SGSEA). The reports were published in 1979 (Department of Trade, 1979a and b). Both groups had wide membership, from several government departments, local authorities, airports and users. John Mulkern, who by this time had become managing director of BAA, told me that the first meeting seemed to him to be lacking direction, so he volunteered that BAA would prepare the first paper which, in effect, set the agenda for the whole study.

The Treasury was again actively involved and, for a while, pushed the idea of 'deliberate restraint', citing a paper by the Central Policy Review Staff that 45 per cent of meetings could be replaced by teleconferencing and noting particular concerns about tourism congestion and lack of hotel accommodation in London (Central Policy Review Staff, 1979). The policy would have involved rationing and investing in alternative transport systems, presumably rail (Monck, 1978). It may seem odd that the Treasury was pursuing such a line but, with much of the aviation industry in the public sector, there were public spending implications and the economic value of air travel had not been established. The line taken by Treasury representatives at ACAP meetings was that it was important to establish the need for airport capacity from first principles, but they received little support (indeed vehement opposition) from other government departments or the local authority representatives, except those from outside the South East (Treasury, 1979a). Internal Treasury memos in April 1979 complained that the airport lobby was always allowed to have things their own way and that the Treasury was in danger of being outmanoeuvred and isolated (Treasury, 1979b).

To find sites for the post-1990 capacity as set out in the 1978 White Paper, SGSEA had a working party on airport sites. Initially this was limited to DoE, DoT, Department of Transport (DTp), BAA, CAA and the Standing Conference on London and South East Regional Planning (SCLSERP), representing local authorities, but was soon widened to include BA, British Rail (BR) and the Ministry of Defence (MoD). The specification was for a two-runway airport capable of accommodating 50 mppa. The working party used the well-established process of looking for sites by first excluding unsuitable areas, such as those that would have airspace conflicts with Heathrow and Gatwick, urban areas and areas with planning designations such as green belt and Area of Outstanding Natural Beauty (AONB). It then created a long list of sites and finally reduced this to a shortlist of six: Hoggeston (Buckinghamshire), Langley (Hertfordshire), Maplin (Essex), Stansted (Essex), Willingale (Essex) and Yardley Chase (Northamptonshire). The working party visited the six shortlisted sites during 1979 and in May 1979 a press release announced them.

Hoggeston was close to the Cublington site that had been recommended by the majority report of the Roskill Commission (see Chapter 3) but would have resulted in employment overheating and the closure of RAF Upper Heyford. Langley, close to Stevenage, would require the closure of RAF Wattisham and Alconbury and would have had difficulty in attracting labour but would require relatively short road and rail spurs. Maplin would require significant new road and rail access and the closure of the Shoeburyness firing range but would result in the least noise disturbance. Stansted would require short road and rail spurs and had the lowest construction costs, but there would be concerns about labour supply, urbanisation and noise. Yardley Chase was within a designated growth area but would require the closure of RAF Upper Heyford and Alconbury and was the furthest from London. Willingale, which was closest to London and would therefore have the shortest access times, was actually within the airspace exclusion area.

SGSEA was chaired by a DoE civil servant, Stan Smith. Geoff Ambrose told me that BAA's stance was not to indicate a preference, but to seek allies among the local authorities who opposed certain sites that BAA was not keen on. The MoD provided information about the closure of defence establishments and at one stage brought as many as eight representatives to a meeting (Department of the Environment, 1979). Other government departments and agencies commented: the Nature Conservancy Council was opposed to Maplin, and the Ministry of Agriculture, Fisheries and Food (MAFF) provided information on bird strikes. The Home Office was concerned about the effect of the Langley site on the Baldock monitoring station and Cambridge University provided information about the Lords Bridge Observatory. BR provided information about rail access. SCLSERP said that Maplin remained the best choice but the International Air Transport Association (IATA) did not support Maplin or Yardley Chase. The GLC sought to promote Maplin as a two-centre site, with a major terminal operation in east London, but BAA criticised the GLC report on its Maplin proposal as 'highly misleading' (Smith, 1979). Geoff Ambrose told me that local community groups did not play a significant role in SGSEA, although Stan Smith took an entirely neutral stance and ensured that all parties were able to present their viewpoints.

Peter Sanders, current chairman of the North West Essex and East Hertfordshire Preservation Association (NWEEHPA), told me something of the history of opposition to Stansted. NWEEHPA had contributed to the 1975/76 consultation and noted that the 1978 White Paper, while setting limits on Heathrow (to four terminals) and Gatwick (to two terminals), had not set a limit on Stansted, although the short-term proposal was for only limited use of the existing runway. The history as set out in Sanders' evidence to the Stansted Generation 1 (G1) Inquiry of 2007 (see Chapter 8), and also in his book on the history of the village of Stansted Mountfitchet (Sanders, 2016), does not mention ACAP or SGSEA. Nor does it mention the subsequent announcement by Secretary of State for Trade John Nott that BAA should be invited to bring forward proposals for a new terminal and outline planning consent for a second runway at Stansted, which may suggest that NWEEHPA was taken by surprise by the announcement.

The airlines were represented at ACAP and SGSEA by IATA – the representative was Tom Carter of BA. He told me that BA was not particularly interested in the location of a third London airport, but wanted to ensure that expansion at existing airports, particularly Heathrow, was not ruled out. Similarly, Laurie Price told me that BCal did not seek greater involvement because its focus was on making Gatwick work, and a second runway was not on the agenda. However, given that the specification for the new airport was for two runways, SGSEA did not consider a fifth terminal at Heathrow or a second runway at Gatwick, which had been ruled out in the 1978 White Paper. This caused BA to complain in a letter from Ross Stainton, then BA's chairman, in November 1979, although by then the committees had completed their work (Stainton, 1979).

BAA's view, given in a letter from Norman Payne also in November 1979, was that a fifth Heathrow terminal would not defer the need for a new airport (Payne, 1979). SCLSERP indicated its continuing opposition to Heathrow Terminal 5 and a Gatwick second runway. The ACAP report (Department of Trade, 1979a) rejected Heathrow Terminal 5 on the grounds of timing, costs, noise and the complexity of the terminal arrangements, and a second runway at Gatwick because of timing, defence issues and the loss of homes (the second runway would have been to the north of the airport).

The issue of not meeting demand anywhere, which had been put forward by the Treasury, was rejected in the ACAP report on the grounds that the reduction in adverse impacts (the loss of agricultural land and reduced noise) would not be sufficient to outweigh the economic benefits of expansion. The report also said that the contribution of regional airports to meeting demand would not be sufficient to affect the basic problem of a shortfall of capacity in the South East. A new airport at Severnside, in south Wales, one of whose proponents was the Ealing Aircraft Noise Action Group, was considered but rejected. SGSEA did not attempt to rank the six shortlisted sites and ACAP also did not make a recommendation on the site.

As BAA and BA were nationalised industries, they had sponsoring departments in government and spent a lot of time keeping close to government, MPs, peers and trade unions. BAA was considered to be less of a problem because of its consistent financial performance, compared with BA, whose finances were less stable. Geoff Ambrose told me that BAA judged that politicians would accept increases in terminal capacity because the noise impact was related to existing runways and independent research had shown no difference in house prices under flight paths compared with neighbouring areas.

While ACAP and SGSEA were busily studying airports policy, there were some major events taking place in the wider world. The 'winter of discontent' in 1978/79 was accompanied by a contracting economy, public spending cuts and high interest rates. MP Airey Neave was killed by an IRA bomb in Westminster and Lord Mountbatten was assassinated in Ireland. Anthony Blunt was revealed as the fourth man in the Cambridge spy scandal. A referendum on Scottish devolution failed to reach the 40 per cent approval threshold. Abroad, a new majority government took over in Rhodesia and, in technology, the first CD appeared. In a general election in May 1979, a Conservative government led by Margaret Thatcher was elected. The National Archives do not reveal any suggestion of a change of policy despite the change of government, and the airports policy proposals were put to the Cabinet on 13 December 1979 (Cabinet Office, 1979). Chaired by Margaret Thatcher, the meeting also considered the transfer of powers of local authorities, British Leyland and Honda, lifting sanctions against Rhodesia, nuclear arms controls, the European Economic Community budget and the UK economic outlook. An internal concern found in the files is a note from another part of the DTp requesting that further expansion at Heathrow (beyond Terminal 4) be ruled out because it could enable objectors to the M25 Staines-to-Heathrow section to force a reopening of the decision (Department of Transport, 1979).

At the Cabinet meeting, the airports item was led by John Nott, Secretary of State for Trade. The key points were that there should be

- an end to uncertainty
- the fullest use of regional airports
- no major new airport for London
- a fourth terminal at Heathrow, but not a fifth
- no second runway at Gatwick
- an invitation to BAA to bring forward proposals for a new terminal and outline planning consent for a second runway at Stansted.

In the discussion, the need for public and parliamentary debate, and for public expenditure on road and rail links, was noted. The minutes record the prime minister's summing up of the discussion and the Cabinet's approval. The announcement was made to Parliament on 17 December 1979, along with the publication of the ACAP and SGSEA reports and the decision on the Heathrow Terminal 4 Inquiry. The subtitle of this book is taken from John Nott's words on that day in Parliament, when he said, 'Years of indecision, decision and counter-decision reflect no credit on this country's capacity to make difficult but necessary choices' (HC Deb 17 December 1979).

Academic comment on this period is limited, but there are a few key papers worth noting. The issue of regional diversion has been studied, with Francis and Humphreys (2001) suggesting that regional 'clawback' would occur if Heathrow charges were higher, although they recognised that such higher charges would threaten the share of connecting traffic and weaken the UK's competitive position. The processes of the Maplin Review, the Airports Strategy for Great Britain consultation, the 1978 White Paper, ACAP and SGSEA were noted by Professor Peter Hall as not having the benefit of a South East Regional Plan to guide them (Hall, 1982). Hall also noted the influence of various parties, although he implied that these may even balance or cancel each other, for example with the pro-expansion airports lobby losing influence during the Roskill Commission period while the Wing Resistance Association (who opposed expansion at Cublington) used resources supplied by some residents to influence the overturning of the Roskill majority recommendation. In an article in *New Society* in January 1979 (Hall, 1979), Hall commented on the campaign by Amsterdam Schiphol Airport to market itself as London's third airport, and suggested that this fortified the arguments for a major new airport

Figure 6.2 A 1979 cartoon from the *Architects' Journal*, published after the shortlisted sites considered by SGSEA were revealed
(Cartoon courtesy of Louis Hellman)

at Maplin. Farrington (1984), commenting on the involvement of local representatives in ACAP and SGSEA, said that people living in the vicinity of sites felt 'dismay and anger at the apparent ineptitude of the decision-making process' (p. 169). Colin Buchanan, responsible for the minority recommendation for the Foulness (Maplin) site in the Roskill Commission, said in 1979 that no major new airport capacity should now be contemplated in the South East because of the 'iniquity of threats reimposed' (Buchanan, 1979). His article in the *Architects' Journal* included a cartoon which likened the situation to *Watership Down* (see Figure 6.2). He went further, saying that travel patterns should be redrawn and scarce fuel used for other purposes.

In later years, we will see a much greater involvement of both support and opposition groups, alongside a decline in the role of civil servants, albeit with ministers still as the decision-makers.

6.5. Inquiries and a White Paper

The 1980s therefore began with a clear statement of policy based on a White Paper, followed by a series of studies, consultations and committees which had involved a wide range of interested parties. Public inquiries had taken place into the plans for Heathrow Terminal 4 and Gatwick North Terminal, and approval had been given to the former. Passenger numbers were growing and there was a relatively new government. Although not directly associated with airport expansion, it is worth noting a significant step in airline competition policy (which, as noted in Chapter 2, is a key driver of airport use). The Civil Aviation Act of 1980, among other things, enabled British Midland Airways to compete with BA at Heathrow and BCal and Cathay Pacific to compete on the route to Hong Kong (which was still then under British control) (Glaister et al., 2006).

The House of Lords debated airports policy on 14 February 1980 (HL Deb 14 February 1980) and the Commons a week later (HC Deb 21 February 1980). Nothing new was raised, and many of the contributions related to personal experiences or constituency concerns.

The next step was the Airports Inquiries of 1981–1983, under Inspector Graham Eyre QC. Initially, this was set up to consider BAA's application for a new terminal at Stansted to accommodate 15 mppa, with potential expansion to 25 mppa based on the existing runway, and the safeguarding of land for a second runway, as identified by SGSEA. However, the inquiries were expanded to cover several other proposals (hence the plural 'inquiries'). Uttlesford District Council (the local authority for Stansted) submitted an application for a fifth terminal at Heathrow. This might be considered a rather bizarre act, but the council, supported by Essex and Hertfordshire county councils and others, opposed the expansion of Stansted and believed that making a planning application was the best way of ensuring that an alternative was considered at the inquiries. Technical support was provided by BA, who, although it had participated in the ACAP and SGSEA studies, had never been happy that further expansion at Heathrow had been ruled out. Tom Carter told me that pressure was put on BA to withdraw its support but that correspondence between Lord King (chairman of BA) and Margaret Thatcher suggested that Heathrow Terminal 5 would assist with BA's forthcoming privatisation. The main anti-Stansted group, NWEEHPA, also supported the application and Sherwood (2009), writing from a perspective of opposition to Heathrow development, alleges that they persuaded Uttlesford District Council to submit the application. Sherwood says that it is understandable for groups to suggest that a development should go elsewhere, but it was 'almost without precedent' to identify a specific alternative (p. 131). Peter Sanders told me that he understood that NWEEHPA had a close relationship with Uttlesford District Council and it was possible that they 'inspired' the application. BAA was put in the awkward position of having to oppose expansion at Heathrow, primarily because the logic of the planning system is that it has to be demonstrated that there is no better alternative than the one being proposed. There were other

Figure 6.3 Quendon Hall in Essex, now a wedding venue; the 1981–1983 Airports Inquiries took place here in a temporary building on the back lawn, and there was a croquet match between the parties on the front lawn, but there is no record of who won
(Photograph: Scott Miller)

technical objections to the Heathrow Terminal 5 application, but the principle was clearly about Heathrow as an alternative to Stansted.

Other proposals were also considered at the 1981–1983 inquiries. The Town and Country Planning Association submitted an application for Maplin, which had been rejected by the government based on the advice of ACAP and SGSEA. Although the association subsequently withdrew the application, the proposal was considered, as was (briefly) Yardley Chase, another of the SGSEA shortlisted sites. A more substantive case was put forward by the North of England Regional Consortium (NOERC), a group of local authorities and others, led primarily by Manchester Airport (itself owned by a group of local authorities). Its case was that Stansted should not be expanded and that, instead, traffic should be either diverted or retained in the regions.

The inquiries lasted for 258 days and were held initially at Quendon Hall, some 6 miles (10 km) north of Stansted Airport (see Figure 6.3). Now a wedding venue, a temporary building was used for the inquiries, with plenty of space for public observers, as well as the legal and support teams for the parties. For the final six months, the inquiries moved to the far less attractive surroundings of the Centre Airport Hotel at Heathrow (now the Thistle Hotel). Prior to the inquiries there were meetings between the parties to try to reduce areas of disagreement, and campaigns to put the cases to the wider public. BAA took a mobile display around villages in the Stansted area and attended meetings at village and town halls. There was plenty of opposition, which could be seen in roadside posters and by the attendance at meetings, but the behaviour of the protestors was always polite, albeit strongly voiced. Peter Sanders told me that he understood NWEEHPA's main concerns were noise, the loss of land and listed buildings, and a general concern about the protection of the rural character of the area and its potential loss to urbanisation. An illustration of differing perspectives came from a debate about agriculture. Evidence was put forward that the highly productive agricultural land led to a 'monoculture' where ecological diversity was limited, but NWEEHPA felt that such high agricultural productivity was what this part of England was good at. Undoubtedly the majority of local opinion opposed expansion at Stansted, but there was a significant minority voice in support, led by a desire for better economic prospects. Geoff Ambrose, who managed many of BAA's inquiry teams over many years, told me that one of the greatest concerns initially was about the acquisition of land through compulsory purchase. A meeting with local farmers had been facilitated by the National Farmers' Union (NFU), which was initially hostile. After the meeting several landowners agreed to sell. In the end, BAA owned a significant number of the properties that would be required, and these were leased or rented out pending their being absorbed into the developed airport.

The range of subjects discussed at the inquiries was much wider than had been the case at the Heathrow Terminal 4 and Gatwick North Terminal inquiries. The need for additional capacity based on the forecasts was examined in much more detail because it would mean airlines moving services to Stansted rather than just growing their existing bases. The expectation was that Stansted would accommodate large aircraft operating mainly on charter flights (after the new terminal opened, it was the LCCs which dominated, which have a very different business model and use smaller aircraft). While BA proposed expansion at Heathrow instead of Stansted, BCal supported Stansted on the basis that, according to Laurie Price, charter airlines would be moved there under the then current IATA slot allocation rules, allowing BCal to expand at Gatwick. However, this strategy was noted by the opponents of Stansted with some glee when BCal agreed that they did not plan to relocate their services to Stansted. The NOERC case questioned the forecasts in terms of meeting regional demand at regional airports. Surface access was a key issue. The M11 had been completed from London's North Circular Road to Cambridge, but the Airport Junction would need to be upgraded from a roundabout to direct links. More significantly, a rail link was needed, involving a new spur from the London–Cambridge West Anglia Main Line, including a tunnel beneath the airport and a new station. In terms of impacts, noise was, of course, an important issue, given that few people were affected by the existing airport. Other environmental impacts were related to the rural nature of the site, with ecology, ancient woodlands and the loss of high-quality agricultural land being discussed. The demolition of several listed buildings was required and this led to discussions about the history of buildings in this part of Essex. The site is on high ground and there was much discussion about visual impact, with the terminal designed on one and a half levels, with the lower level being partly below ground. One of the more bizarre site visits involved the inspector and key witnesses touring the area in a minibus looking through binoculars to see a quartet of helium-filled tethered balloons which simulated the height of the terminal building (see Figure 6.4). The visual impact of long-term car parks would be softened by planting along contours, and a huge number of trees and shrubs would be planted to mitigate the visual and ecological impacts. Off site, there were major concerns that there would not be sufficient labour supply and therefore that new urban areas would be required, for example by extending Harlow or Bishops Stortford. Much of this wider concern was debated in the context of the lack of a clear regional strategy for the London–Cambridge corridor.

Alastair McDermid was part of BAA's team at the 1981–1983 Airports Inquiries and one of his responsibilities was to counter the NOERC case. He told me that BAA's knowledge of the data about passengers' origins and destinations, combined with the expertise of Professor Rigas Doganis, who was called as an expert witness on aviation economics, was able to punch holes in NOERC's contention that restricting growth in the South East would help regions outside the South East grow faster. Stan Maiden was BAA's forecasting manager and gave BAA's evidence on the subject, and he recalled briefing QCs to cross-examine the NOERC witnesses after a major

Figure 6.4 Balloons over Essex: demonstrating the visual impact of the new Stansted terminal by flying a helium-filled giant hamburger
(Author's photograph collection)

flaw was found in their evidence. Lionel Read QC was BAA's lead counsel and had a habit of swinging his fob watch into his waistcoat pocket when he completed a series of questions and did so at the end of cross-examination of NOERC to emphasise the conclusive nature of his questions.

Inspector Graham Eyre's massive report was published in December 1984 (Eyre, 1984) and recommended that approval should be given for the new terminal at Stansted, with growth controlled by Parliament through a limit on aircraft movements. The case for safeguarding land for a second runway had been limited, and Eyre rejected it. He also rejected the Heathrow Terminal 5 application, but he recommended that the limit on aircraft movements (which had been imposed as a condition of the Terminal 4 Inquiry) should be scrapped and that studies should be made of how to re-provide the sludge works that occupied the site and improve surface access. Eyre's logic for scrapping the limit was that it would make no difference to the noise climate, but this was based on forecasts of aircraft movements which turned out to be significant underestimates, again showing the difficulty of predicting average aircraft loads. He rejected the NOERC case.

Eyre's conclusions referred to 'ad hoc expediency, unacceptable and ill-judged procedures, ineptness, vacillation, uncertainty and ill-advised and precipitate judgments' and stated that 'the paramount need is for the identification of a coherent strategy for the future' (Bailey, 2007: p. 251). Given this view, it was strange that Eyre had concluded that a second runway at Stansted (which was government policy since 1979) should not be pursued, whereas Heathrow Terminal 5 (which had been ruled out by the 1979 statement) should be. Eyre had an obvious concern for the loss of valuable countryside at Stansted but he seemed to be more concerned, in making a controversial decision to allow the initial development at Stansted, to provide a 'cushion' for the opponents so that the decision would not be a total failure for them. It can be argued that there was a contradiction in the recommendation to simultaneously remove the cushion from the Heathrow objectors, although the particular application for Terminal 5 was rejected.

Peter Sanders told me that NWEEHPA was naturally disappointed with Eyre's recommendation for the initial development but pleased that he recommended against a second runway in such strong language as 'nothing less than a catastrophe in environmental terms'. NWEEHPA thought there was political pressure to approve expansion and that all Eyre could do was to strongly resist a second runway.

The report was debated in Parliament in the early part of 1985 (HC Deb 30 January 1985; HL Deb 11 February 1985), with many MPs and peers repeating the various cases put forward at the inquiries. The government's decisions were announced together with a White Paper in June 1985 (Department of Transport, 1985a). The National Archives files show civil servants being very cautious in preparing the White Paper because of the Secretary of State for Transport's statutory role in deciding the applications on the basis of the evidence alone, so there was no consultation outside government (Department of Transport, 1985b). Transport Secretary Nicolas Ridley's preliminary view was more or less in line with Graham Eyre's recommendation, although he seemed to be particularly keen on expansion at Luton, but opposed to more at Gatwick. These were not issues that had been discussed at the inquiries, but the Luton expansion seems to have been scotched by concerns about airspace and the effect on defence establishments. A paper on Heathrow reveals a concern that its runway capacity matched the capacity of the four terminals and therefore that a fifth terminal would require more runway capacity to be in balance. It was recognised that average loads were a critical factor in the forecasts. The files include notes that 133 MPs might oppose a decision, based on signatures to Early Day Motions, the majority of whom supported the NOERC argument and many of whom were Conservatives. However, after a debate in the House of Commons on 17 June 1985, the government's airports policy as set out in the White Paper (the principal elements of which were the expansion of Stansted, studies of Heathrow and the privatisation of airports) was supported by 326 MPs, with 190 voting against (HC Deb 17 June 1985).

Although the Cabinet had been informed in January 1985 of the forthcoming debate on the inspector's report, the decision and the White Paper does not appear to have been discussed at a Cabinet meeting, but a letter from the prime minister's Private Secretary, dated 20 May 1985, says that the prime minister 'subject to any comments colleagues may have, is content for the White Paper to be finalised and published' (Turnbull, 1985). A note on the same file may give a clue to Mrs Thatcher's thinking, as it requests a briefing on Perry Oaks, asking 'if it is realistic to say that, subject to full engineering studies, the relocation/replacement of the Perry Oaks installation would be feasible if it were found necessary in the 1990s to rationalise and/or expand the terminal facilities at Heathrow'. The note adds, 'This need not imply major extension of the airfield such as the Inspector envisaged or the kind of development proposed by Uttlesford DC/BA at the inquiry: all that is necessary at this stage is to keep open the option of further development at Heathrow' (Delafons, 1985). It could be surmised that keeping the option of further development at Heathrow open would be sufficient to meet BA's wishes without a complete reversal of the previous policy of no further expansion.

Iryna Terlecky was a civil servant in the DTp at the time and told me that it appeared that the decision not to support the second runway at Stansted was 'purely political, based on the map of blues and reds' and that ministers were very sensitive to political issues in constituencies around Stansted and they had already established some red lines before considering the inspector's report. Although there were environmental concerns about a second runway at Stansted, mainly associated with the amount of land take, the NOERC lobby was seen as more of a political threat. Heathrow Terminal 5 was seen as a development whose time would come, but a step too far at the time. Terlecky was complimentary about Nicholas Ridley's intellect and principles and his highly developed political awareness, believing him to be someone who focused on getting things done in the right way, rather than just wanting to be seen in a good light. Ridley was, of course, very keen on privatisation, and a close, trusted colleague of Prime Minister Margaret Thatcher.

John Mulkern, BAA's managing director at the time, said that, although the BAA board was pleased with the approval for the new terminal at Stansted, they were dismayed by the decision not to go ahead with the second runway, believing it was a 'cop out'. BAA had bought many of the properties required for the second runway, and one of the first actions after publication of the White Paper was for the Department of Transport to ask BAA to sell these. The board was content with the Heathrow decision, and had firmly in their minds that Terminal 5's time would come as a logical step in the long-term sequence after Heathrow Terminal 4, Gatwick North Terminal and Stansted. The board was not surprised by the privatisation proposals and had considered many options through a 'Quo vadis?' ('Where are you going?') group of key BAA people and civil servants.

I also asked Geoff Ambrose about the Stansted second runway and why BAA had not put up a stronger case at the 1981–1983 inquiries. Geoff said that the arguments for using the existing runway at Stansted included being able to create a very modern twenty-first-century terminal without the space constraints at Heathrow and which would enable new airlines to grow away from the dominance of BA at Heathrow. Against a second runway were arguments ranging from the engineering challenges (the amount of earthworks) to airline opposition and the need for major airspace reorganisation. BAA was also keenly aware of public and parliamentary opinion, which included the NOERC and local groups. Within government, the MoD was keen on an alternative to Maplin (which would have resulted in the loss of the Shoeburyness range) but not on a two-runway Stansted, which would have meant the closure of RAF Wattisham. There was clearly support within government for the second runway, which Geoff Ambrose described as 'their baby, not ours'. But once BAA and BA had been privatised, the two organisations, led by Norman Payne and Lord King respectively, reached an understanding that they could present a united front by focusing the next expansion at Heathrow, with the need for additional runway capacity being a long way off.

Tom Carter, formerly of British Airways, gave me an interesting perspective on the Heathrow aircraft movement limit. The proposed limit had come 'out of the blue' in the T4 Inquiry inspector's report (and the subsequent government decision) and BA spent many years trying to get it reversed. BAA had accepted the limit (which was set by the government decision at 275 000 ATMs) because its forecast was that this would be the capacity of the existing runways. A Civil Aviation bill, which would have included the powers to impose such limits, was promoted in Parliament in 1984 and, at its second reading in the House of Commons on 21 November 1984, Nicholas Ridley, Secretary of State for Transport, said:

> In 1979 the Government gave a pledge that air transport movements at Heathrow would be limited to 275 000 movements a year. We would be wrong to go back on that pledge, first, because those who live around Heathrow expect us to honour it. It seems straightforward to me that a pledge should be honoured. It is they who have suffered the noise and disturbance and we are right to seek to limit it for their sakes.
>
> (HC Deb 21 November 1984).

However, Tom Carter told me that, at the committee stage, three Conservative MPs, having been briefed by BA, used a procedural motion to postpone the committee meeting. Although the government had a majority on the committee and would normally be expected to ensure the bill's progress, the three MPs took the opportunity of the absence of a number of other Conservative MPs to propose the motion. Subsequently, the Secretary of State withdrew the bill, although the powers to impose limits were included in the later Airports Act of 1986. In the meantime, the Airports Inquiries Inspector's Report had recommended the scrapping of the limit at Heathrow, and the government had accepted this recommendation in the 1985 White Paper. Tom Carter suggested that Nicholas Ridley was reluctant to go back on the promise to impose the limit, but was persuaded by the logic of the inspector's report.

As well as agreeing with the inspector's recommendations on Stansted, Heathrow and the other issues, the White Paper also proposed the privatisation of airports. BAA was to be privatised as a single company, and local-authority airports were required to become arm's length or sold off. This radical change in ownership was in line with the Conservative government's general policy of privatisation, but it is remarkable that the policy of development of additional capacity was considered in almost total isolation from ownership. The National Archives files indicate that the prime minister had been briefed on privatisation in February 1985 and had been advised that there were powerful reasons for keeping the London airports together as a system. Some time after the White Paper in December 1985, but before the privatisation took place, there is a letter from Nicholas Ridley to Chancellor Nigel Lawson noting that opponents to Stansted may seek to have that airport privatised separately, so as to frustrate its development (Ridley, 1985).

Roy Griffins had been the secretary to the Airports Inquiries of 1981–1983 and was head of airports policy in the DTp in 1986 when the Airports Bill was going through Parliament and then parliamentary private secretary (PPS) to the Secretary of State for Transport for the rest of the decade. Griffins agreed that the privatisation was coincidental to the policy issues, but that the fact that there was policy certainty meant that a good price was obtained for BAA. Iryna Terlecky was the bill's manager and told me that there was little effective opposition to the privatisation of BAA as a whole in the debates or the committee stages, but instead the amendments tended to focus on how the monopoly would be regulated. There was, ironically, more concern about opposition from within the Conservative Party than from Labour and the focus was on keeping government backbenchers on side. A briefing note for a meeting between the prime minister and the transport secretary on 12 March 1986 noted, 'So far so good on the Airports Bill, but the Prime Minister may want Nicholas Ridley's latest assessment of the possible threat from those who advocate splitting up the ownership of the London airports – supposedly as a spoiling tactic against the development of Stansted' (Wybrew, 1986).

Reaction to the White Paper was as expected. BAA naturally welcomed the decision, while opponents were disappointed. BA was content that Heathrow Terminal 5 was back on the agenda. In the debate in the House of Commons on 17 June 1985 (HC Deb 17 June 1985) the usual constituency issues were raised, and there were numerous media reports. There is very little academic comment, except on the issue of privatisation. On the process, the only paper published is by Mike Toms, who was part of the BAA Inquiry Team. Toms argued that the 'process has not constrained debate, no party was deprived of the opportunity to air its views, environmental issues have been balanced with economic and operational matters, following political decision' and that 'the common view that the Stansted proposal is the manifestation of the narrow sectional interest of the BAA alone is therefore a false representation because it was preceded by ACAP and SGSEA etc.' (Toms, 1984).

David Starkie has written extensively about privatisation, and wrote (with others) that Stansted was loss-making and unlikely to make a return on investment, so that the 'financial viability of the

Stansted proposal is very questionable' (Hill *et al.*, 1986: p. 13). The authors did not believe that Stansted should be cross-subsidised and therefore argued for splitting up BAA. The forecasts in the 1985 White Paper were criticised as underestimating the extent to which market forces will reduce demand because of the costs of accessing and developing Gatwick and Stansted. In effect, the argument was that if BAA had been separately privatised, the development would not have been promoted (thus echoing the concern noted in the Ridley/Lawson correspondence mentioned above). Sir Alan Haselhurst, the MP for Saffron Walden, told me that he was also opposed to BAA being privatised as a single entity, not just because it had promoted Stansted as part of a London system, but also because of a natural Conservative desire to enable competition and prevent monopolies. He noted that Norman Payne, chairman of BAA at this time, was a very powerful figure and so his views on the form of privatisation prevailed. Haselhurst's dislike of the BAA monopoly continued through his time on the Transport Committee in the 1990s and he believes that the eventual break-up of BAA has brought significant benefits. Also, more recently, Starkie has monitored the changes in the relationships between airlines and airports and the break-up of BAA and, as we will see later, there is now a very altered situation where the airports, under different ownership, have competed for the right to expand. However, the arguments about airport systems were not just about London, but also applied to as many as about 30 multi-airport locations around the world, including New York, Paris, Tokyo, Washington and Moscow (de Neufville and Odoni, 2003).

Within BAA, there was also concern about the financial viability of Stansted. John Phillips, who was BAA's chief economist for many years and was involved in setting airport charges and BAA's strategy, recounted that many airlines objected to increases in charges and, in particular, to any restructuring designed to better reflect asset use (for example, through peak and off-peak differentials, and weight-related and passenger-related elements), and this included non-Stansted airlines having to pay for its development. Forecasts were again crucial as the build-up of traffic would have a significant effect on Stansted's viability.

Sherwood (2009) argues that when BAA and the Thames Water Authority, which owned the Perry Oaks site on which Heathrow Terminal 5 was proposed, were both in the public sector, there was no real incentive for the site to be transferred to the airport, as it would have been merely a paper transaction. However, when they were privatised, this completely changed and Thames Water could 'gain a huge windfall profit' (p. 41).

The wider context at the time of the 1985 White Paper is worth considering. In the UK, the miners' strike ended and unemployment was falling. The first mobile phones were seen and Microsoft Windows appeared. The Antarctic ozone hole was discovered. The Big Bang (deregulation in the financial sector) took place in 1986, unemployment continued to fall (although it was still high by current levels) and inflation was decreasing. Other events that occupied politicians and the media were the Bradford City stadium fire and the Brixton and Tottenham riots (1985) and the fall of the Berlin Wall (1989). In transport, the M25 was completed in 1986, the *Herald of Free Enterprise* ferry disaster and the King's Cross fire happened in 1987, the Clapham rail crash and the Lockerbie disaster were in 1988 and the Kegworth air crash was 1989. Privatisation continued, with BA in 1986 and BAA in 1987. BA and BCal swapped routes as part of the 'spheres of influence' policy. The first long-haul twin-engine operations began (using Extended-range Twin-engine Operational Performance Standards, or ETOPS) and there were several hijacks and aviation disasters (including the Manchester aircraft fire), as well as terrorist attacks at Rome and Vienna airports. Passenger numbers had grown after a hesitant start in the early 1980s.

After the 1985 White Paper, for the rest of the decade public debate on airports policy was limited, given the openings of Heathrow Terminal 4 (1986), Gatwick North Terminal (1988) and

Figure 6.5 Sir Norman Payne (1921–2010); a civil engineer with Sir Frederick Snow, he joined the newly formed BAA as engineering director in 1966, became director of planning, then chief executive and finally chairman, retiring in 1991
(BAA, 1982)

Stansted's new terminal (1991), which provided significant new capacity. However, as well as the studies on the Perry Oaks site and rail access for Heathrow, BAA was actively considering its next steps. Alastair McDermid told me that he was involved in a group reviewing BAA's strategy in its newly privatised state, and was particularly interested in the views of the then regulator, Cliff Paice of the CAA. It was felt that more should be done for BA, which was facing strong competition from Air France, Lufthansa and KLM, all of whom were perceived as having the support of their home-base airport. The review was particularly driven by Norman Payne, by then chairman of BAA (see Figure 6.5). There were three options: Heathrow Terminal 5, Stansted second terminal and a strategy of dispersed growth at all the airports, but none of these would involve new runway capacity. BAA decided to pursue the Heathrow option.

6.6. London City sneaks under the radar

The story of London City Airport could fill a whole book (for example, Ginsberg, 2017) given its role within the development of the docklands area, but the timing of its opening coincided with this period of incremental additions to London's airports capacity, so it was not seen as a major development in aviation terms. It is not mentioned in the chapter of the 1985 White Paper on London airports, but is covered in a separate section on 'Business Aviation, STOLports and Heliports' (Department of Transport, 1985a). STOL was the acronym for Short Take-Off and Landing and suitable aircraft at the London City Airport could use the short length of runway available between the disused docks. There had been a public planning inquiry in 1983 and permission was granted in 1985, and the White Paper described the plan as a new and imaginative concept in air travel. Being developed by the private sector, it no doubt also appealed to the

Conservative government of the day. The initial plan was for a capacity of 1 mppa and such a small increment would make no material difference to the White Paper's main conclusions on the need for additional capacity. This capacity of 1 mppa was reached by the mid 1990s but growth significantly beyond this began in the mid 2000s and, with a number of extensions and additions to the infrastructure, passenger throughput had risen to 4.5 million by 2017. Expansion has not been without controversy and a number of planning applications have been opposed by some local communities, but policy support has been generally positive.

6.7. Railways and airports

The subject of rail access to airports could also fill a book (if not several) but this is a brief summary related to my personal involvement. There is sometimes a debate about which airport was the first to be served by rail, the contenders being Gatwick and Brussels, but Gatwick certainly had a rail station at its original 'beehive' terminal in the 1930s. A new station immediately next to the new terminal was built as part of the development that opened in 1958, and was a key factor in the growth of the airport from the 1960s onwards. A dedicated service of trains serving just the airport began in 1975 and the Gatwick Express brand began in 1984. Michael Schabas's excellent book on railways in London (Schabas, 2017) describes how London Underground's Piccadilly line got to Heathrow in 1977, with a subsequent extension to Terminal 4 in 1986. Schabas recalls that a BR link to Victoria was originally selected for a Heathrow link in the late 1960s, but did not get airline support. Stansted's rail link was planned and built by BR as a result of the 1985 White Paper approving the airport's expansion.

Also following the 1985 White Paper, I became involved with the Heathrow Express project. The 1985 White Paper had recommended that Heathrow's expansion beyond four terminals should be considered by first looking at how the Perry Oaks site could be released and second how a main-line rail link could be established. The Heathrow Surface Access Study (Howard Humphreys and Partners, 1988) looked at options including an express Tube and various routes for a main-line link, concluding that Paddington Station and the Great Western Main Line should be used. Michael Schabas again describes how this was developed as a joint venture between BR and BAA. I was BAA's project manager, appointed because I had experience with getting approvals. But railways were promoted by the parliamentary bill process, and my opposite number in BR, David Beynon, and his colleagues had that expertise.

The Heathrow Express Railway Bill took two and a half years to get through Parliament. It got stuck with the House of Lords Committee, who insisted on tunnelling the line from close to the main line all the way to the airport beneath open land and the M4. We had planned a surface line with a vision of a seven-span viaduct sweeping over the M4, but in the end had to bury it beneath a rubbish tip in order to ensure that the open land (which is green belt) was not subject to development pressure. By contrast, the House of Commons Committee did not delay the process. I recall that the Commons Committee was chaired by Bernie Grant MP, who had a reputation as a firebrand but, in committee, was most polite, gentlemanly and fair.

BAA had become a partner in the Heathrow Express project in part because it had recently been privatised, which enabled it to be involved in non-airport activities. By the time the project was being built, BR was beginning its privatisation process and, partly as a result, steadily reduced its involvement from 50/50 to nothing, except the provision of train paths on the main line. The cost of electrification and junctions was met by BAA, along with the major costs of tunnelling, stations and rolling stock.

Rail access had thus become a key factor in permitting expansion at the major London airports and it will also be discussed in later chapters in relation to Heathrow Terminal 5 and the plans for additional runways.

6.8. Step by step: the strategy is rebuilt

In 1974, after the cancellation of the Maplin project, there was a clear need to create new policy and, despite the downturn in air travel that was essentially the reason for the cancellation, the need for additional capacity returned quickly. This was perhaps because all the policy eggs had been in the one Maplin basket, which then broke. The civil service reacted quickly and set up a wide-ranging study, trying to apply the lessons from the previous Stansted inquiry of 1965–1966 and the Roskill Commission by considering the needs of the whole country and involving local authorities and some environmental groups. Short- and medium-term strategies were devised, which were then tested at public inquiries at Heathrow and Gatwick. The outcomes of these inquiries, while they did not satisfy everyone, seemed to get a degree of acceptance from most stakeholders, perhaps because they provided for medium-term growth but with (at the time) clear limits for the longer term. At Heathrow, a limit on aircraft movements combined with clear policy statements enabled a fourth terminal to be approved, while at Gatwick, a second terminal became possible in part because BAA and West Sussex County Council signed a legal agreement.

It can be argued that it is relatively easy to find a short- or medium-term policy solution by this combination of permitting some growth while setting limits, but it is much more difficult for this to provide long-term certainty. This was tested in the next stage, with the ACAP and SGSEA exercises leading to decisions in December 1979, the Airports Inquiries of 1981–1983 and the White Paper of 1985. ACAP, and particularly SGSEA, on the face of it, may have appeared to include wider representation, open agendas and sound analysis, but there are one or two indications that those seeking expansion were able to impose their views, for example by seeking favourable alliances and, despite policy statements to the contrary, reintroducing ideas that had previously been ruled out. Thus the Airports Inquiries of 1981–1983 considered not just the scheme that had evolved from the ACAP/SGSEA process (Stansted with two runways), but also the regional case for no South East expansion and a fifth terminal at Heathrow, both of which had been ruled out in the 1978 White Paper.

The Airports Inquiries of 1981–1983 were a thorough examination of the details of the Stansted proposals but, it could be argued, the regional and Terminal 5 cases were less well covered. The regional case had probably been included for essentially political reasons, to ensure that the final decisions received sufficient parliamentary support. The Heathrow Terminal 5 case was put forward primarily by BA and succeeded in principle, despite opposition (at least on timing and the details) from BAA, probably because of the airline's influence within government. The corollary of the recommendation to support Terminal 5 was the recommendation to abandon the second runway at Stansted, thus overturning the 1978 White Paper/SGSEA/1979 decisions. However, criticism of this recommendation and the subsequent 1985 decisions should be tempered by the fact that BA has been consistent in its views on Heathrow expansion while BAA blew with the wind and, in so doing, was rightly accused of breaking promises.

The approval of the development of Stansted with its existing runway, plus the approvals for Heathrow Terminal 4 and Gatwick's North Terminal, enabled BAA to expand significantly in all its markets and, for a while, the pressure for more expansion was relieved. The Stansted decision (to approve development with a single runway) was a blow to the opponents there (probably more so than at Heathrow or Gatwick, given that expansion would be from virtually zero to a major operation) but nevertheless was placated by the no-second-runway policy.

The 1985 White Paper also included the policy of privatisation and, although in some respects I have sought to show that it was not directly connected to the airport development elements, there are clearly some links, such as the ability to fund the development of Stansted from the profits made at Heathrow, using the argument that the London airports were a system. The form of privatisation continued to be an issue for the next 20 years until BAA eventually was broken up.

6.9. Themes for 1974–1991

Given the more detailed consideration given to this and subsequent time periods, it is possible to look for themes and patterns in the evolution of airports policy. These will be brought together in Chapter 10, but for the moment are identified as follows.

- **Forecasts**, which are the basis of proving the need for developments, were subject to much debate and criticism, in particular the relationship between passenger numbers and aircraft movements (i.e. average aircraft loads) and the issue of regional diversion.
- The development of Heathrow Terminal 4, Gatwick North Terminal and Stansted's new terminal can be seen as a series of **incremental steps**. The process was also incremental in the sense of seeking short- and medium-term solutions before looking at the longer term. This contrasts with the single, long-term strategy sought by the Roskill Commission.
- The main London airports were considered as a **system**.
- There was less analysis than Roskill, but more **consultation**.
- There were attempts to remove uncertainty about the future by setting **limits**.
- **Environmental issues**, always important at inquiries, always included noise, but other impacts varied according to location.

Notes

1. An Air Transport Movement (ATM) is a landing or take-off of an aircraft engaged in commercial air transport. It could be a passenger or cargo flight, scheduled or charter, but excludes private/business aviation and military aircraft movements.

REFERENCES

Ashpole H (undated) *The Gatwick–Heathrow Airlink*. www.british-caledonian.com/BCalLGW-LHRirlinkP1.html accessed (11 October 2016).

BAA (1978) *Annual Report and Accounts 1977–1978*. British Airports Authority, London, UK.

BAA (1982) *Annual Report and Accounts 1981/82*. British Airports Authority, Gatwick, UK.

Bailey J (2007) An assessment of UK Government aviation policies and their implications. *Journal of Airport Management* **1(3)**: 249–261.

Buchanan C (1979) Third Airport: the morality. *Architects' Journal*, 8 August 1979. TNA file AT 63/35.

Cabinet Office (1978) Conclusions of a meeting of the Cabinet on 19 January 1978. TNA file CAB 128/63.

Cabinet Office (1979) Conclusions of a meeting of the Cabinet on 13 December 1979. TNA file CAB 128/66/25.

Central Policy Review Staff (1979) Paper on aviation forecasts. TNA file T 370/1323.

de Neufville R and Odoni A (2003) *Airport Systems Planning, Design and Management*, 2nd edition. McGraw-Hill, London, UK and New York, USA.

Delafons J (1985) Note from John Delafons to Mr Gunn on Stansted/T5 – Perry Oaks, 21 March 1985. TNA file AT 94/108.

Dell E (1978) Note to the prime minister from the Secretary of State for Transport on moving US airlines' flights to Boston to Gatwick, 29 June 1978. TNA file T 370/1327.

Department of the Environment (1979) Minutes of the third meeting of the SGSEA working party on airport sites held on 19 February 1979. TNA file AT 94/15.

Department of Trade (1975) *Airport Strategy for Great Britain: Part 1 The London Area.* HMSO, London, UK.
Department of Trade (1976) *Airport Strategy for Great Britain: Part 2 The Regional Airports.* HMSO, London, UK.
Department of Trade (1978) *Airports Policy.* Cmnd 7084, HMSO, London, UK.
Department of Trade (1979a) *Report of the Advisory Committee on Airports Policy.* Department of Trade, HMSO, London, UK.
Department of Trade (1979b) *Report of the Study Group on South East Airports.* Department of Trade, HMSO, London, UK.
Department of Transport (1979) Note warning of M25 issues, 20 November 1979. TNA file AT 63/35.
Department of Transport (1985a) *Airports Policy.* Cmnd 9542, London, UK.
Department of Transport (1985b) *Skeleton White Paper.* TNA file AT 94/107.
Eyre G (1984) *The Airports Inquiries 1981–1983.* Department of the Environment, London, UK.
Farrington JH (1984) A third London airport: options and decision-making. *Built Environment* **10(3)**: 168–180.
Finlay A (1976) Letter from Alec Finlay, group planning director, British Airways, on airport strategy for Great Britain. TNA file BT 338/70.
Francis G and Humphreys I (2001) Airport regulation: reflecting on the lessons from BAA plc. *Public Money & Management* **21(1)**: 49–52.
Ginsberg M (2017) *London City Airport: 30 Years Serving the Capital.* Crecy Publishing, Manchester, UK.
Glaister S, Burnham J, Stevens H and Travers T (2006) *Transport Policy in Britain,* 2nd edition. Palgrave Macmillan, Basingstoke, UK.
Hall P (1978) *Paper to the ICE, 6 February 1978.* TNA file AT 94/12.
Hall P (1979) Article in *New Society,* 11 January 1979. TNA file AT 63/34/1.
Hall P (1982) *Great Planning Disasters.* University of California Press, Berkeley, CA, USA.
HC Deb 1 February 1978, vol. 943, col. 456.
HC Deb 17 December 1979, vol. 976, col. 35.
HC Deb 21 February 1980, vol. 979, col. 684.
HC Deb 21 November 1984, vol. 68, col. 301.
HC Deb 30 January 1985, vol. 72, col. 291.
HC Deb 17 June 1985, vol. 82, col. 29.
Hill R, Starkie D and Thompson D (1986) Some comments on the 'Airports Policy' White Paper. *IFS Working Paper 77.* Institute for Fiscal Studies, London, UK.
HL Deb 14 February 1980, vol. 405, col. 320.
HL Deb 11 February 1985, vol. 460, col. 9.
HMG (Her Majesty's Government) (1980) Civil Aviation Act 1980. Chapter 60. HMSO, London, UK.
HMG (Her Majesty's Government) (1986) Airports Act 1986. Chapter 31. HMSO, London, UK.
Howard Humphreys and Partners (1988) *Heathrow Surface Access Study.* Department of Transport, London, UK.
Hutton AC (1974) Note of dinner with BAA held on 9 December 1974. TNA file AVIA 112/250.
Melville R (1977) Letter from Sir Ronald Melville to Sir Ian Bancroft, 15 June 1977. TNA file AT 94/2.

Monck N (1978) Letter from N Monck, Treasury, to S Steele, Department of Trade. TNA file T 370/1323.
Payne N (1979) Letter from Norman Payne, 22 November 1979, on ACAP. TNA file AT 94/105.
Ridley N (1985) Letter to Nigel Lawson from Nicholas Ridley, 30 December 1985. TNA file AT 94/108.
Ritchie JM (1976) Letter from JM Ritchie, British Caledonian Airways, on airport strategy for Great Britain. TNA file BT 338/70.
Sanders P (2016) *On the Beaten Track – A History of Stansted Mountfitchet*. Stansted Mountfitchet Local History Society, Stansted Mountfitchet, UK.
Schabas M (2017) *The Railway Metropolis: How Planners, Politicians and Developers Shaped Modern London*. ICE Publishing, London, UK.
Sherwood P (2009) *Heathrow: 2000 Years of History*. The History Press, Stroud, UK.
Smith S (1979) Memo to Mr Shearer, Department of the Environment, from Stan Smith, 8 March 1979. TNA file AT 94/15.
Stainton R (1979) Letter from Ross Stainton, 21 November 1979, on ACAP. TNA file AT 94/105.
Toms M (1984) Airport development and the planning process: the Stansted case. *Built Environment* **10(3)**: 181–186.
Treasury (1979a) Progress note on ACAP, 9 July 1979. TNA file T 370/1325.
Treasury (1979b) Internal memos on ACAP. TNA file T 370/1328.
Turnbull A (1985) Letter to Richard Allan, Department of Transport, from Andrew Turnbull, 20 May 1985. TNA file AT 94/108.
Walters A (1978) Airports – an economic survey. *Journal of Transport Economics and Policy* **12(2)**: 125–160.
Webber M (1977a) Memo from M Webber, Department of the Environment, to S Smith, Department of Trade. TNA file AT 94/2.
Webber M (1977b) Minute by M Webber, Department of the Environment, 17 May 1977. TNA file AT 94/1.
Wilks J (1974) Letter from the Department of the Environment to local authorities, 15 August 1974. TNA file AT 94/9.
Wybrew J (1986) Briefing note to Mr Wicks, 25 February 1986, ahead of prime minister's bilateral meeting with Nicholas Ridley. TNA file PREM 19/3496.

Chapter 7
1991–1997: policy vacuum

7.1. Introduction

At the start of the 1990s, new capacity had been opened at Heathrow (Terminal 4) and Gatwick (North Terminal) and would soon be completed at Stansted. There is a slight overlap between the last chapter and this one as the first key study (RUCATSE) began before the opening of the new Stansted terminal.

There had been continuous growth in passenger numbers in the late 1980s, although growth halted in 1990 and 1991. BAA plc was now in the private sector, with a new chief executive, John Egan (see Figure 7.1). Norman Payne, who had led the strategy through the 1970s and 1980s, retired as chairman in 1991. The US airlines Pan Am and TWA fell by the wayside but were replaced at Heathrow by United Airlines and American Airlines. This required the removal of Traffic Distribution Rules (which prevented new airlines from starting operations at Heathrow) and this had the effect of undermining growth at Gatwick and Stansted. In 1992 Air Europe ceased operations and British Airways (BA) acquired Dan-Air. Airline liberalisation had begun in the USA in the 1980s and was beginning in Europe. Three packages of EU regulations between 1987 and 1993 opened up the European market (Budd, 2007) and low-cost carriers (LCCs) such as Ryanair and EasyJet began operations, initially at the less busy Luton and Stansted airports. The next generation of jet aircraft was beginning to appear, either as developments of existing types (Boeing 737 and 747) or new types (Airbus A320 and A330). Throughout the 1990s, passenger numbers grew at the London airports, albeit slowly at Stansted and Luton until the LCCs became established.

Margaret Thatcher was replaced as prime minister by John Major in November 1990 and the Conservatives retained power in the 1992 general election. In the early 1990s, a recession was taking place in the UK and there were riots over the poll tax. Canary Wharf, in London, began to be developed and the M40 motorway was completed. The Maastricht Treaty was signed in 1992 and the UK left the EU Exchange Rate Mechanism. Internationally, 1989 had seen the fall of the Berlin Wall and Germany was reunited in 1990. The USSR collapsed in 1991 and the Baltic states began to separate. After the recession of the early 1990s, most of the rest of the decade saw economic growth, with unemployment falling from 3 million to 1.3 million. There were continuing IRA attacks until the Good Friday Agreement in 1998, and internationally there were hijacks and the Balkan conflict. Global warming began to be discussed, with the UN Framework on Climate Change following the Rio Earth Summit and a World Meteorological Organisation report on ozone depletion. At the general election of 1997, the Conservatives were replaced by a New Labour government.

The two major airports policy events of the 1990s were the Runway Capacity to serve the South East (RUCATSE) study and the Heathrow Terminal 5 Inquiry. The decision on Terminal 5 was made in 2001 but the subject is dealt with in this chapter. (The next stage of airports policy began in the late 1990s, but is covered in the next chapter.) The RUCATSE study and Heathrow

Figure 7.1 Sir John Egan, the former chairman of Jaguar who became BAA's chief executive in 1990 (Photograph: BAA, 1998)

Terminal 5 Inquiry resulted in publications that are a key source for this chapter. The National Archives (TNA) files are generally only released after 30 years, so there is little of this material available. However, interviews with key individuals have revealed some issues. There is also more academic and general comment on this period than on the 1970s and 1980s.

7.2. The inconclusive search for a strategy for the next decade

Although the Stansted terminal development had enabled that airport's runway to be used more, concerns about runway capacity at Heathrow, and to a lesser extent at Gatwick, remained. After the privatisation of BAA, the government turned to the Civil Aviation Authority (CAA) instead of BAA for advice. The CAA published three papers, CAP 548, 559 and 570. CAP 548, published in 1989 (CAA, 1989), was the report of a committee on runway utilisation, which recommended ways to increase capacity within environmental constraints at Heathrow and Gatwick. CAP 559 and 570 were specifically about runway capacity and forecasts of aircraft movements and suggested a need for more capacity by 2005 (Humphreys, 1994). CAP 570 identified ten existing airports where more runway capacity could be provided, including Heathrow, Gatwick and Stansted.

Forecasts of aircraft movements once again raised the issue of average aircraft size. The 1970s had seen the introduction of wide-bodied aircraft – the Boeing 747, McDonnell Douglas DC10, Lockheed TriStar and Airbus A300, with seats for 300–500 passengers compared with less than 200 in the aircraft they replaced. Average seat numbers grew as shown in Figure 7.2.

However, the aircraft size trend changed in the early 1980s to a much more modest growth rate of less than 1 per cent per annum, much lower than the rate of growth of passengers. Academic research shows that, generally for transport, as traffic volume grows, vehicle size would be

Figure 7.2 Change in average aircraft size in the global fleet in terms of average number of seats per departure
(Source: Global Market Forecast 2006–2026, Airbus, 2007, France, in Lee et al., 2009)

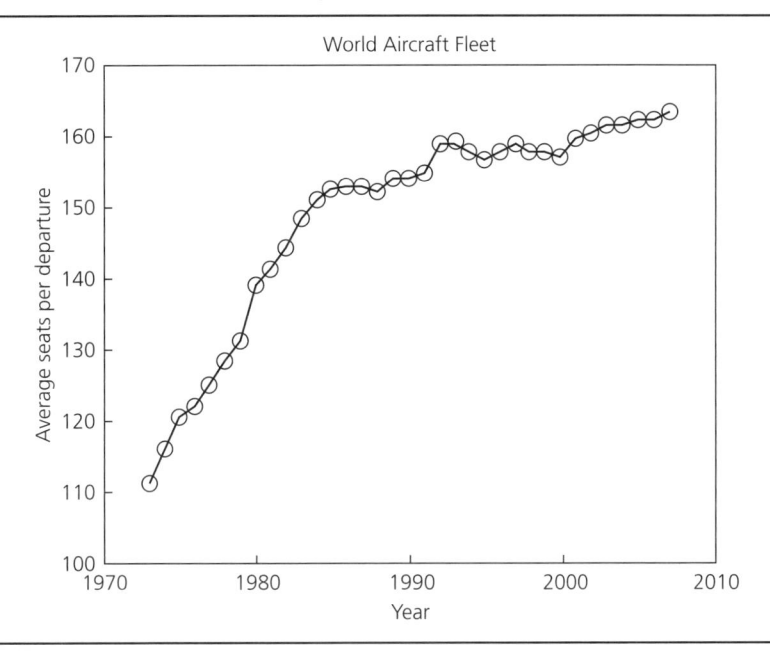

expected to increase also. However, this has not been the case for air transport, because airlines find it more profitable to increase load factor and frequency (Givoni and Rietveld, 2009). This is also described as 'the puzzle of aircraft size' by Zhang (2014).

John Phillips, then BAA's head of airport strategy, told me that BAA was monitoring the CAA activity throughout this period, noting the difference in forecasts of aircraft movements, which had also been the case in earlier studies, and, in particular, the assessment of the capacity of the runways in terms of passengers. BAA was anxious that the runway debate did not overshadow the need for more terminal capacity. BAA's strategy was to continue to develop the existing terminals at Heathrow, Gatwick and Stansted, and then the next major tranche of terminal capacity would be either at Stansted (Terminal B) or Heathrow (Terminal 5). Stansted B would be cheaper, but Terminal 5 would be better value. Advice was also received that it would not be possible to pursue both at the same time. The board decided on the latter.

The RUCATSE study was set up by the government in response to the CAA's advice. Its terms of reference were to follow CAP 570, but to have regard to the 1985 White Paper policy of no second runways at either Gatwick or Stansted, and to look again at regional diversion. It was set up in late 1990 and was led by a senior Department of Transport (DTp) civil servant, Russell Sunderland. Essentially a working group, it included representatives from government departments, the South East Regional Planning Conference (SERPLAN), the CAA, the Joint Airport Committee of Local Authorities (JACOLA), the British Air Transport Association (BATA), BAA plc, the Airport Operators Association (AOA) and community groups. In total there were 90 members in a number of groups. Politicians were not directly involved but there is correspondence from Cecil Parkinson in 1990 (Parkinson, 1990), when he was Transport Secretary, notifying other ministers about setting up the study. This provoked some replies, but there was little parliamentary activity until the report was published in 1993. I asked Russell Sunderland what was meant by the phrase 'have regard to' in the terms of reference in relation to the previous policies of no second runway at either Gatwick or Stansted. He said that RUCATSE's interpretation was that it was meant as a warning that, if you wanted to change these policies, you had better have a very good reason to do so, but they were not absolute rules. Sunderland also recalled that the community representatives from the Gatwick area made a particularly strong case against the idea of a second runway at that airport.

As RUCATSE's remit included regional diversion, it sought to forecast how runway capacity would be used at several airports in England. These forecasts were criticised because they did not question the economic growth assumptions, or the effect of liberalisation, or test the effect of constraining capacity (Humphreys, 1994). A regional subgroup considered diversion and 'clawback' but the overall conclusion was that additional runway capacity would be needed in the South East by 2010 (five years later than suggested in CAP 570). Sunderland told me that ministers clearly wanted to see a case for a new runway and it would therefore have been a waste of time to consider a scenario with no new development in the South East. However, RUCATSE did study the possibility of making better use of airports in Bristol and Birmingham to see if it would defer the need, but their initial enthusiasm for the Bristol site (Filton) dissipated when they visited the area and discovered that major housing developments were planned nearby. In considering sites for this additional capacity, RUCATSE had the particular benefit of advice from SERPLAN on regional planning guidance and there was a focus on the East Thames corridor and constraints to the south and west of London. As well as considering the ten existing airports from CAP 570, RUCATSE also looked at seven military bases and the Thames Estuary, but not at 'greenfield' sites. Heathrow options included both a short and a full-length runway. Gatwick options included a second runway to the south of the existing one, as well as the northern runway from previous studies.

The study listed the benefits and impacts for all the options but did not attempt to rank them, although the Heathrow options showed the greatest benefits and impacts. Sunderland told me that the report was near completion when he was given a firm instruction by the Secretary of State, Cecil Parkinson, that the report should leave it open to ministers to decide on how to proceed with the options. This had been triggered by Parkinson having picked up the fact that a second runway at Stansted would have affected a historic house. It is not clear which house this was (although there are a number in the area), or why the Secretary of State should express concern about a particular house, but it is an indication of ministers' desires not to be put in a position of having to disagree with a recommendation. Sunderland suggests that this instruction could be regarded as a classic case of ministers seizing a chance to slow down the inevitably difficult progress towards a decision.

The RUCATSE report was published in July 1993 (Department of Transport, 1993). There were various debates in Parliament raised by constituency MPs and there was a consultation about the report. In one such debate in July 1993, Steven Norris replied to a debate on a petition from Sir Alan Haselhurst (HC Deb 27 July 1993). Norris was Minister for London at the time but, because the Aviation Minister (Lord Caithness) sat in the House of Lords, Norris spoke on aviation matters in the Commons. Alan Haselhurst was the MP for Saffron Walden, the constituency that includes Stansted Airport. The debate included references to RUCATSE, Heathrow Terminal 5 and the then current issue about additional rights to fly between the USA and the UK under the Air Services Agreement (with TWA turning down an offer to use Stansted), showing how the ASA is inextricably linked to airports policy. In February 1995, Transport Secretary Brian Mawhinney gave the government's response in a written answer, which was to agree that there was a strong case for more runway capacity but that more work was needed to inform decisions, which would take between two and three years. However he confirmed that, in these further studies, BAA should not consider the options studied in RUCATSE for a third runway at Heathrow or for a second runway at Gatwick, although he did ask BAA to examine whether there might be less damaging options for development, such as a close parallel runway at Gatwick (HC Deb 2 February 1995). The House of Commons Transport Committee published a report on airport capacity in May 1996 (Ares et al., 2009), which noted BAA's reluctance to make plans for future runway capacity and called for the government to prepare a longer-term strategy. By this time the Heathrow Terminal 5 Inquiry was under way.

Tom Carter, formerly of British Airways, told me of his continued efforts to keep expansion of Heathrow on the agenda. One of the less damaging options referred to by Brian Mawhinney may have been a close-spaced parallel southern runway at Heathrow (about 400 metres south of the existing southern runway), which Tom Carter was pushing. This would not provide as much additional capacity as an additional wide-spaced runway, but would keep flight paths close to existing ones. RUCATSE had not examined a close-spaced runway and Brian Mawhinney had been clear that the government rejected any third runway. However, the proposal did not go away and has reappeared both in the 2000s (see Chapter 8) and more recently (see Chapter 9).

7.3. 'A little yellow at the edges': policy at the Terminal 5 Inquiry

Heathrow Terminal 5 had been rejected in the 1978 White Paper, ACAP, the government decision in 1979 and the 1985 White Paper, although in the last case, it was only the particular planning application that was rejected. The 1985 White Paper, based on Graham Eyre's recommendations, which in turn had been based on evidence from BA, recognised the arguments in favour of Terminal 5 and called for studies of the acquisition of the Perry Oaks site and on main-line rail links. The Perry Oaks site was occupied by Thames Water's sludge disposal works, and a study on how this could be cleared took place between 1986 and 1988 (Pellman, 2008). Sludge is a product of the sewage treatment process (the other product being clean water) and Perry Oaks was a large site, established well before the airport, where sludge dried out over a number of years such that it could then be taken elsewhere for use or disposal. The study identified how and where an alternative process could be provided. The sludge works was also an important ecological site and mitigation for its loss would also need to be made. Tom Carter told me that he went to see Roy Watts on Watts' first day as the chairman of Thames Water (having moved from BA), to remind him of his previous support for the Terminal 5 plan. Regarding rail access, the Heathrow Surface Access Study took place between 1985 and 1987 and resulted in a recommendation for what became the Heathrow Express, which by 1991 had received parliamentary approval.

However, BAA's application for Terminal 5 was not submitted until 1993. In part, this was due to the fact that BAA, newly in the private sector, was finding its way in terms of non-aeronautical businesses such as property, hotels, freight and railways. The level of policy support was also unclear, given the previous rejections. BAA took a long time to prepare its case, consulting widely and meeting with many stakeholders, and also looking at the key issues such as the size of the terminal and therefore the amount of land to be acquired. In 1990, BAA decided to keep the development to the east of the A3044/Perimeter Road (Pellman, 2008). Although the Perry Oaks site was designated as green belt, it was felt that this constrained site, essentially between the two runways, would be easier to justify than if the development extended to the M25 (which had an additional designation as the Colne Valley Regional Park). This meant that the terminal and its car parks would have to be multi-level (in contrast to Stansted, where space had enabled a much lower-profile design). There was also a question of which airlines should occupy Terminal 5, although the decision was perhaps the obvious one, that it should be BA.

Figure 7.3 The author, who was a member of the BAA team preparing for the Heathrow Terminal 5 Inquiry, standing at a windswept Perry Oaks sludge works

I was part of the team preparing for the Terminal 5 Inquiry from 1991 to 1993 (see Figure 7.3). My particular role was to consider how to communicate the proposals to a range of audiences. It was a frustrating period because we took a long time to decide what to propose, but it was also somewhat uncomfortable personally, given that I had been part of the team that ten years previously had opposed Terminal 5.

The initial application for Terminal 5 was submitted in February 1993 and was accompanied by a number of supplementary applications and draft orders, which eventually numbered 37, including for associated road and rail schemes. The Inquiry ran over 525 days between May 1995 and March 1999 under Inspector Roy Vandermeer QC and took place at the Renaissance Hotel, at Heathrow.

The inspector's report (Vandermeer, 2001) recognised the history of previous government statements about Terminal 5, in particular the 1978 White Paper and the statement following the Terminal 4 decision, which had said that Heathrow should be limited to four terminals, and then the reversal of this in the 1985 White Paper following the Airports Inquiries' inspector's recommendation that Heathrow should be permitted to grow. Vandermeer's report said, 'This background goes a long way towards explaining the widespread distrust of Government policy towards the development of Heathrow that I encountered throughout the inquiry' (Vandermeer, 2001: paragraph 9). The then Department of the Environment, Transport and the Regions (DETR) appeared at the inquiry to explain government policy, and it was recognised that the 1985 White Paper had been affected by subsequent changes, such as a growing recognition of the importance of sustainable development. The 1985 White Paper had been at best equivocal in its support for Terminal 5 and, in the words of the then Minister for Aviation, Lord Caithness, was 'beginning to look a little yellow at the edges' (Pellman, 2008). Regional Planning Guidance, although concerned with the balance between the eastern and western parts of the South East, did not suggest a preference for growth at Gatwick or Stansted over Heathrow. The forecasts used to justify the case indicated that Terminal 5 would not satisfy all the demand and therefore there would be opportunities for other airports to grow. Overall, policy and need issues took 117 of the 525 days.

Reflecting the previous pledges on limiting capacity, the question of a third runway was discussed at the inquiry. The case was that a fifth terminal would balance the capacity of two runways (in segregated mode[1]), but opponents argued that it would result in calls for a third runway. The inspector noted that 'the environmental costs of further growth at Heathrow would quickly become unacceptable but the only effective and conclusive means of protecting against the provision of an additional runway would be through a legal agreement similar to that in force at Gatwick' (Vandermeer, 2001: paragraph 75). After a public meeting in Richmond in 1994 and various opinion polls, BAA decided to declare publicly that Terminal 5 would not lead to a call for another runway (Egan and Wilson, 2002), a pledge that was (much) later described by the CEO of Heathrow, John Holland-Kaye, as a commitment that should never have been made (Westcott, 2016).

Michael Maine was BAA's director of technical services responsible for the planning and design of Terminal 5 and was the company's main policy witness at the inquiry. He told me he had expected to be in the witness box for a few days but it ended up taking over four weeks, with several reappearances. Part of the reason for this extended time was that the inspector went out of his way to ensure that all parties had an opportunity to cross-examine and, as the first witness, this gave opponents their first chance to attack BAA's case. One of the most difficult areas was the question of aircraft size, which, of course, is fundamental to the question of the balance of terminal and runway capacity, and therefore to whether or not Terminal 5 would lead to a third runway. Stan Maiden was BAA's witness on forecasts and his evidence was that the replacement of smaller aircraft by larger types would lead to the capacities of five terminals and two runways being in balance. The arithmetic is quite simple – approximately 80 million passengers divided by 500 000 aircraft movements is 160 passengers per aircraft. In 1995, the average was 130 and had risen by about 3 per cent per year since 1990. To reach an average of 160 by 2015 required annual growth of just over 1 per cent. However, opponents did not believe that this would happen as very large aircraft, such as the Airbus A380, were still some way away (it first flew in 2005) and there were still many small aircraft operating short-haul flights. The actual average in 2015 was 159, so the prediction was good. Tom Carter told me that, when preparing BA's evidence for the inquiry, his colleagues were reluctant to accept any proposed limits on aircraft movement numbers, noting that market share is determined primarily by frequency.

Nevertheless, Stan Maiden recalled that, when John Egan made the no-third-runway statement, there was a sharp intake of breath. BAA's request that the Secretary of State should rule out the prospect of a third runway was not supported by BA and, in the event, the inspector placed only limited reliance on it, noting instead a government commitment to a review of national aviation policy.

Another aspect that added to the concern that a third runway was inevitable was Prospect Park. In 1991, BA proposed that it should build a corporate headquarters on land to the north-west of Heathrow. The development would require only 5.3 hectares but another 104 hectares would be acquired and laid out as public parkland. The local authority, the London Borough of Hillingdon, owned some of this land and supported the proposal, even though it would be contrary to green belt and local policies, because it would provide the public park (Sherwood, 2009). Objectors feared that the proposal was a Trojan Horse and the building site would become a new terminal and the land would be used for the third runway. Since then, a number of third-runway schemes have been considered, some of which did not use this land, but the latest plan (as of 2018) would require the complete removal of the building for a new runway.

om the no-third-runway pledge, BAA's case for Terminal 5 was supported by BA, ...e representatives, Luton Airport, business organisations and trade unions. Local authorities argued that Terminal 5 would be contrary to local and regional policies and that the employment generated would result in excessive demand for housing. They also argued that the forecasts and the economic benefits had been overstated and that greater use could be made of other airports. Hertfordshire and Essex county councils appeared, not specifically in support of Terminal 5 but to explain their opposition to further expansion at Stansted. Other opponents were residents' and environmental groups, including the Heathrow Association for the Control of Aircraft Noise (HACAN), which initially supported expansion at Stansted (Griggs and Howarth, 2004). There was virtually no evidence presented on regional diversion, which had been a strong element of previous inquiries.

It was accepted that the development would be inappropriate in the green belt and therefore the test would be, as required by the planning legislation, that 'very special circumstances' applied. BAA argued that those very special circumstances were the national interest. There were arguments about the visual impact of a tall building and the impact on the Colne Valley Regional Park and BAA suggested a contribution to the then-proposed Barn Elms wetlands reserve as mitigation for the ecological impact. Those opposing argued that the development would cause significant harm to the green belt and the regional park.

Surface access was a key issue at the inquiry. A new spur from the M25 was promoted by the Highways Agency. BAA accepted that car parking should be limited. The opponents argued that public transport would be inadequate and that road traffic congestion would increase. There was much discussion about whether the M25 and M4 would need to be widened, with BAA again making a pledge that it would not lead to a 14-lane M25.

Some of the history of the Heathrow Express rail link is covered in Chapter 6. By the start of the inquiry, it was under construction and opened to Terminals 1, 2 & 3 and Terminal 4 in 1998, while the inquiry was still in progress. The inquiry considered applications under the Transport and Works Act of 1992, which by then had replaced the parliamentary bill process for some transport schemes, for extensions of both the Heathrow Express and Piccadilly line links to Terminal 5. It was accepted that these would be provided as a key part of the project but the inquiry spent some time discussing options for additional rail links. The London Airports Surface Access Study had been initiated in 1995 by Brian Mawhinney when Secretary of State for Transport and suggested a number of schemes for Heathrow, including a 'sister' service to St Pancras Station and a southern rail link. These schemes were not definitive enough at the time (and, indeed, only a part of the 'sister' service, Heathrow Connect, has been implemented to date) but it was agreed that the station at Terminal 5 should be built with space for additional platforms to take such additional services at a later date. This was no small commitment, requiring a chamber the same size as the current station to be built beneath the terminal, which is now ready to be fitted out.

Westminster City Council appeared at the Terminal 5 Inquiry to express concern about the impact of the additional Heathrow Express on road traffic at Paddington. The council had previously petitioned against the original Heathrow Express Bill, and had been developing schemes for the redevelopment of the area around the station. It used the process to elicit various commitments, including funding, for these schemes.

Crossrail, the project to build a new east–west rail route through London, had originally been promoted in a 1991 parliamentary bill but, as noted by Schabas (2017), a link to Heathrow had been added as an afterthought. In any event, the bill was rejected in 1994 so, by the time of the Terminal 5 Inquiry, it was not on the agenda (although the underground route through central London continued to be safeguarded, in the same way as land for Gatwick's second runway). Schabas reviews a number of alternatives to Crossrail which emerged in the 1990s, including a

Heathrow Southern Link. Eventually, a revised Crossrail scheme did receive parliamentary assent in 2008 and is opening in stages, including to Heathrow, from 2018.

As in all previous inquiries, noise was a major issue, occupying 73 days. BAA argued that noise was reducing, and would reduce even with Terminal 5, albeit a lesser reduction than without Terminal 5. Most of the reduction would come from the assumed removal of Concorde from service. Michael Maine told me that opponents, as well as not accepting that smaller aircraft would be replaced with larger types, would not accept that newer aircraft would be less noisy. There was much discussion about the appropriate measure of noise, night movements and sleep disturbance. Many local residents said that the noise climate around the airport was intolerable and had not improved. The inspector accepted some of the criticisms but, in turn, his views were criticised by technical noise experts, who claimed they were not based on research but instead took account of the views of unrepresentative opposition groups (Brooker, 2004).

The inquiry also considered air quality, which at this time was beginning to be recognised as an issue (although EU limits, which were to become much more important in later years, were not then in place), as well as public safety. Noise, air quality and public safety were linked by opponents because of the constant passing of aircraft overhead.

The inspector's recommendation was based on the overall balance of harm against benefits. He accepted the need case and said that the economic benefits would be so fundamental and wide-ranging that it would be in the national interest, and therefore demonstrated the very special circumstances required for otherwise inappropriate development in the green belt. He also accepted the other elements of BAA's case in terms of surface access, noise and other environmental impacts, recommending conditions to ensure that measures would be implemented.

During the four years of the inquiry there was, not surprisingly, relatively little aviation-related activity in Parliament. There were several debates about aircraft noise from Heathrow, in particular relating to night flights, and a petition opposing Terminal 5. There were also wider debates about European air transport and the UK–US Air Services Agreement and, on 20 July 1998, John Prescott introduced the White Paper *A New Deal for Transport: Better for Everyone* (Department of the Environment, Transport and the Regions, 1998), which was the precursor to the next stage in the evolution of airports policy.

The decision to approve the Heathrow Terminal 5 application was made by the Deputy Prime Minister and Secretary of State for Local Government and the Regions, John Prescott (Neve, 2001). So, while the policy in support of Terminal 5 had first appeared in 1985 under a Margaret Thatcher-led Conservative government, it continued through four general elections and two changes of prime minister before the decision was made. Prescott agreed with most of the inspector's conclusions and imposed a number of conditions on the approval, including an annual ATM limit, a noise-contour-size limit and the requirement for both Heathrow Express and the Piccadilly line to be extended, plus a number of recommendations about operations, and a number of Section 106 agreements.[2] On the third runway, the decision letter notes that 'it is unnecessary in the context of these decisions for the Secretary of State to reach a conclusion on such matters' (paragraph 18). It should also be noted that the length of the Terminal 5 Inquiry was a key factor in a review of the planning regime, which eventually led to new procedures of the Planning Act of 2008.

Griggs and Howarth (2013) provide a comprehensive commentary on the Heathrow Terminal 5 Inquiry, noting that Heathrow was always the 'jewel in the crown' of the aviation industry and that its expansion 'flowed inexorably' (p. 88) from the decision to enshrine Heathrow as the preferred choice for expansion at the end of World War 2. However, this commentary is somewhat confused, suggesting, for example, that the Terminal 5 Inquiry opened despite the RUCATSE study, whereas in fact RUCATSE said nothing about Terminal 5, and the authors also ignore the

1981–1983 Airports Inquiries and the 1985 White Paper's (admittedly weak) endorsement of Terminal 5. The commentary is also contradictory, for example suggesting that liberalisation fuelled demands for expansion at Heathrow while noting that other airports benefited more from liberalisation. Nevertheless, the authors describe how the 'fantasmic narrative' of 'the (future) competitiveness of the aviation industry – and the growth of air travel itself – was portrayed as an essential ingredient on the economic modernisation and improved social well being of the UK' (p. 112), with failure to meet need a horrific dimension of overloaded capacity.

7.4. The 1990s: not much happened (apart from the Terminal 5 Inquiry)

With plenty of new capacity in the pipeline in the late 1980s and early 1990s, the need to make decisions about the long term remained distant, especially for those with shorter-term political horizons. Others in the industry, in particular in the CAA, did want to look further ahead and persuaded the civil servants to study the issues further, but it never really got beyond a few forays into Parliament. Instead, the much bigger issue of Heathrow Terminal 5 emerged without any real policy support and, indeed, a mixed history of being ruled out in earlier White Papers. The inspector for the Terminal 5 Inquiry was perhaps fortunate that he could make a recommendation without having to comment on long-term strategy because by that time (the early 2000s) a whole new process was ongoing.

7.5. Themes for the 1990s

What were the key themes and issues during the RUCATSE studies and the Heathrow Terminal 5 Inquiry, and were they any different from the previous decades? These are examined in detail in Chapter 10, but can be identified as follows.

- **Forecasts** were again a key issue. Both RUCATSE and the Terminal 5 Inquiry struggled with the relationship between passenger demand and runway capacity, as had been the case in the 1970s. RUCATSE considered regional diversion but to a lesser extent than previously, and the Terminal 5 Inquiry heard virtually no evidence on this issue.
- Both RUCATSE and the Terminal 5 Inquiry considered very large increments of capacity, so were an attempt to provide a **longer-term strategy**.
- While RUCATSE attempted to look at the whole of the South East, the Terminal 5 Inquiry was much more **local** in its consideration of benefits and impacts.
- There was a real problem with **promises to limit expansion**. RUCATSE was supposed to 'have regard for' previous policies to limit expansion at various sites, while the Terminal 5 Inquiry exposed differences of view of the idea of limiting development at Heathrow.
- **Environmental issues** remained important, with noise particularly significant at Heathrow, but local air quality was rising up the agenda.
- Overall, both key events of the 1990s exposed a **policy vacuum**.

Notes

1. Segregated mode means that one runway is used for landings and the other for take-offs. Mixed mode is where both runways are used for landings and take-offs at the same time.
2. An Air Transport Movement (ATM) is a landing or take-off of an aircraft engaged in commercial air transport. For explanations of noise contours, see Chapter 5.2. A Section 106 agreement between a planning authority and an applicant covers matters including obligations to provide benefits for the local community when planning permission is granted.

REFERENCES

Ares E, Barclay C, Butcher L and Mellows-Facer A (2009) *Expansion of Heathrow Airport*. Research paper RP09/11, House of Commons Library, London, UK.

BAA (1998) *BAA Annual Report 1997/98*. BAA plc, London, UK.

Brooker P (2004) The UK Aircraft Noise Index Study: 20 years on. *Proceedings of the Institute of Accoustics* **26(2)**: 20–30.

Budd L (2007) *Producing Airspace: The Contested Geographies of Nottingham East Midlands Airport*. PhD thesis, Loughborough University, Loughborough, UK.

CAA (1989) *Traffic Distribution Policy for the London Area and Strategic Options for the Long Term*. CAP 548, Civil Aviation Authority, London, UK.

Department of the Environment, Transport and the Regions (1998) *A New Deal for Transport: Better for Everyone*. HMSO, London, UK.

Department of Transport (1993) *Runway Capacity to Serve the South East: A Report by the Working Group*. TSO, London, UK.

Egan J and Wilson D (2002) *Private Business, Public Battleground*. Palgrave, Basingstoke, UK.

Givoni M and Rietveld P (2009) Airlines' choice of aircraft size: explanations and implications. *Transportation Research Part A: Policy and Practice* **43(5)**: 500–510.

Griggs S and Howarth D (2004) A transformative political campaign? The new rhetoric of protest against airport expansion in the UK. *Journal of Political Ideologies* **9(2)**: 181–201.

Griggs S and Howarth D (2013) *The Politics of Airport Expansion in the United Kingdom: Hegemony, Policy and the Rhetoric of 'Sustainable Aviation'*. Manchester University Press, Manchester, UK.

HC Deb 27 July 1993, vol. 229, col. 1011.

HC Deb 2 February 1995, vol. 253, col. 859.

Humphreys I (1994) Review of runway capacity to serve the South East: the RUCATSE report. *Journal of Air Transport Management* **1(3)**: 183–184.

Lee D, Fahey D, Forster P, Newton P, Wit R, Lim L, Owen B and Sausen R (2009) Aviation and global climate change in the 21st century. *Atmospheric Environment* **43(22–23)**: 3520–3537.

Neve E (2001) *Terminal Five Decision Letter*. Office of the Deputy Prime Minister, London, UK.

Parkinson C (1990) Letter to Chris Patten and others, 14 November 1990. TNA file AVIA 112/296/2.

Pellman R (2008) Heathrow Terminal 5: gaining permission. *Proceedings of ICE* **161**: 4–9.

Schabas M (2017) *The Railway Metropolis: How Planners, Politicians and Developers Shaped Modern London*. ICE Publishing, London, UK.

Sherwood P (2009) *Heathrow: 2000 Years of History*. The History Press, Stroud, UK.

Vandermeer R (2001) *The Heathrow Terminal 5 and Associated Public Inquiries: Summary Report*. Department of Transport, Local Government and the Regions, London, UK.

Westcott R (2016) Heathrow Airport communities wary of more promises. BBC News website, 18 May 2016. www.bbc.co.uk/news/business-36315344 (accessed 28 December 2016).

Zhang Y (2014) The puzzle of aircraft size and traffic growth. *Journal of Transport Economics and Policy* **48(3)**: 465–482.

Le Blond, P
ISBN 978-0-7277-6365-5
https://doi.org/10.1680/ilap.63655.087
ICE Publishing: All rights reserved

Chapter 8
1997–2010: a new deal for air transport

8.1. Introduction

As this book progresses to consider more recent years, the sources of information change. Because The National Archives only opens files more than 30 years old as a rule, this source is no longer available. On the other hand, there are more people around to interview, and their memories could be fresher. There is also a much larger body of academic study of such issues as the environmental impact and the activities of pro- and anti-expansion groups.

The new millennium brought celebrations and the fear that aircraft would fall out of the sky when affected by the millennium bug (which didn't happen). Although unemployment was relatively low, there were anti-capitalist riots and fuel protests in the UK. Ken Livingstone was elected as London mayor. As well as warnings from scientists about climate change, there were a number of extreme weather events. The EU Emissions Trading System began in 2005 and the Stern report on the economics of climate change was published in 2006. Technological developments included DVDs overtaking VHS tapes, internet access reaching 70 per cent of the UK population and chip-and-PIN credit and debit cards being launched. The Iraq war dominated foreign affairs. The terrorist attacks in the USA on September 11, 2001 had a dramatic effect on aviation and there were bombings in London in July 2005. Labour won general elections in 2001 and 2005. A major world financial crisis began in 2007–8 and continued into the next decade.

After strong growth in the 1990s, the events of September 11, 2001 resulted in a drop in passenger numbers at London's airports, although this recovered in 2002. A much bigger drop in passenger numbers occurred in 2008 as a result of the financial crisis – passenger numbers took six years to recover. However, early in the decade, the airline industry responded to the downturn with mergers (such as Air France/KLM), the formation of alliances, code-sharing, bankruptcies (Swissair, Sabena) or bankruptcy protection in the US (Doganis, 2006). The low-cost carriers (LCCs) had become established in the 1990s at secondary airports, in particular EasyJet at Luton and Ryanair at Stansted (Francis *et al.*, 2004). The last commercial Concorde flight took place in 2003 but new aircraft included the Airbus A380, Embraer 170 and Boeing 787. As well as September 11, there were other security scares affecting aircraft (including the 'shoe bomber' in 2001 and the liquids plot in 2006).

This chapter begins with the consultations that followed from the 1998 White Paper *A New Deal for Transport*, then considers the 2003 *Future of Air Transport* White Paper, a 2006 Progress Report and the 2009 decision to proceed with a third runway at Heathrow. The chapter ends with the general election of 2010, which reversed the decisions on new runways.

8.2. National consultations on a long-term strategy

Following the election of a New Labour government in 1997, a transport White Paper (*A New Deal for Transport: Better for Everyone*) was published in 1998 (described in Docherty and

Shaw, 2003). It was promoted by John Prescott, then deputy prime minister and leading a very large Department of the Environment, Transport and the Regions (DETR). This White Paper had suggested that a long-term, integrated approach should be established for aviation, after a wide-ranging consultation. The government initiated this consultation in 1999, and published a wide-ranging document called the *Future of Aviation* in 2000 (Department of the Environment, Transport and the Regions, 2000). The *Regional Air Services* documents were a suite of reports published in July 2002, one for each region of the UK, including for the South East and Eastern regions (SERAS).

Chris Cain, a senior civil servant involved with the SERAS exercise, told me that the previous policy, the understanding of how the industry worked and the forecasting methodology were out of date and it was therefore necessary to start from scratch. Previous forecasts, particularly in the 1985 White Paper and RUCATSE in 1993, had been lower than the actual outturn and the previous model of demand overspilling from Heathrow to Gatwick to Stansted was considered to be too simplistic and did not reflect airline decision-making. The 1979 Gatwick Second Runway Agreement was noted and, although a second runway was considered, the subsequent White Paper did not suggest that the agreement should be overturned. The Heathrow Terminal 5 condition limiting Air Transport Movements (ATMs) was not considered to be binding on SERAS as there were other environmental conditions that would apply. There appears to have been no consideration of the previous policy limiting Stansted to one runway, or indeed to the previous rejections of new sites.

Forecasting average aircraft size was again critical when assessing the need for more runway capacity. As we saw in the previous chapter (Figure 7.2), the rate of growth of average aircraft size had slowed in the 1980s and 1990s. Load factors grew significantly (around 75 per cent in 2007 compared with 55 per cent in 1970) and Lee *et al.* (2009) suggested that there might not be much scope for further growth in this element. A study that modelled airline choice of aircraft size in US duopoly markets (based on actual airline behaviour) demonstrated that flight frequency is more important than other factors (Wei and Hansen, 2005), although the same authors had noted previously that, for any particular length of flight, aircraft operating costs per seat mile would be lower for US airlines if larger aircraft were used (Wei and Hansen, 2003). The use of grandfather rights[1] for slots and the pricing of landing charges may also affect airlines' choice of aircraft size, and airlines may offer 'excessive' frequencies to protect their market share (Givoni and Rietveld, 2009: p. 500). The remedy suggested by Givoni and Rietveld is to change the way runway capacity is allocated. However, in the UK, as 'aircraft size is considered an exogenous factor in the planning process of air transport infrastructure, the strategy of meeting future demand through larger aircraft and current runway capacity is ignored' (ibid: p. 509). Stan Abrahams, who was responsible for forecasting for the Civil Aviation Authority (CAA) in its early years, accepts that forecasts of aircraft size can be a self-fulfilling prophecy, as airlines will use the aircraft best suited to a range of factors, including any limits on capacity at an airport. If they cannot obtain an additional slot, they will use a larger aircraft to accommodate growth. On the other hand, the grandfather rights noted earlier in this chapter may result in airlines using a smaller aircraft in order to retain the slot, an activity known as 'slot warming'. An Airbus forecast had average aircraft size increasing from 179 seats in 1999 to 219 in 2019, along with higher load factors, but there are also counter-trends, such as British Airways' strategy of downsizing aircraft to focus on high-yield markets in the late 1990s (Humphreys and Francis, 2002).

One of the key points about the 2000 *Future of Aviation* and 2002 *Regional Air Services* consultation documents is that they seek to reflect a commitment to a sustainable airports policy that balances benefits with environmental effects. They should be noted as the first major government publications to highlight aviation's impact on climate change, possibly because the Kyoto

Protocol had been agreed in 1997. The South East document highlighted the economic benefits of air travel, discussed the need for a hub airport and suggested that the forecasts would only be 'predict and provide' if unconstrained demand is met,[2] but nevertheless indicated what a 30-year unconstrained forecast would be. Although there was one document for each region, there was also an attempt to coordinate the options through the Regional Air Services Coordination study (RASCO).

The South East document reviewed the options of Heathrow, Gatwick, Stansted, Luton, Cliffe (a Thames Estuary site) and other smaller airports in the South East, comparing a number of combinations with a base case and a maximum-use case. The proposal for Heathrow was for a 2000-metre runway which would take 260 properties and 230 hectares of green-belt land, would increase the area and the number of people within a specified noise contour and result in exceedences of EU local air-quality limits. Road and rail access would be provided by widening motorways and new rail links. No Gatwick options were included in the first edition of the document but, following a legal challenge, options for a second runway were considered in a second edition published in February 2003, some of which would require up to 300 properties and 200 hectares of land, but the numbers of people within specified noise contours or poor-air-quality areas would be much fewer than for Heathrow. Stansted was considered for either one, two or three additional runways, requiring up to 1200 hectares of land, but with few people within noise contours or in poor-air-quality areas. Road and rail access would have to be significantly enhanced. The Cliffe option was for a completely new four-runway airport, requiring the acquisition of 1100 residential properties and 2000 hectares of land, with significant ecological effects but very few people affected by noise.

The initial *Future of Aviation* consultation had resulted in 550 responses and the SERAS consultation had led to over 500 000 responses, including many through an opinion-polling exercise, as well as by exhibitions, seminars, workshops and individual submissions. By far the largest number (almost half) of the responses were from a campaign organised by the Royal Society for the Protection of Birds (RSPB) against the Cliffe option. The Gatwick second-runway option resulted in around 5000 objections, Heathrow third runway 8000 and Stansted second runway 24 000.

Peter Sanders and Brian Ross, of the campaign group Stop Stansted Expansion (SSE), a working group of the North West Essex and East Herts Preservation Association (NWEEHPA), told me that NWEEHPA had been less active through the 1990s in terms of airport policy activity. However, it had been actively involved with 'bread and butter' activities at the Stansted Airport Consultative Committee, establishing a working relationship with BAA. But the publication of the SERAS report in July 2002 led to the setting up of the SSE campaign, with 800 people attending the first public meeting in August 2002. SSE was a party to the legal challenge that resulted in the second edition of the SERAS report including Gatwick options, and this did create some tensions with Gatwick community groups.

In Parliament in the early years of the decade there were a few debates and questions on air transport, covering issues such as international flights from regional airports, aircraft noise, climate change impacts and airport regulation. After the attacks in the USA on September 11, 2001, there were a number of debates and a select committee inquiry expressing concern about the effect on the aviation industry, even from opponents of expansion such as John McDonnell, the MP for Hayes and Harlington, the constituency which includes Heathrow. Although the timing was coincidental, approval for Heathrow Terminal 5 came in November 2001, and acceptance of the decision was no doubt eased by concerns about the downturn. The SERAS consultation stirred up MPs to ask questions, initiate debates and present petitions throughout 2002 and 2003, in particular relating to greenfield sites such as the Midlands, North Bristol, Cliffe and Severnside, which had been noted as options in the consultation documents. The House of Commons Transport Committee report on aviation of July 2003 (House of Commons Transport Committee, 2003) concluded that more capacity would be needed even though the approach was not 'predict and provide'. However, it was highly critical of BAA for hiding behind the government on the choice of options and for its statements that a fifth terminal at Heathrow would not require a third runway (see Chapter 7), calling the company 'at best culpably short sighted... at worst wilfully misleading' (p. 75). However, the committee concluded that, as a third Heathrow runway would require the closure of RAF Northolt, it might be better to realign the Northolt runway and use it as a third runway for Heathrow, and to plan for a second runway at Gatwick. The committee also noted that, despite previously supporting the case for aviation environmental taxes, this would not be feasible on an international basis.

The 1990s had seen a growing awareness of global warming and climate change (for example, see Lee and Raper, 2003). Upham (2003) criticises the use of unconstrained forecasts and a mitigation approach in the 2000 *Future of Aviation* and the 2002 *Regional Air Services* consultation documents, suggesting that greenhouse gas reduction should be the start point, from which government should allocate part of the target to aviation to see if there is space for growth. A similar conclusion was reached by Graham (2003), who suggested that, despite the consultation documents including constraint scenarios, there seemed to be a move away from the 1998 White Paper approach and back to 'predict and provide'. There was criticism of the consultation process from Griggs and Howarth (2013a), who suggested that it had the appearance of an inclusive democratic process, but the playing field was not level, because it was technocratic, elitist, managerial and top-down and denied access to objectors. On the other hand, support for the process came from Rhodes (2008), who described it as 'an exemplary approach, with unprecedented consultation' (p. 22) and 'ownership blind' (p. 24).

8.3. A 30-year national strategy: the 2003 White Paper

Following the major consultation in the 2002 SERAS study and as promised in the 1998 Transport White Paper, *The Future of Air Transport* White Paper, published on 16 December 2003, proposed a 30-year strategy for the whole of the UK (Department for Transport, 2003; see Figure 8.1). The foreword was signed by Alistair Darling, Secretary of State for Transport. The executive summary says that the policy takes account of the views expressed in the consultation exercise which have closely informed the conclusions (and there are many references to these views throughout the document), and that further consultation will be started on the proposed developments.

The White Paper repeated the statement that the forecast was not 'predict and provide' if unconstrained demand is not fully met. The difference between the unconstrained demand and the proposals for the UK as a whole was 30 mppa (millions of passengers per annum) and, as it is likely that the constraints would bite only in the South East, this represented about 10 per cent of unconstrained South East demand. Griggs and Howarth (2017) analysed statements in a large number of texts and, for this period, they characterise the policy as: a balanced approach, which first appeared in the 1997 White Paper, challenged predict and provide, resonated with New Labour's third way, but assumed growth was a good thing that required mitigation, with government as the judge.

The headlines of the White Paper were two new runways in the South East, at Stansted and Heathrow, but the strategy provided some policy certainty for even the smaller airports. The second runway at Stansted was seen as being deliverable first, by around 2011 or 2012. Land and homes, including listed buildings, would have to be acquired and BAA was invited to put in place a blight scheme, which would enable property owners to sell at an unblighted price. The noise

Figure 8.1 *The Future of Air Transport* White Paper of 2003: the Labour government's attempt at a 30-year, UK-wide strategy

contours would grow to encompass more people, but operational controls (using segregated mode[3]) could reduce the impact. EU air-quality limits would not be exceeded. Stansted is in a designated growth corridor and urbanisation could be accommodated. It was recognised that surface access would need significant improvement, increasing capacity on both the M11 and the West Anglia Main Line. A third and fourth runway at Stansted, which had been considered in the consultation, were ruled out.

The proposal for Heathrow was a third, short (2000-metre) runway to the north of the existing airport. Recognising the noise environment around Heathrow, the proposal required no net increase in the area within a specified noise contour compared with the 2002 situation. Local air quality was considered the most difficult issue to deal with, and the White Paper reiterated the policy that the third runway could operate only if EU limits were met. In part, this was the reason for suggesting that the delivery of the third runway should be in the 2015–2020 period, when the limits could be met. As there were no plans for further road capacity (other than what was already in the pipeline), future demand for surface access would have to be based on significant rail improvements. However, the benefits of expanding Heathrow were said to be so great that it would be possible to overcome any adverse effects in terms of noise, air quality and road traffic. BAA was invited to take steps to safeguard the land and put a blight scheme in place.

The White Paper's position on Gatwick was to support a second runway to the south if a third runway at Heathrow could not meet the required conditions noted above, and then only after 2019 when the BAA/West Sussex County Council agreement expired (see Chapter 6). The noise and other environmental impacts, which would be much less than at Heathrow, were noted. BAA was invited to take steps to safeguard the land required. At Luton, a replacement runway option was supported. This would have provided a longer runway with more capacity than the existing arrangement, enabling growth to 30 mppa. The White Paper rejected all the options for new airport sites, including in the Thames Estuary.

Alistair Darling would have been briefed extensively before publication and, although papers from this period have not been released, it is likely that the briefings would have included all the options, in various combinations. One particular issue likely to have been considered is how the viability of a second runway at Stansted would be adversely affected if a Heathrow third runway was also supported. Despite this concern, this was the policy chosen and, as will be seen later, this difficulty did arise and contributed to the delay in implementing the second runway at Stansted.

It appears that ministers were open-minded about the options but there was instinctive prejudice by officials in various departments to ensure that Heathrow was favoured. However, it was clear that the air-quality issue would not be resolved quickly and so Stansted's second runway was put forward as the first tranche of new capacity.

The 2003 White Paper said that master plans for major airports should include: proposals for development of the airport to 2015, with indicative land-use plans for the period 2016–2030; detailed proposals for surface access, environmental controls and mitigation; measures to address blight; and reference Regional Spatial Strategies and local transport plans. They were supposed to facilitate participation and therefore be a useful tool for communicating to a range of stakeholders, including airlines, funding institutions, local-authority and other local interests, to allow them to make well-informed investment decisions (Rawson and Hooper, 2012).

Although this book is about airports policy for London, it is worth noting that the 2003 White Paper also supported significant growth around the UK, including safeguarding for second runways at Edinburgh, Glasgow and Birmingham, and runway extensions and terminal developments at a number of airports. It indicated roles for virtually every airport in the UK, including for business and general aviation. It was therefore both comprehensive and long term. As noted above, the total capacity to be provided would not have matched the long-term forecasts of demand but, as will be shown in Chapter 10, these forecasts were particularly high and the White Paper has therefore been seen as very pro-growth.

When the White Paper was introduced to the House of Commons on 16 December 2003 by the Secretary of State for Transport, Alistair Darling, the Shadow Secretary of State was Theresa May, the current (as of 2018) prime minister. May's response was to criticise the White Paper as 'a fudge from an incompetent government' (HC Deb 16 December 2003), noting that initially the consultation had not included Gatwick, that the Environmental Audit Committee had criticised the lack of an environmental impact assessment and the lack of consideration of a short runway at Birmingham, as well as a general lack of joined-up thinking. Darling's response was to suggest that the opposition had no aviation policy. The first opportunity for a debate on the White Paper took place in Westminster Hall on 11 February 2004 (HC Deb 11 February 2004). Westminster Hall debates are more limited than the full Chamber, but in 90 minutes MPs spoke of their constituency interests as well as more general concerns about the environmental impact of aviation.

8.4. Progress checked by increasing environmental concerns

Lobbying and briefing seem to have stepped up a gear both before and following the 2003 White Paper. The development of groups supporting and opposing airport expansion in this period has been explored in some detail by Griggs and Howarth (2004, 2006, 2013a, 2013b), who note that there were links between New Labour, civil servants and the aviation industry, and that pro-expansion groups such as Freedom to Fly, led by Brenda Dean, a former trade union leader, were created which gave the government ideological cover to make decisions. Future Heathrow was formed in 2005, led by Labour peer Clive Soley, to be followed by Flying Matters, led by another former Labour MP, Brian Wilson. Sustainable Aviation, described by some as an oxymoron (Budd et al., 2013; O'Doherty, 2015) and Greener by Design were other industry-led groups seeking to deal with the environmental impacts. A senior official involved with the White Paper told me that some parts of the DfT were clear supporters of Heathrow expansion, in part because these officials dealt with international negotiations where access to Heathrow was always the key issue for foreign airlines, but also because the Government needed BAA to fund airport expansion and Heathrow would always be the most fundable. Of those opposing expansion, after the failure to stop Heathrow Terminal 5 (and a second runway at Manchester), Airport Watch was formed, which dismissed the neutrality of inquiries and sought to change the rhetoric away from Nimbyism to economic and global arguments. These opposition groups also agreed not to support expansion at other sites, although some groups continued to support Thames Estuary sites.

John Stewart joined the Heathrow Association for the Control of Aircraft Noise (HACAN) in 1995 and has been its chairman since 2001. He told me that HACAN had its origins in residents' groups in Kew and Richmond, which had objected to aircraft noise since the 1960s, when jets had started appearing in significant numbers. ClearSkies was set up in the mid 1990s in the Stockwell/Clapham area by residents concerned about changes in flight paths. These changes had initially been denied by the CAA and National Air Traffic Services (NATS), but it emerged later that the point at which aircraft joined the Instrument Landing System (ILS) had moved eastwards. HACAN and ClearSkies merged in 1999. Historically, HACAN had been most active at the T4 and T5 Inquiries but became active again in the SERAS consultation and the follow-up to the 2003 White Paper. The long-term, UK-wide nature of the White Paper meant that many groups worked more closely together to put forward common arguments against the levels of growth proposed (two new runways in the South East, plus new runways at Birmingham, Edinburgh and Glasgow and expansions at virtually every UK airport), for example on climate-change or economic-benefit grounds. HACAN commissioned research on the economic benefits of a Heathrow third runway from CE Delft, which challenged the almost universal (until then) view about the scale of benefits from airport expansion. Although it was not always easy to reconcile the different approaches of the groups, this gave the groups strength, or at least a perception of strength.

The positive (for the air transport industry) policies set out in the 2003 White Paper enabled significant progress to be made on the developments proposed in the South East. Passenger numbers were growing strongly, although Heathrow was clearly under strain until Terminal 5 opened in 2008. A judicial review of the White Paper in 2006 supported the government's position and a progress report (Department for Transport, 2006) was published in December 2006.

For Heathrow, the government set up the Project for the Sustainable Development of Heathrow (PSDH) in 2004. This was led by government because of the policy requirement that air-quality limits would have to be met, as the penalty for non-compliance would fall on the government. PSDH therefore concentrated on the air-quality issues, although BAA was also refining the layout plans and subsequently proposed a slightly longer third runway (2200 metres instead of 2000 metres) and additional terminal facilities. As well as considering local air quality, the progress report noted that plans for mixed mode were being prepared,[4] which would provide more capacity with the existing two runways, although there would be some loss of runway alternation. The progress report also reported on noise issues and public transport plans. A consultation on Adding Capacity at Heathrow began in November 2007 and resulted in around 70 000 responses. A large majority of the responses (including 43 000 in campaigns and petitions) opposed the third runway, but these were dismissed because the government had already decided this in principle. Nevertheless, significant majorities of responses did not agree that the environmental conditions were appropriate, or that mixed mode should be implemented.

Terminal 5 opened in 2008, but the opening was marred by operational difficulties. A number of other operational issues had affected the airport, including the 2006 liquids plot that resulted in increased security requirements and subsequent delays, and bad weather. A British Airways Boeing 777 crash-landed at Heathrow in January 2008 (the passengers and crew escaped). There had been calls for the break-up of BAA, with Humphreys *et al.* (2007) noting that regulation of the BAA airports and the single till (see Chapter 2) continued to distort the timing and nature of capacity investments. David Starkie had criticised the privatisation of BAA as a single entity and the form of regulation for many years (see Chapter 2) but by 2008 he was arguing that the system was working well and had produced a dynamic and profitable industry, free of subsidy (Starkie, 2008). BAA was bought by Ferrovial in 2006. Regulation included regular reviews of BAA by the CAA and the setting of limits for aeronautical charges and one of these reviews led to an investigation by the then Competition Commission. Although there were a number of appeals, the end result was that BAA sold off all its airports (except Heathrow), with Gatwick going first in December 2009, followed by Stansted in February 2013. A comprehensive review of regulation and the effect on capacity provision is provided by Anne Graham (2008). Although all of these events were independent of the proposals for a third runway at Heathrow, it is probably the case that they were linked by politicians, anti-expansion groups and the media to strengthen the case against expansion. And, of course, the economic recession that started in 2008 led many to question the need for additional capacity.

Despite these difficulties and the negative response to the consultation, on 15 January 2009 Geoff Hoon, Secretary of State for Transport, announced that the conditions set for a third runway on air quality, noise and surface access would be met and therefore it could go ahead, although he decided against mixed mode (HC Deb 15 January 2009a). The announcement was made as part of a package of transport infrastructure proposals, including road investments and the setting up of High Speed Two Ltd. However, the Heathrow third runway decision was by far the most controversial element. Roy Griffins, who by this time had left the civil service but was still very much involved with aviation as the chairman of London City Airport, suggested that the 2009 decision was 'a bit finagled' in relation to the air-quality predictions. The announcement of the decision in the House of Commons was greeted by much opposition, including from those who would become transport ministers and others in the next government. John McDonnell was suspended for 'having conducted himself in a grossly disorderly manner' (HC 15 January 2009b) after he grabbed hold of the mace, as I was reminded by Sir Alan Haselhurst, who was chairing the session. A debate took place on 28 January 2009 when an opposition motion to rethink policy was defeated by 297 to 278 votes (HC Deb 28 January 2009). The House of

Commons Transport Committee had been one of the most critical voices calling for the break-up of BAA but nevertheless continued to support the third runway (House of Commons Transport Committee, 2009).

John Stewart of HACAN told me that Geoff Hoon was a 'gift' to the opposition to a Heathrow third runway, given his previous controversial involvement in the Iraq conflict as Defence Secretary and other events. He was criticised in the media as part of the MPs' expenses scandal and subsequently sanctioned by the Standards and Privileges Committee and suspended from the Parliamentary Labour Party. He was Transport Secretary for only eight months and, after his resignation, he was involved in a failed bid to oust Gordon Brown as prime minister.

Because the White Paper had proposed a second runway at Gatwick only as a 'standby' in case the Heathrow third runway did not proceed, there was little related activity. An Interim Master Plan in 2006 focused on the existing runway, but noted the land that would be required for a second runway to the south, which the White Paper had proposed should be safeguarded. That safeguarding was implemented in the Crawley Local Plan, and remains so in the latest version of the plan. The Transport Committee's December 2009 report had suggested that a second runway at Gatwick would be preferable to one at Stansted. However, it is worth noting that, since the BAA/West Sussex County Council agreement of 1979 and the North Terminal Inquiry of 1980, BAA Gatwick had successfully overseen significant growth through the 'contract with the community'. Alastair McDermid, who led Gatwick's planning team in the late 1990s, told me that this had enabled developments to be approved without public inquiries by ensuring that the local communities were fully involved in decision-making. It is noticeable that the 'contract with the community' and the second runway legal agreement seem to have resulted in more positive relationships than arose from the adversarial inquiry process based on changing government policies.

The 2003 White Paper had proposed that the first new runway should be at Stansted. At the time, the airport had been growing rapidly and the immediate need was to build more terminal capacity. Expanding the existing terminal became known as the Generation 1 (G1) project, but it proceeded slowly and was considered at a public inquiry, eventually being approved in 2008. The slow progress of the G1 project may have been in part due to the fact that it was being planned at the same time as the plans for the proposed second runway, known as Generation 2 (G2), were being considered. However Dixon (2014), in a study of a number of master plan consultations, notes the poor relationship between BAA Stansted and the local authorities, which compared unfavourably with more positive relationships at other airports (as noted above for Gatwick). A consultation on a second runway took place in 2005 on four options with different spacings, and significant work was undertaken on plans for improved road and rail access. However, the Highways Agency and Network Rail were not particularly enthusiastic about their respective responsibilities, and intervention was required from the DfT. The 2006 progress report said that a new runway would not be operational before 2015, three to four years later than the White Paper timetable. The airlines were not keen to fund the expansion and, although LCCs had grown strongly in the early 2000s, the doubling of air passenger duty in 2007 added to concerns about their viability. These concerns were particularly noted by Ferrovial, BAA's new owners from 2006. Then came recession and passenger numbers declined sharply, and the Competition Commission recommended that BAA should be broken up. A planning application for the G2 project, which included 36 applications under eight different pieces of legislation, was submitted in 2008 and two pre-inquiry meetings were held ahead of the scheduled start of the inquiry, which had been programmed to last 21 months. But the perfect storm of delays, downturns, uncertainty, negativity and potential change of ownership resulted in work on G2 being put on hold in 2009 and the application was withdrawn in March 2010.

Peter Sanders and Brian Ross told me how SSE campaigned through this period. Immediately after the publication of the White Paper in December 2003, BAA had written to local householders in the Stansted area. SSE believed that the letter backfired as it seemed to suggest that expansion was a fait accompli, and it led to many people joining the campaign. SSE decided to campaign against G1 and G2, on the basis that G1 was a step towards G2, and they pledged to 'fight every inch of the way'. Money was raised, a campaign manager was appointed, and the use of email and the internet made gathering evidence and communications for the campaign much easier. They received helpful input from BA and Virgin, which were opposed to Stansted being cross-subsidised from Heathrow revenues. SSE sought to inflict reputational damage on BAA by raising the issue of free car parking at airports for MPs, by briefing city institutions on the funding issues, and by challenging BAA's monopoly. Campaign materials included posters and the 'Monopoly beer mat', which was distributed at political party conferences (see Figure 8.2). For the G1 proposal, even if it was approved, a delay would be considered a success, given the political adages that 'a week is a long time in politics' (attributed to Harold Wilson) and things being affected by 'events, dear boy, events' (Harold Macmillan). G1 was eventually approved, but the delay to G2 meant that it was overtaken by the recession of 2008, the break-up of BAA and then the 2010 general election.

The White Paper had proposed significant expansion at Luton, based on a relocated runway. The airport, which is owned by Luton Borough Council and was operating under the terms of a 30-year lease, published a draft master plan in 2005, but withdrew the plan later that year, probably because the 30-year term of the lease would not enable the investment to provide a return. Luton had grown rapidly in the late 1990s and had quadrupled in size in the decade to 2006, but then suffered a significant downturn in 2009. Although Luton's reputation is as an LCC

Figure 8.2 SSE's 'BAA Monopoly beer mat'
(Courtesy of Peter Sanders, SSE)

airport serving mainly short-haul leisure flights, it is less well known but very important as a business aviation base, handling more business aviation aircraft movements than any other London airport.

The White Paper had required the preparation of master plans for airports, and many smaller South East airports took the opportunity to put forward contributions to meeting the need for more runway capacity in the short term. The White Paper had noted support for 5 million passengers per annum at London City (it handled 1.6 million in 2002), and the rest of the decade saw it linked to the Docklands Light Railway, various extensions were undertaken, transatlantic flights began and it was acquired by Global Infrastructure Partners (which also bought Gatwick).

Other airports, including Southend and Biggin Hill, were noted for their potential in the White Paper and sought to expand on the basis of this policy support. Southend was acquired by the Stobart Group in 2008, which invested over £100 million in a new terminal and rail station and obtained agreement with EasyJet to base a number of aircraft there. Passenger numbers quickly rose to about 1 mppa. Biggin Hill sought to operate scheduled flights to a limited number of short-haul destinations but was prevented from doing so by the terms of its lease, and so concentrated on its core activities of business aviation, flying training and private aircraft. Farnborough, the home of the biennial air show, was acquired by TAG Aviation in 2003, which has invested heavily for business aviation. Use of RAF Northolt as a satellite runway for Heathrow had been rejected in the White Paper, but it is used for a limited number of business aviation flights, and the proposals to use it as a satellite re-emerge from time to time. Manston, in Kent, had a particularly long runway from its wartime and post-war use and has had commercial operations, particularly by freighter aircraft but, despite several proposals to develop air services, it has not been able to attract airlines and is currently closed. These airports have played a part in the strategy for the South East by accommodating aircraft movements that have been squeezed out of the larger airports and thus enabling them to grow their air-transport activities.

The 2006 progress report noted that the operators of Edinburgh, Glasgow and Birmingham airports had decided not to take forward proposals for new runways in the timescale envisaged in the 2003 White Paper. Edinburgh identified the land needed for a second runway but did not pursue the plan, instead concentrating on expanding its terminal and improving access with the Edinburgh tram. Similarly, Glasgow, having identified the land required for a second runway, did not pursue the plans. Birmingham Airport dropped the plan for a second runway and implemented a plan to extend the existing runway. Subsequently, a different location has been identified for a second runway in the long term, integrated with plans for HS2 and other major developments in the area. Many other non-London airports implemented improvements to their facilities, although the recession of the late 2000s dampened demand and investment for a while. Manchester Airport had constructed a second runway, which opened in 2000, and had enough capacity to accommodate growth.

During this period there was continuing criticism of the forecasts, in part related to those who opposed the growth of aviation on environmental, in particular climate-change, grounds. Riddington (2006) criticised the White Paper forecasts for not allowing for environmental costs or increased oil prices and Brian Graham (2003) suggested that they represented a move away from the 1998 policy back to 'predict and provide', although he also noted that the studies had included constrained scenarios. On the other hand, Bailey (2007) noted that, historically, DfT forecasts had been too low. Trends in the airline sector had been closely linked to the economic climate, plus September 11, SARS[5] and the Gulf War, but liberalisation had continued (enabling LCCs to grow) and alliances developed (concentrating traffic at hub airports) (Doganis, 2006; Francis et al., 2004). Anne Graham (2000 and 2006) asked if leisure traffic was moving towards maturity, but the evidence was inconclusive. There was much less emphasis on regional diversion than in previous periods, although there were arguments for higher aeronautical charges at Heathrow to encourage regional clawback (Francis and Humphreys, 2001). Givoni and Rietveld (2009) reviewed the aircraft-size element of the forecasts, which had been significant in the previous period, and suggested that it should not be an exogenous factor, but rather should be part of the strategy for meeting future demand.

Some of these criticisms were taken on board in the forecasts that were updated in the 2006 progress report, in particular to reflect environmental costs, including the cost of carbon, although the unconstrained forecasts were only slightly below those in the 2003 White Paper, and the effect of constraints was similar.

Forecasts were challenged at the Stansted G1 Inquiry in 2007. Although this inquiry was limited to looking at an increase from 25 to 35 million passengers per annum at Stansted, it illustrates some of the uncertainties. SSE sought to show that the forecasts were too low, such that the impact was being underestimated; the Stansted airlines, concerned that the facilities they would have to pay for would be too large, said the forecasts were too high. There was also much debate about average aircraft size, as had been the case at every other inquiry. The inspector ruled that the forecasts were satisfactory for considering the impacts (Boyland, 2008) but then, of course, the actual numbers declined rather than grew for six years, rendering all the forecasts outdated.

The policy clash between aviation growth and carbon reduction became apparent through a number of studies (for example, Bows and Anderson, 2007; Lee et al., 2009; Upham et al., 2003). These scientific studies were echoed by the House of Commons Environmental Audit Committee and the Tyndall Centre (Bailey, 2007) and used by airport opponents, who had previously concentrated on local issues, and fed into the debate on airports policy (Griggs and Howarth, 2013a). The Stern Review of the economics of climate change was published in 2006 (Graham, B., 2008). Proposals to include aviation in the EU Emissions Trading System (ETS) were criticised because they would not significantly reduce air travel (Anger, 2010; Anger-Kraavi and Köhler, 2013), because of the ETS's uncertainty, and because it did not include non-carbon-dioxide (CO_2) effects (Dessens et al., 2014). Proponents of expansion sought to widen the argument by noting the Bruntland definition of sustainable development (as reported in Budd et al., 2013), which includes economic development and social progress, as well as environmental issues. Groups such as Airport Watch countered with arguments about taxation and tourism deficits and questioned the value of aviation (Graham, 2003; Griggs and Howarth, 2013a). The social-progress element is explored by Adey et al. (2007).

As in previous periods, noise continued to be a matter of major concern, although progress had been achieved in reducing the noise footprint of individual aircraft and the design specification of the Airbus A380 met particular Heathrow night-noise criteria (Girvin, 2009). However, aircraft movement numbers were growing faster than aircraft were becoming quieter (Graham, 2003) and noise remained the single most important local environmental impact (Thomas and Lever, 2003). An EU Directive on noise had also been implemented, which required the mapping of noise at airports (and other locations) (King et al., 2011).

Acceptable local air quality was a key condition of the support for a third runway at Heathrow and was considered in depth in the subsequent studies (Graham, B. 2008; Peace et al., 2006). It is difficult to separate airport and non-airport sources of NO_x (see Chapter 5) but, close to the airport boundary, where emissions exceeded EU limits, airport sources accounted for 27 per cent of the total, and were diluted further away (Carslaw et al., 2006).

Although the support groups such as Freedom to Fly and Future Heathrow seemed to be achieving their aims in the mid 2000s, the combination of academic, institutional and local opposition enabled HACAN and Airport Watch to provide 'ideological cover' for the Conservative and Liberal Democrat parties to oppose expansion (Griggs and Howarth, 2013a), as is apparent in their parliamentary activity. In the late 2000s, the Conservative Party undertook a review of its environmental policies which challenged the pro-expansion policies and led to the manifesto for the 2010 general election, which included a commitment to cancel the additional runway plans and to make Heathrow 'better not bigger'. Steven Norris, a Minister of Transport in the 1990s, had remained involved in politics despite standing down as an MP in 1997 and stood as a Conservative candidate for London Mayor in 2000 and 2004. He chaired the Transport Working Group of the Quality of Life Policy Group, which in turn was led by John Gummer and Zac Goldsmith, whose views on environmental matters were certainly green. Their report, titled *Blueprint for a Green Economy* (Gummer, 2007), is more than 500 pages long, with a 50-page transport chapter. Steven Norris told me that David Cameron had wanted a wide-ranging environmental study, which he certainly got, which asked fundamental questions including 'Why travel?' and 'How is travel linked to land use?' On aviation, the objective of the proposals was to reduce carbon emissions and to 'head off air-dependent lifestyles facilitated by cheap flights, based on second homes abroad or even international commuting' (p. 351). The policy measures proposed included taxation, promoting high-speed rail as an alternative to flying and limiting airport capacity. Steven Norris expressed criticism of David Cameron's later reversal of some of these policies, which Cameron was reported as calling 'green crap' (Mason, 2013).

Therefore, at the end of this period, there had been some progress with the Heathrow third runway plans and the government had reiterated its policy support, having demonstrated to its satisfaction that the environmental tests would be met. However, the level of opposition remained high. The Stansted second runway plans had clearly not made good progress. In the words of Griggs and Howarth (2013b: p. 515), 'Despite valiant efforts lasting more than ten years, New Labour's persistent attempts to broker a "balanced" policy of "sustainable aviation" ended in disarray.' Then came the 2010 general election.

8.5. The New Deal ended by a perfect storm

The period covered by this chapter started with the New Labour government, from 1997, seeing the lack of policy support for airport expansion as an example of Tory laissez-faire government. This may have helped to push the already-open door of long-term transport policy wider. John Prescott was nothing if not ambitious for all elements of transport, and the idea of a 30-year aviation policy, supported by extensive research and public involvement, undoubtedly appealed to him and was enthusiastically supported by his civil servants and advisers. The aviation industry also supported the process, as did many of the local communities and others concerned about airport expansion, because of the degree of public involvement, for example in the SERAS studies and consultations. However, this latter group must have been bitterly disappointed when the 2003 White Paper proposed expansion at Stansted, then Heathrow, with Gatwick as a fallback, such that all three airports would then be seen as having potential for development. Despite its attempt to describe a balanced approach to growth, with expansion tempered by concerns about climate change and local environmental issues, opponents saw it as 'predict and provide', with almost no recognition of either the local or global impacts.

Nevertheless, the plans were progressed through the 2000s despite the concerns, so much so that in 2009 decisions were announced that both Stansted and Heathrow developments would proceed, albeit somewhat delayed compared with the original timescales.

Perhaps the plans for Stansted and Heathrow would have proceeded to fruition had a number of other events not intervened to create the perfect storm. One of these events was indeed a storm in 2006, when snow caused significant delays and cancellations at Heathrow. The airport's reaction to this was considered to be slow and there was much media criticism, which politicians also echoed. There had also been criticism at the opening of Terminal 5, when there were inevitable teething troubles and, again, it was the reaction of the airport that was seen to be at fault. Increased security requirements added to the impression that the management of the airport was not coping. All this had come not long after BAA had been bought by Ferrovial, a Spanish-based infrastructure company. Those who had long criticised BAA for its near-monopoly were now able to point to the company's foreign ownership and alleged management failings and press for the break-up of the company. As if this wasn't enough, the economic downturn, which began in 2007, then undermined the growth forecasts. The Conservative Party, preparing for a general election in 2010, seized the opportunity to present a policy which was different from that of the Labour government, whose popularity was declining. Such policies also appealed to a number of local constituencies around the airports that had been earmarked for expansion, as well as those concerned with the climate-change effects of aviation growth. After the election, the Conservatives formed a coalition government with the Liberal Democrats, whose longstanding opposition to airport expansion meant it was a 'no brainer' to implement the manifesto commitments to cancel the new runways proposed for Stansted and Heathrow.

8.6. Themes for the 2000s

Some of the themes of previous decades continued into the 2000s, but there were also new approaches.

- **Forecasts** were again significant, but the challenge was whether they took account of environmental costs, or were 'predict and provide'.
- The SERAS and PSDH consultations resulted in the largest amount of **public involvement** ever, although the majority of responses were opposed to the expansion policy that resulted.
- The 2003 White Paper was clearly an attempt to provide a **long-term, UK-wide strategy**.
- The White Paper supported significant **regional expansion**, and there were fewer calls for regional diversion.
- There were some policies to limit expansion, but many of the policies **overturned previous commitments**.
- **Environmental issues** now included climate change, as well as local air quality and noise.

Notes

1. Effectively, 'grandfather rights' are that if an airline uses a time slot at an airport for a service in one year, it has the right to use the same time slot in the next year.
2. For an explanation of 'predict and provide', see Chapter 10.2.
3. Segregated mode means that one runway is used for landings and the other for take-offs.
4. Mixed mode is where both runways are used for landings and take-offs at the same time.
5. An outbreak of SARS (severe acute respiratory syndrome) took place in the early 2000s. Air passengers travelling from affected countries were screened for the infection.

REFERENCES

Adey P, Budd L and Hubbard P (2007) Flying lessons: exploring the social and cultural geographies of global air travel. *Progress in Human Geography* **31(6)**: 773–791.

Anger A (2010) Including aviation in the European emissions trading scheme: impacts on the industry, CO_2 emissions and macroeconomic activity in the EU. *Journal of Air Transport Management* **16(2)**: 100–105.

Anger-Kraavi A and Köhler J (2013) Aviation and the EU Emissions Trading System. In *Sustainable Aviation Futures* (Budd L, Griggs S and Howarth D (eds)). Emerald Group Publishing, Bingley, UK, pp. 109–130.

Bailey J (2007) An assessment of UK government aviation policies and their implications. *Journal of Airport Management* **1(3)**: 249–261.

Bows A and Anderson K (2007) Policy clash: can projected aviation growth be reconciled with the UK Government's 60% carbon-reduction target? *Transport Policy* **14(2)**: 103–110.

Boyland A (2008) *Report to the Secretary of State for Communities and Local Government & the Secretary of State for Transport on the Appeal by BAA plc and Stansted Airport Ltd Stansted Airport, Stansted, Essex*. The Planning Inspectorate, Bristol, UK.

Budd L, Griggs S and Howarth D (2013) Sustainable aviation futures: crises, contested realities and prospects for change. In *Sustainable Aviation Futures* (Budd L, Griggs S and Howarth D (eds)). Emerald Group Publishing, Bingley, UK, pp. 3–35.

Carslaw D, Beevers S, Ropkins K and Bee M (2006) Detecting and quantifying aircraft and other on-airport contributions to ambient nitrogen oxides in the vicinity of a large international airport. *Atmospheric Environment* **40(28)**: 5424–5434.

Department for Transport (2003) *The Future of Air Transport*. Cmnd 6046, HMSO, London, UK.

Department for Transport (2006) *The Future of Air Transport Progress Report*. Cmnd 6977, HMSO, London, UK.

Department of the Environment, Transport and the Regions (2000) *The Future of Aviation: The Government's Consultation Document on Air Transport Policy*. HMSO, London, UK.

Dessens O, Köhler O, Rogers H, Jones R and Pyle J (2014) Aviation and climate change. *Transport Policy* **34**: 14–20.

Dixon S (2014) *Managing the Master Planning Process: How do airport managers incorporate stakeholder contribution in their final master plans?* PhD Thesis, Cranfield University, Cranfield, UK.

Docherty I and Shaw J (eds) (2003) *A New Deal for Transport*. Blackwell, Oxford, UK.

Doganis R (2006) *The Airline Business*, 2nd Edition. Routledge, London, UK.

Francis G and Humphreys I (2001) Airport regulation: reflecting on the lessons from BAA plc. *Public Money & Management* **21(1)**: 49–52.

Francis G, Humphreys I and Ison S (2004) Airports' perspectives on the growth of low-cost airlines and the remodelling of the airport–airline relationship. *Tourism Management* **25**: 507–514.

Girvin R (2009) Aircraft noise-abatement and mitigation strategies. *Journal of Air Transport Management* **15(1)**: 14–22.

Givoni M and Rietveld P (2009) Airlines' choice of aircraft size – explanations and implications. *Transportation Research Part A: Policy and Practice* **43(5)**: 500–510.

Graham A (2000) Demand for leisure air travel and limits to growth. *Journal of Air Transport Management* **6(2)**: 109–118.

Graham A (2006) Have the major forces driving leisure airline traffic changed? *Journal of Air Transport Management* **12**: 14–20.

Graham A (2008) Airport planning and regulation in the United Kingdom. In *Aviation Infrastructure Performance: A Study in Comparative Political Economy* (Winston C and Rus G de (eds)). Brookings Institution Press, Washington DC, USA, pp. 100–135.

Graham B (2003) Air transport policy: reconciling growth and sustainability? In *A New Deal for Transport* (Docherty I and Shaw J (eds)). Blackwell, Oxford, UK.

Graham B (2008) UK air travel: taking off for growth? In *Traffic Jam: Ten Years of Sustainable Transport in the UK* (Docherty I and Shaw J (eds)). Policy Press, Bristol, UK, pp. 139–159.

Griggs S and Howarth D (2004) A transformative political campaign? The new rhetoric of protest against airport expansion in the UK. *Journal of Political Ideologies* **9(2)**: 181–201.

Griggs S and Howarth D (2006) Metaphor, catachresis and equivalence: the rhetoric of freedom to fly in the struggle over aviation policy in the United Kingdom. *Policy and Society* **25(2)**: 23–46.

Griggs S and Howarth D (2013a) *The Politics of Airport Expansion in the United Kingdom: Hegemony, Policy and the Rhetoric of 'Sustainable Aviation'*. Manchester University Press, Manchester, UK.

Griggs S and Howarth D (2013b) 'Between a rock and a hard place': the Coalition, the Davies Commission and the wicked issue of airport expansion. *The Political Quarterly* **84(4)**: 515–526.

Griggs S and Howarth D (2017) Discourse, policy and the environment: hegemony, statements and the analysis of UK airport expansion. *Journal of Environmental Policy & Planning*. Published online 5 January 2017.

Gummer J (2007) *Blueprint for a Green Economy: Submission to the Shadow Cabinet*. Conservative Party Quality of Life Policy Group. https://conservativehome.blogs.com/torydiary/files/blueprint_for_a_green_economy110907b.pdf (accessed 13 August 2018).

HC Deb 16 December 2003, vol. 415, col. 1438.

HC Deb 11 February 2004, vol. 417, col. 429WH.

HC Deb 15 January 2009a, vol. 486, col. 355.

HC Deb 15 January 2009b, vol. 486, col. 367.

HC Deb 28 January 2009, vol. 487, col. 408.

House of Commons Transport Committee (2003) *Aviation, Sixth Report of Session 2002–03*.

House of Commons Transport Committee (2009) *The Future of Aviation, First Report of Session 2009–10*.

Humphreys I and Francis G (2002) Policy issues and planning of UK regional airports. *Journal of Transport Geography* **10**: 249–258.

Humphreys I, Ison S and Francis G (2007) UK airport policy: does the government have any influence? *Public Money & Management* **27(5)**: 339–344.

King E, Murphy E and Rice H (2011) Implementation of the EU environmental noise directive: lessons from the first phase of strategic noise mapping and action planning in Ireland. *Journal of Environmental Management* **92**: 756–764.

Lee D and Raper D (2003) The global atmospheric impacts of aviation. In *Towards Sustainable Aviation* (Upham P, Maughan J, Raper D and Thomas C (eds)). Earthscan, London, UK, pp. 77–96.

Lee D, Fahey D, Forster P, Newton P, Wit R, Lim L, Owen B and Sausen R (2009) Aviation and global climate change in the 21st century. *Atmospheric Environment* **43(22–23)**: 3520–3537.

Mason R (2013) David Cameron at centre of 'get rid of all the green crap' storm. *The Guardian*, 21 November 2013. www.theguardian.com/environment/2013/nov/21/david-cameron-green-crap-comments-storm (accessed 23 July 2018).

O'Doherty D (2015) Missing connexions: the politics of airport expansion in the United Kingdom. *Organization* **22(3)**: 418–431.

Peace H, Maughan J, Owen B and Raper D (2006) Identifying the contribution of different airport related sources to local urban air quality. *Environmental Modelling & Software* **21(4)**: 532–538.

Rawson R and Hooper P (2012) The importance of stakeholder participation to sustainable airport master planning in the UK. *Environmental Development* **2**: 36–47.

Rhodes J (2008) *The Planning System and Airports Policy*. Report to the Competition Commission on behalf of BAA, RPS.

Riddington G (2006) Long-range air traffic forecasts for the UK: a critique. *Journal of Transport Economics and Policy* **40(2)**: 297–314.

Starkie D (2008) *The Airport Industry in a Competitive Environment: A United Kingdom Perspective*, Discussion Paper No. 2008-15. OECD and International Transport Forum Joint Transport Research Centre, London, UK.

Thomas C and Lever M (2003) Aircraft noise, community relations and stakeholder involvement. In *Towards Sustainable Aviation* (Upham P (ed)). Earthscan, London, UK.

Upham P (2003) Climate change and planning and consultation for the UK Aviation White Paper. *Journal of Environmental Planning and Management* **46(6)**: 911–918.

Upham P, Thomas C, Gillingwater D and Raper D (2003) Environmental capacity and airport operations: current issues and future prospects. *Journal of Air Transport Management* **9(3)**: 145–151.

Wei W and Hansen M (2003) Cost economics of aircraft size. *Journal of Transport Economics and Policy* **37(2)**: 279–296.

Wei W and Hansen M (2005) Impact of aircraft size and seat availability on airlines' demand and market share in duopoly markets. *Transportation Research Part E: Logistics and Transportation Review* **41(4)**: 315–327.

/ Chapter 9

2010 onwards: policies reversed, reviewed and reinstated

9.1. Introduction

On 7 May 2010, the UK general election resulted in the Conservatives winning 306 seats, Labour 258 and the Liberal Democrats 57. After several days of negotiation, a coalition government between the Conservatives and the Liberal Democrats was formed. In the coalition agreement, under the heading 'Energy and Climate Change', it was stated, 'We will cancel the third runway at Heathrow' and 'We will refuse permission for additional runways at Gatwick and Stansted' (HMG, 2010: 16).

The work on Heathrow that was led by the government was immediately halted and BAA also ended its actions. Safeguarding the land had never been formally implemented by the local authorities but BAA had bought a number of properties. Similarly, at Stansted, BAA withdrew its planning application and ended its property purchases. At Gatwick, where only minimal planning had been undertaken for a second runway, the safeguarding, which had been implemented by the local authority, Crawley Borough Council, remained in place, despite the coalition agreement. In fact, having implemented the safeguarding through the statutory planning process, it remains in place unless a subsequent plan deletes it and, as I argue in Chapter 12, safeguarding land for future use is a good long-term strategy.

Sherwood (2009) had correctly predicted that the 2010 general election would result in the cancellation of the Heathrow third runway, but, in a chapter called 'The last battle', suggested the 'recent developments should decide the controversy once and for all' (p. 158). It was certainly not the last battle and the controversy continues to this day.

The decade had started with the economic recession, with unemployment at 2.5 million. Following the general election there was an emergency budget, when VAT was raised to 20 per cent and public spending cuts began. Students demonstrated, in particular against the raising of university fees, which the Liberal Democrats had pledged in their manifesto not to let happen. As the decade continued, there was a referendum on an alternative voting process which was rejected, there were riots in the cities and, after some economic improvement from quantitative easing, a double-dip recession occurred in 2012. Other domestic issues occupying the government included the Jimmy Savile scandal, the West Coast rail franchise debacle, the Leveson Inquiry into the culture, practices and ethics of the press, strikes by firemen and other public sector workers over pensions, the Scottish independence referendum and, on a positive note, the London Olympic and Paralympic Games. Internationally, the Syrian civil war began, the Ebola outbreak took place in West Africa, and there were terrorist attacks in France, Tunisia and Egypt, as well as migration flashpoints all across Europe, including Calais. UK climate records were broken in 2012 (wettest) and 2015 (hottest). The UK population and the economy were growing again by 2015, when a general election, to the surprise of many, brought a majority Conservative government into power, with the Liberal Democrats reduced to seven MPs. Then came a referendum on leaving the EU in 2016, after which David Cameron was replaced as prime minister by Theresa May. She called a general election in June 2017, at which the Conservatives won the largest number of seats but not an overall majority, but formed a government with Northern Ireland's Democratic Unionist Party. In 2017, the UK faced terrorist attacks in London and Manchester, and the tragedy of the Grenfell Tower fire.

Overall, air passenger numbers recovered from the 2008 recession and have grown by 20 per cent since 2010, although the Eyjafjallajokull volcanic eruption in Iceland in 2010 dented that year's traffic and numbers at Stansted did not grow again until 2014. Delta and Northwest Airlines merged in the USA in 2010, American Airlines and US Airways in 2013, and British Airways (BA) and Iberia in Europe in 2011. The European Union's Emissions Trading System (ETS) was extended to aviation in 2012, but was subsequently put on hold when many non-EU airlines refused to be bound by it. There were large aircraft orders, in particular from Middle East airlines, and jet fuel prices reduced. The Boeing 787 entered service and the Airbus A350 and Bombardier CS300 had their first flights.

9.2. A coalition government implements its manifesto commitments

The new Secretary of State for Transport, Philip Hammond, announced the setting up of the South East Airports Taskforce (SEATF) on 15 June 2010 (HC Deb 15 June 2010) which, following the cancellation of the additional runway capacity proposals, had a remit to explore ways of making better use of existing capacity in the short term. The taskforce was chaired by the Aviation Minister Theresa Villiers and included representatives from Heathrow and Gatwick airports, the Civil Aviation Authority (CAA), National Air Traffic Services (NATS), airlines, Air Transport Users Council, London First, Aviation Environment Federation and Airport Operators Association. The taskforce did not consult wider than its membership but, once published, it promised consultation with local communities. The report was published on 14 July 2011 (Department for Transport, 2011).

Given its short-term remit, the taskforce did not include new forecasts. It concluded that a number of measures should be implemented to make more flexible use of Heathrow's runways, known as Tactically Enhanced Arrivals or Departures Measures. These measures were primarily aimed at improving flight punctuality (delays had been apparent in recent years, particularly during bad weather). It also recommended that customer service at security checks and border controls should be improved and that the airport community should lead representations and provide evidence on the importance of surface access. The taskforce did not consider environmental issues, although its remit required it to take account of the government's commitment to a low-carbon and eco-friendly economy.

9.3. Short-term policies established quickly

By this time, Gatwick and Stansted had been sold, Heathrow Terminal 5 was working well and the new Terminal 2, eventually replacing Terminal 1 and the old Terminal 2, was under construction. However, there were continuing concerns about resilience, delays and customer service at Heathrow, the issue being the subject of a number of questions and debates in Parliament. The Civil Aviation Act of 2012 was enacted to modernise key elements of the regulatory framework for civil aviation, with a main aim being to deliver better outcomes for passengers and cargo shippers.

The coalition government elected in May 2010 was to be 'the greenest government ever' (Connelly, 2013) and initial ministerial appointments, such as Chris Huhne as Energy and Climate Change Secretary, seemed to confirm this (although he was later jailed for perverting the course of justice). Secretary of State for Transport Philip Hammond said that the 2003 White Paper had failed to give sufficient weight to climate change. Justine Greening, whose Putney, Roehampton and Southfields constituency is affected by aircraft noise from Heathrow, took over from Philip Hammond in October 2011 and confirmed the decision not to have a third Heathrow runway. Boris Johnson had been re-elected as London Mayor in May 2011 and also played a significant role, opposing expansion at Heathrow and indeed proposing its closure, to be replaced by a major new four-runway airport, either in the Thames Estuary or at Stansted. Griggs and Howarth's 2017 analysis of government statements for this period characterised them as 'a genuinely sustainable framework', which note that the 'balanced approach' of the previous decade failed to give sufficient weight to the challenge of climate change. Griggs and Howarth then suggest that this allowed Conservative MP Justine Greening, whose view was that we had reached peak oil and that technological fixes would not be sufficient to prevent dangerous climate change, to be appointed as Secretary of State for Transport and to implement a policy of no additional runway capacity.

The climate change impacts of aviation expansion, which had come to the fore in the previous period, continued to be a key issue. The influential House of Commons Environmental Audit Committee, chaired by Tim Yeo, said that the EU ETS would transform the picture (Griggs and Howarth, 2013a) and aviation was included from 2012, but the carbon price had collapsed and therefore had only a small impact (Anger-Kraavi and Köhler, 2013). International support for the EU ETS was limited, and the Chicago Convention had prohibited tax on aviation fuel (Ryley, 2014), and the inclusion of aviation in the EU ETS was suspended in 2013 pending action by the International Civil Aviation Organisation (ICAO). Bows-Larkin and Anderson (2013), noting various scenarios for how carbon budgets might be used, concluded that 'until technological and operational solutions can decarbonise air travel at rates well beyond the pace of expansion in the industry, policy measures must place a constraint on growth, for example, through delaying plans for increased airport capacity' (p. 81). Griggs and Howarth (2017) used the statement that the government was looking for 'a genuinely sustainable framework' as an example of how a theoretical approach (see Chapter 4) can be used as a tool to investigate the changes of policy. In this case, the statement seemed to relegate aviation growth beneath climate change, or at least recognise that there would have to be a trade-off between them.

The impact of aviation on health (through air quality and noise impacts) was raised in comments on the draft Aviation Policy Framework (APF) of 2011 by Banatvala and Rao (2013), who noted that the consultation was not sent to the Department of Health.

Looking to the future in terms of environmental impacts, Budd and Budd (2013) commented that, 'while aircraft can be made to be significantly quieter *or* less polluting, achieving both at the same time is a much harder prospect' (p. 106). According to Graham *et al.* (2014), targets of 50 per cent reductions in fuel burn and noise and 80 per cent in nitrous oxides (NO_x) by 2020 from 2000 levels will not be achieved, so demand management is still needed.

9.4. The longer term kicked into the long grass

The government began the process of creating a new White Paper by the publication of a scoping document in March 2011. More than 600 responses were received and a draft Aviation Policy Framework was published in July 2012. The draft APF discussed the economic benefits as well as the climate change and local environmental impacts but, in relation to the long term, noted only that beyond 2020 there would be 'a capacity challenge' at the biggest airports in the South East of England.

A National Infrastructure Plan had been initiated by the Treasury in November 2011 which included a reference to exploring ways of maintaining the UK's international aviation connectivity. Then, in September 2012, Justine Greening was replaced as Secretary of State for Transport by Patrick McLoughlin; Theresa Villiers, who had also been associated with opposition to Heathrow expansion, was moved from the Department for Transport (DfT). This was described by Connelly (2013: p. 233) as a 'textbook masterpiece of political manoeuvring' by the Chancellor, George Osborne, and his allies in government. As in the early 1970s, the Treasury's role was significant and it was able to dominate without the need to persuade (ibid). By 2013, Connelly writes, 'the Treasury remains supreme; radical, green and powerful ministers prepared or able to challenge the Treasury have resigned or been sidelined and replaced by weaker or actively hostile ministers; public opinion is indifferent and believes the claims of green government to be bogus; the deep lying assumption that economic growth is paramount is triumphant' (p. 235). Connelly suggests that this was a 'descent to politics as usual', or perhaps the period 2010–2012 was more of 'a temporary ascent from politics as usual'.

I asked John Stewart, of the Heathrow Association for the Control of Aircraft Noise (HACAN), why he thought the government had changed its stance on additional capacity between 2011 and 2012. His view was that the aviation industry had been shocked by the 2010 decision and began to drive a media campaign while, at the same time, the opposition groups reduced activity as they did not have specific proposals that the community would object to, and the large environmental groups withdrew from Airport Watch. 'Control of the narrative' was lost to the aviation industry, which, noting that the economy was still struggling, was able to push the economic benefits of growth. HACAN continued to be active in current issues, such as night flights, the possibility of mixed mode, the removal of the Cranford Agreement, etc.[1] John Stewart was also generous enough to acknowledge a change in Heathrow Airport Ltd's attitude to engage more with the local community, as he thinks they reassessed their approach following the loss of trust that came after their changes of stance on Terminal 5 and the third runway in previous decades.

One of the first actions of Patrick McLoughlin was to set up the Airports Commission in the autumn of 2012, with a remit similar to the Treasury's National Infrastructure Plan statement about maintaining international aviation connectivity. McLoughlin oversaw the completion of the APF begun by his predecessor but, when published in March 2013 (Department for Transport, 2013), it deferred all discussion about the long term to the Airports Commission. Nevertheless, it replaced the 2003 White Paper with a framework that sought to indicate how airport expansion proposals would be considered, without specifying which ones would be approved.

Regional issues were covered in the APF, but to a significantly lesser extent than in the 2003 White Paper. New forecasts had been prepared which were some 7 per cent below the 2030 numbers in the previous forecast. However, this still led to South East airports being full by 2030, although under various scenarios this could be between 2025 and 2040. Heathrow was assessed as being full from 2011. The document was considerably less prescriptive than the 2003 White Paper in terms of individual airport developments, noting instead a number of case studies.

The APF confirmed a number of the short-term measures that had been proposed in the 2011 South East Airports Taskforce report. As well as short-term measures, the APF also referred to the medium term, noting the development of HS2. A considerable proportion of its pages (about one third) were devoted to environmental issues. It referred extensively to the government's climate change strategy, which followed the Climate Change Act of 2008, and which included seeking emissions trading initially through the EU and eventually through ICAO. In particular, it noted a 2009 report from the Committee on Climate Change, which had indicated how UK aviation would contribute to the target reduction for carbon dioxide (CO_2) to below 2005 levels by 2050. The APF noted a range of management measures for noise, but had little to say on local air quality. Neither did it say much about surface access, other than to confirm the role of Airport Transport Forums and Airport Surface Access Strategies.

The APF said very little about the long term, as the Airports Commission had been set up. Interestingly, it noted the ability of planning authorities to safeguard land for long-term airport use, although it did not identify particular airports.

9.5. HS2: a diversion?

One element of the Heathrow issue was high-speed rail. The Conservatives and Liberal Democrats, when in opposition, had suggested that high-speed rail would be able to replace many short-haul flights as, indeed, had been the case on the London–Paris and London–Brussels routes since the opening of the Channel Tunnel in 1994 and on other routes around the world. High Speed 2 (HS2), the high-speed rail project between London, the Midlands and the North, had been initiated by the Labour government in 2009 with cross-party support and the coalition government continued with the policy after the 2010 general election. Lord Mawhinney, a former Conservative Transport Secretary, was asked to review the route and recommended that a Heathrow spur (which would cost between £2 and 4 billion) should not be included in Phase 1 of the project, but should be safeguarded for Phase 2. Also, as the HS2 project developed, it became clear that the potential for diversion from air to rail would be limited. Phase 1 of HS2, which continues to receive cross-party support and has now received parliamentary approval (royal assent was granted in February 2017) is planned to be operational in 2026. The initial link to Heathrow will then be by Crossrail and Heathrow Express services, which will connect with HS2 at Old Oak Common, in north-west London. These views were confirmed by the Airports Commission in its Final Report (2015). The Commission also noted that the alternative of a second runway at Gatwick would not be connected to HS2 except via central London. The direct link to Heathrow, which was to have been safeguarded, is not in the current plans for Phase 2.

It is also worth noting how other airport rail links had developed in this period. Heathrow Express was now well established and, together with the Piccadilly Tube line, had been extended to Terminal 5. Heathrow Express was being used for 9 per cent of air passenger trips and the Piccadilly line for 18 per cent, with the latter also serving many employees. Plans for additional links had not progressed in the previous decade, other than Heathrow Connect, providing a stopping service between Paddington and the airport, which started as a joint venture between BAA and Great Western in 2005. As noted in Chapter 7 and described in detail by Schabas (2017), a Crossrail bill went through Parliament in 2008 and the Elizabeth line will open to Heathrow in 2019. Gatwick Express received new trains from 1999, but these were replaced with refurbished units and then by new trains in 2016. The franchise, which had been separately run, was merged into the large Southern franchise in 2008. Many new trains were introduced on Southern at this time and the merger led to the Gatwick Express becoming less distinctive as a premium, dedicated service. Nevertheless, the overall rail share of air-passenger journeys grew from around 22 per cent to 36 per cent. Stansted Express is operated as part of the West Anglia franchise. Longer trains were introduced and the frequency increased in the early 2000s. New trains were delivered in 2011 but the journey time increased as additional stops were made for commuters. The share of Stansted air passengers using rail has remained relatively steady at around 25 per cent.

Rail access, and surface access in general, remains a key element in the consideration of options for airport expansion, as discussed in the remainder of this chapter on the Airports Commission and subsequent events.

9.6. The Airports Commission: a comprehensive review?

The Airports Commission's remit was 'to identify and recommend to government options for maintaining the UK's status as an international hub for aviation'. The chairman was Sir Howard Davies and the other commissioners were Sir John Armitt, Professor Ricky Burdett, Vivienne Cox and Professor Dame Julia King, supported by an expert advisory panel. The terms of reference required an interim report by the end of 2013. A series of discussion papers were published and two public evidence sessions were held in Manchester and London. In addition, the Commission took evidence from airport operators, airlines, environmental organisations, local campaign groups, business organisations, tourism representatives and others, and received research and reports from a wide range of bodies, including committees, academic bodies and interest groups. Submissions were invited on specific issues, such as making best use of existing capacity, and outline proposals were invited on long-term options. All of the documentation was published, including the responses and submissions.

To meet its remit, the Airports Commission undertook an analysis of the way in which global aviation works, and the UK market, and in particular how the London airport system operates. It considered the value of aviation and argued that the wider economic impacts of a failure to address capacity constraints would be between £30 and 45 billion between 2021 and 2080. The Commission prepared its own forecasts, which included options for carbon capping or trading, and unconstrained and constrained capacity. It also prepared scenarios to test the sensitivity of the forecasts.

In terms of proposals, the Interim Report (Airports Commission, 2013) reiterated the previous optimisation strategy of the Airports Policy Framework and developed a number of proposals further for the short and medium term, in particular relating to surface access.

Initially, rather than developing its own proposals, the Commission invited them from developers. There were 52 submissions on long-term options: seven for Heathrow, two for Gatwick, six for Stansted, eleven for Thames Estuary sites, and many others for a range of solutions, including greenfield sites, military airfields, alternatives to new runways and surface access proposals. The submitters included airport operators, architects, planners, Transport for London and private individuals. The Commission then performed a series of 'sifts', using criteria it had developed.

One of the submissions that was sifted out by the Airports Commission was for a close parallel southern runway at Heathrow, similar to that proposed by the airlines during RUCATSE in the 1990s (see Chapter 7). Tom Carter, by now retired from BA, worked with consultant Aras Global on this scheme. The Commission rejected it because it did not provide the full capacity of a wide-spaced runway, and therefore would require a fourth runway, also close-spaced parallel but north of the existing northern runway. Carter continues to argue that this would be a better operational solution, matching similar layouts at Los Angeles and Atlanta, although he accepts that it would not provide the type of respite valued by the local community.

The main submissions to the Airports Commission were reviewed by Bentley (2014), who noted support for the various options from MPs, airlines and regional interests. The main options were analysed by Irvine et al. (2015) using a Monte-Carlo approach to show the relationship between cost and capacity,[2] with an additional runway at Stansted providing the lowest cost/capacity ratio. Janic (2015) undertook a multi-criteria evaluation, under different weightings, which concluded that an additional runway at Heathrow was ranked first. The Airports Commission also used the technique of Computable General Equilibrium (CGE) to assess the options in terms of the overall effect on the economy, in particular the benefits of tourism and the effect of a constrained airport system (Forsyth, 2014).

Although most of the options were submitted by developers, the Airports Commission did evaluate two additional sites, one between Maidenhead and Reading and the other between

Table 9.1 Airports Commission options after the second sift (Department for Transport, 2017a)

Proposal	Proposer	Result of second sift
Heathrow north-west runway	Heathrow Airport Ltd	Shortlisted
Heathrow south-west runway	Heathrow Airport Ltd	Sifted out because of effect on reservoir/SPA[a]/Ramsar[b] site and flooding issues
Heathrow four runways	Airports Commission	Sifted out because of airspace, excess capacity, highway costs and loss of houses
Heathrow extended northern runway	Heathrow Hub Ltd	Shortlisted
Gatwick second runway	Gatwick Airport Ltd	Shortlisted
Stansted second runway	Manchester Airports Group	Sifted out because of smaller catchment than Heathrow or Gatwick, long rail access, heritage issues and funding
Stansted five runways	Mayor of London	Sifted out because of large surface access requirements and funding
Thames Hub Airport	Foster + Partners	Elements of each of these options were combined and further assessed, but then rejected because of very large costs, impacts on SPA and Ramsar sites and funding
London Gateway Airport	International Aviation Advisory Group	
Metrotidal Tunnel and Thames Reach Airport	Metrotidal Ltd	
London Britannia Airport	Gensler/TESTRAD	
Isle of Grain	Mayor of London	

[a] SPA is Special Protection Area, an EU designation for the conservation of wild birds
[b] A Ramsar site is a wetland of international importance designated under the Ramsar Convention

Milton Keynes and Bedford. They also took some features of different submissions for similar sites and combined them. After their first 'sift' there was a list of 12 options, which was then reduced to a shortlist of three, as shown in Table 9.1.

Peter Sanders and Brian Ross, of the group Stop Stansted Expansion (SSE), told me of their involvement with the Airports Commission. They responded to every discussion paper and consultation, appeared at the public hearings and met with the Commission's staff. Most of their submissions were related to the Stansted proposals, but in addition they objected to the appointment of Geoff Muirhead as one of the commissioners. Muirhead had been chief executive of Manchester Airport and, although he retired from that post in 2010, he was still involved with the Manchester Airports Group when it acquired Stansted in 2013, having been appointed to the Airports Commission in 2012. Muirhead stood down from the Commission later in 2013. Sanders and Ross also co-signed a request to the Commission to make the shortlist as short as possible, so as to minimise blight. John Stewart, of HACAN, was generally complimentary about the Airports Commission, although he noted that the terms of reference (to maintain the UK's status as an international hub) made Heathrow expansion almost inevitable. However, Sir Howard Davies and the other commissioners directed that the process should engage with stakeholders and be

Figure 9.1 Gatwick Airport (Google Maps): the proposed second runway would be located to the south of the existing main runway in the land safeguarded between the airport and Crawley

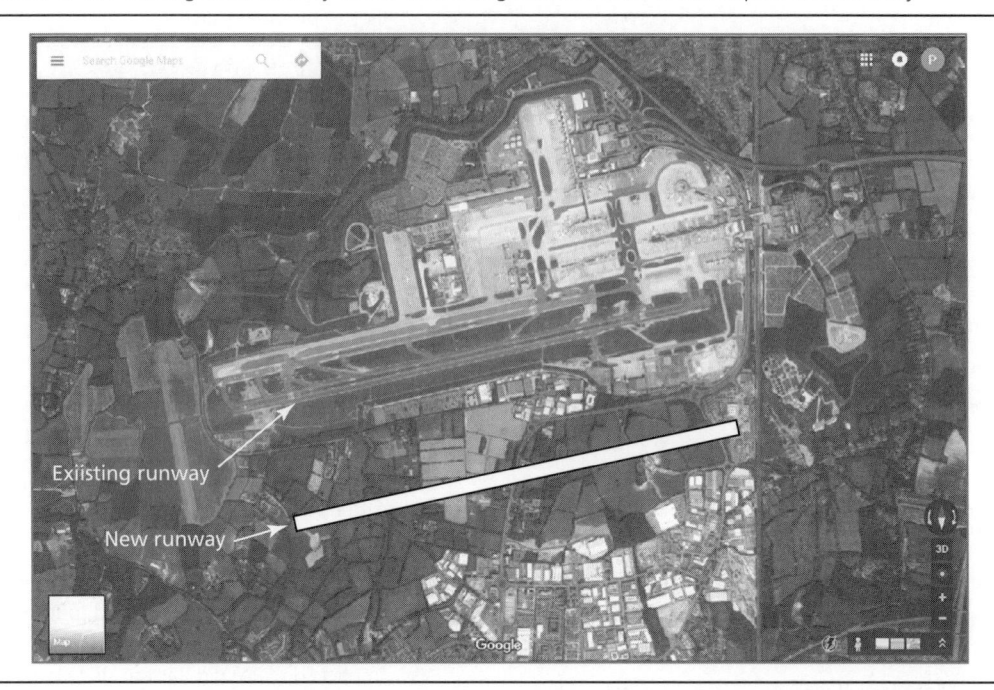

transparent, and the seconded civil servants administered the process in this way. Engagement was through briefings, discussions and meetings rather than public inquiries, and this was more constructive than the adversarial public inquiry format. HACAN was particularly pleased with the Commission's work on noise, which had been HACAN's initial reason for being. This resulted in recommendations to use a range of noise metrics, to create an independent noise body, to have a night ban, and to ensure that respite is a key mitigation strategy, all of which HACAN had been pressing for but had achieved little in the previous decade.

The Commission proposed a shortlist of three options, two at Heathrow (with different runway arrangements) and one at Gatwick, as shown in Figures 9.1, 9.2 and 9.3. The three proponents promoted their proposals in advertisements in the press, for example as shown in Figure 9.2. In a separate report, the Commission considered proposals for Thames Estuary sites and ruled these out. As well as the Interim Report, many supporting technical reports were published.

Local environmental issues were covered at length in the Interim Report, as well as in the technical support papers. Table 9.2 summarises the key impacts of the shortlisted options but is by no means comprehensive. The Interim Report also provided many other details about the shortlisted options, including their costs and economic benefits.

Discussing the processes adopted by the Airports Commission, Budd *et al.* (2013) noted that it was committed to an open and consultative approach, with discussion papers, visits and meetings and an advisory panel, but the contested evidence base may have weakened the Commission's task to create consensus. O'Doherty (2015) saw an inevitability of the Commission's work as they were inundated with economic data and unlikely to come to any other conclusion but that the expansion of aviation must be supported with an additional runway at Heathrow or Gatwick. The Interim Report concluded that some net additional runway capacity would be needed in the

2010 onwards: policies reversed, reviewed and reinstated

Figure 9.2 Heathrow extended northern runway advertisement
(Picture: Heathrow Hub Ltd/Runway Innovations Ltd)

113

Figure 9.3 Heathrow north-west runway proposal (Picture: Heathrow Airport)

Table 9.2 Key environmental issues at shortlisted sites (Data source: Airports Commission 2013)

Issue	Gatwick second runway	Heathrow north-west runway	Heathrow extended northern runway
Number of homes to be acquired	200	1500	720
Land required[a]	624 hectares (safeguarded)	569 hectares	336 hectares
Population within 57 dB L_{Aeq} noise contour	6300	150 000	180 000
EU air-quality limits	Not exceeded	Exceeded	Exceeded

[a] Land areas from the Final Report (Airports Commission, 2015)

South East and followed a 'high modernist' scenario in which continued expansion was permitted while there was human and scientific progress, with risks mitigated (Budd et al., 2013). On the Commission's forecasts, de Neufville (2013), in evidence presented on behalf of Gatwick Airport, noted that the airline and airport industries were in the midst of convulsive organisational changes and suggested that 'the runway debate has become overly entangled in numbers of little meaning. Indeed, detailed debate about 20-year aviation forecasts appears to be a waste of time, when retrospective experience shows that we are lucky to get such estimates right within 20 or 30 per cent' (p. 159). He also suggested that, while Heathrow is a hub for north Atlantic traffic, it is on the periphery of Europe and therefore does not serve intra-Europe travel and that the growth of Asian traffic will favour Gulf and Turkish hubs.

Alastair McDermid, who is noted in Chapters 6 and 8 for his involvement in many inquiries, was by this time working for Gatwick Airport Ltd. He believes that the Airports Commission was set up on the initiative of George Osborne, then Chancellor of the Exchequer, who clearly wanted a third runway at Heathrow, despite David Cameron's and his coalition partners' objections. The choice of Howard Davies as chair and the terms of reference meant that the final recommendation was inevitable, even though the shortlist had included Gatwick. The terms of reference referred to maintaining the UK's hub status but McDermid reported that neither the DfT nor the Airports Commission replied when asked what this meant, and it was only several years later, at the end of the process, that the Revised Draft National Policy Statement stated that it effectively means 'a big hub airport'. McDermid queried that if that's the case, what was the point – the whole process was a sham. McDermid believed that Osborne's 'kitchen logic' that the Heathrow option was best was based on a longstanding perception held by the Treasury that Heathrow would produce the greatest economic benefits for the country as a whole. McDermid suggested that while this may have been true historically, the world of aviation has changed out of all recognition; and neither the Treasury nor the Airports Commission were willing to explore this with an open mind. He suggested that subsequent evidence from government (see the next section of this chapter) showed Gatwick producing greater economic benefits, but he believed that a political change of heart is unlikely. Steven Norris, a Minister of Transport in the 1990s, believes that the outcome of the Airports Commission was pre-determined, and he also claimed that setting the deadline for the final report after the 2015 general election was one of the most cynical acts in politics of recent years.

The issue of average aircraft size, which had been critical in the 1970s Maplin Review and the 1990s RUCATSE study, continued to be analysed. Although Heathrow's Capacity Utilisation Index (a measure of the use of runway capacity) was the highest in the world, there was little difference in the growth in the average number of seats per aircraft between congested and uncongested airports (Berster et al., 2015). Zhang (2014), building on his earlier work, showed how the economies of operating larger aircraft did not always result in larger aircraft being operated as passenger demand grows over time. The acquisition of British Midland Airways by BA in 2012 included a number of slots at Heathrow, which enabled BA to open new routes or retain high frequencies with smaller aircraft. In order to meet their slot regulations, the EU required some of the former British Midland slots to be provided to competitors. Initially, this was an operation by Virgin's Little Red airline but this did not prove sustainable, and now Flybe is operating a number of domestic routes using smaller aircraft. It is possible also that some airlines are 'slot warming', as discussed in Chapter 8.

Griggs and Howarth (2017) use one of Sir Howard Davies' statements at the time of the Interim Report as another example of using a theoretical approach as an investigative tool. Sir Howard said that the challenge was to 'deliver the maximum connectivity bang for each of our carbon bucks' and this indicated that expert opinion had provided the cap (the government's carbon targets) within which aviation should be expanded, and that connectivity had become the key criteria for choosing between options.

The House of Commons Transport Committee undertook an inquiry into aviation strategy in the spring of 2013 and published its report in May 2013 (House of Commons Transport Committee, 2013). It was a particularly thorough inquiry, with 137 pieces of written evidence and 57 witnesses. The committee concluded that expansion at Heathrow was required and that a new hub should not be developed, and a split hub, high-speed rail and regional airport expansion would not replace the need for expansion in the South East. The report was debated in the House of Commons on 24 October 2013 (HC Deb 24 October 2013), with contributions from the committee as well as from MPs with constituencies near airports. The Aviation Minister, Robert Goodwill, said little other than to await the Airports Commission's reports. The Environmental Audit Committee, which had pointed to the contradiction between the Labour government's aviation and climate change policies in 2008, did not consider the matter again until after the Airports Commission's final report, when it noted that the recommendation for a third runway at Heathrow should not be approved unless the Commission's recommended environmental conditions were met.

The Airports Commission published its Final Report in July 2015, again along with a range of supporting technical reports. A full list of the contributors is acknowledged, as well as a number of organisations. In addition to the consultations noted in the Interim Report, the Final Report notes two public evidence sessions at Heathrow and Gatwick, 150 meetings with stakeholders and visits.

The Final Report describes in detail how airport hubs operate, the structure of the industry and the market for air travel. It sets out the economic benefits and the need to limit carbon before presenting updated forecasts, albeit based on the same sensitivities and used in the Interim Report. On this basis, the Commission recommended that there would be a need for one additional runway by 2030. It then described in detail the appraisal process for the shortlisted sites, with much of the detail in the supporting technical reports. The proposals had been modified by the promoters, and the impact assessments were refined compared with the Interim Report. In conclusion, the Commission unanimously recommended the Heathrow north-west runway option, with strict conditions, but noted that all three options would be feasible. The conditions included a ban on night flights, noise management measures, compensation for the loss of homes and community compensation, training opportunities, a major shift in the proportion of staff using sustainable transport modes, and acceptable air quality. In addition, the Commission recommended that a fourth runway should be firmly ruled out.

David Starkie, writing about changes in the airline industry that had taken place in the years leading to the Airports Commission, noted that low-cost carriers (LCCs) were accounting for 40 per cent of passengers, meaning that the balance of power between airlines and airports had undoubtedly shifted and *ex-ante* regulation of airports was generally unwarranted (Starkie, 2012). The attitude of incumbent airlines to expansion was reported by Gillen and Starkie (2016), with IAG (British Airways, Aer Lingus, Iberia and Veuling) saying that a Heathrow third runway is not wanted and is a vanity project with outrageous costs, and EasyJet saying that a second runway at Gatwick would be very onerous and quite worrying to their economic case. The authors conclude that EU slot regulation 'throws further grit into the wheels of hub airport expansion; it exacerbates the incumbent airline's reluctance to embrace runway expansion because it retards the ability of those airlines to take advantage of capacity expansion' (p. 162).

9.7. Government decisions and further steps

In December 2015, the government announced that it accepted the Commission's recommendations that a new runway would be needed and that it should be one of the shortlisted schemes. However, more work would be commissioned on the environmental impacts before a decision would be made. The government confirmed that, once a decision was made, it would prepare a National Policy Statement (NPS) under the Planning and Localism Acts and that the development would proceed by the promoter submitting a Development Consent Order (DCO), which would then pass through the prescribed process before permission to build could be given. A decision was then interrupted by the EU referendum in June 2016, following which David Cameron resigned and Theresa May took over as prime minister, appointing a new Secretary of State for Transport, Chris Grayling.

The matter was considered by the Cabinet on 18 October 2016 and then by the Economic and Industrial Strategy (Airports) sub-committee. In a letter from the prime minister seen on the Airport Watch website (May, 2016), an exception to the normal rules of collective responsibility was proposed. The decision was announced by the government on 25 October 2016 (HC Deb 25 October 2016) and it was to support the Airports Commission's recommended option for a third, north-west runway at Heathrow. The conditions would include compliance with air-quality obligations, a ban on night movements from 11pm to 5.30am and compensation for affected residents.

Roy Griffins, an advisor to GIP, the owners of Gatwick, told me that the process of setting up a commission, followed by an NPS and a DCO under the 2008 Planning Act, is a good thing as it should enable matters of principle to be properly dealt with in Parliament. However, Griffins believes that the terms of reference and the appointment of Sir Howard Davies showed that minds had already been made up that Heathrow should emerge as the favoured option. Griffins' view is that, in comparing the Gatwick and Heathrow options, the economic benefits are close, but that the environmental case against Heathrow should have been overwhelming, except that the adversely affected areas can be seen as 'pollution havens'[3] where the environmental costs are outweighed by the economic benefits, primarily in terms of jobs.

In early 2017, the DfT published a draft NPS for consultation (Department for Transport, 2017b). The process was again interrupted, this time by the general election of June 2017, when the Conservative Party did not gain an absolute majority but held on to power by reaching an agreement with the Democratic Unionist Party.

A draft revised NPS was published in October 2017 (Department for Transport, 2017c). It included updated forecasts and a revised economic appraisal, but continued to conclude that the

Heathrow north-west runway was the best option. There was a parliamentary debate in Westminster Hall in January 2018 (HC Deb 24 January 2018) initiated by Liberal Democrat leader Vince Cable, which enabled some of the objectors to voice their views, while the main support for the government view came from Northern Ireland and Scotland. The Labour spokesman Karl Turner indicated conditional support and the response from Parliamentary Under Secretary of State for Transport, Jesse Norman, concentrated on the way the NPS had been consulted upon. The House of Lords debated the draft NPS in March 2018 (HL Deb 15 March 2018). The House of Commons Transport Committee undertook an inquiry, which received 87 written submissions and heard evidence from 30 witnesses. Its report, published on 23 March 2018, concluded that the government was right to pursue development at Heathrow and accepted the arguments it had made in favour of its preferred scheme. However, it suggested a number of changes to the NPS to minimise any chance of successful legal challenge and to address a number of concerns relating to air quality, surface access, costs, airspace implications and mitigation measures. It also recommended that government should fill several policy gaps relating to airspace and airport capacity across the UK (House of Commons Transport Committee, 2018).

On 5 June 2018, the government published the final version of the NPS (Department for Transport, 2018), and this was debated in Westminster Hall on 7 June 2018 (HC Deb 7 June 2018) and in the full House of Commons on 25 June 2018 (HC Deb 25 June 2018). The full House of Commons debate lasted four hours, with contributions from more than 70 MPs. The NPS was approved by 415 votes to 119, with MPs opposing from Conservative, Labour and Liberal Democrat parties. Subject to legal challenges, the DCO process can be started and, at the time of writing, it is expected that the DCO could be approved by 2021, enabling the new runway to be opened by the mid 2020s. Heathrow Airport has also begun a pre-DCO consultation exercise, mainly related to airport layout issues, and expects to consult further in 2019. The government is also continuing consultations on a national strategy, which it had started in 2017 with an initial call for evidence.

9.8. What happened to the support and opposition groups?

At the end of the 2000s, the anti-expansion groups had managed to use the argument of climate change as a key factor in persuading the Conservatives and Liberal Democrats to oppose new runways. Griggs and Howarth (2013a) said, 'Local campaigners and environmentalists had pulled off the biggest victory in transport policy since the roads movement of the 1980s and early 1990s' (p. 276). However, the victory was short lived, given the ministerial changes and the setting up of the Airports Commission in 2012. It is not clear what role various groups had in this policy swing, although many views were made clear in the submissions to the Commission, all of which were published. Flying Matters had been wound up in 2011, but Sustainable Aviation and Greener by Design continued their specific work on environmental issues. The aviation industry also supported specific campaigns such as 'Fair Tax on Flying' (on the issue of air passenger duty) and, of course, the various trade associations such as the Airport Operators Association (AOA) and International Air Transport Association (IATA) continued to make their views known. A Heathrow support group called 'Back Heathrow' was launched, with funding from the airport, and now claims to have 100 000 supporters. Groups with many fewer members also supported other options submitted to the Airports Commission.

Local opposition groups had mixed fortunes. HACAN and the Gatwick Area Conservation Campaign (GACC) were unable to sustain their cases against expansion at Heathrow and Gatwick respectively, but SSE and groups opposing Thames Estuary sites were content when their sites were not shortlisted. The role of the Royal Society for the Protection of Birds (RSPB) is worth noting in relation to the Thames Estuary sites, as a well-managed campaign energised many of their two million-plus members. More direct action has come from the Climate Camp and Plane Stupid campaigns. The former was concerned with a number of industries, including power generation as well as aviation, and also had international links, but ended its coordinated action in 2011. Plane Stupid is focused on UK aviation and has held a number of protests at airports, including occupying a runway at Heathrow in July 2015. It also unveiled a banner at one of the Airports Commission's public hearings. Some details of the activities of the various protest groups are described by Hayden (2014), who also links the arguments to wider environmental issues. However, the title of the article is prophetic, noting that it is 'Stopping Heathrow Airport expansion (for now)'.

John Stewart of HACAN told me that there is a dilemma in engaging with Heathrow Airport Ltd on the assumption that a third runway will be approved, as this could be seen as making the final approval easier. HACAN could stick its head in the sand and oppose it outright, but the group recognises the parliamentary arithmetic (even after the 2017 general election) and, while always stating its opposition to the third runway, will then engage with the airport on any proposals which could potentially improve the situation for local communities. HACAN's current focus is on flight paths, which will be changing in any event with the introduction of Performance Based Navigation, basically better technology that enables aircraft to follow routes more precisely.

9.9. It's not over yet

The decade started with a policy reversal but slowly yet surely the old policies are returning, with further expansion at Heathrow some way through the approval process. Those in favour of expansion have been able to advance their case, while the opponents have not been able to convince the inquiries, studies and commissions, and in particular the government. But the government is wary, based on previous experience, and is taking it very slowly and deliberately to try to ensure it does not get tripped up. There are still potential stumbling points for the government and indeed for Heathrow Airport as promoters, so it would be foolish to predict that we are definitely seeing the end of this current period of policy-making.

9.10. Themes for the 2010s

Since 2010, airports policy has swung from 'better not bigger', with no additional runways, to a December 2015 statement of support for one additional runway by 2030 and an October 2016 decision that the new runway should be at Heathrow. Many of the themes of the previous decades kept their high profile, with some changes, as follows.

- **Forecasts** were key, as always, and the issue of average aircraft size re-emerged, in particular in relation to the timing of the need for additional runway capacity. The Airports Commission also sought to take account of previous criticisms by exploring different scenarios for carbon limits, as well as for different global situations.
- **Public involvement** took a different form from previous studies and inquiries, with relatively few public meetings, but much more in terms of direct submissions.
- There was a huge amount of **research and analysis**, not only into the direct effects of the options, but also into the context of and background to the need for additional capacity.
- At the beginning of the decade, there was a **policy vacuum**, at least for the longer term, with little prescription and only a policy framework for the shorter term. Currently

(2018), apart from the key runway decision, this vacuum remains, but may be filled by the National Policy Statement and a new White Paper.
- David Cameron, when campaigning for the 2010 general election, said 'No ifs, no buts', there will be no third runway (Wickham, 2009), so the decision to approve it is a clear **policy reversal**.
- There was little debate about regional diversion, but significant discussion about **regional access** to new London airport capacity.

Notes

1. Mixed mode is where both runways are used for landings and take-offs at the same time. The Cranford Agreement was established in the 1950s and prevented aircraft taking off over the community of Cranford, which is at the eastern end of the northern runway at Heathrow.
2. A Monte-Carlo approach uses random numbers in certain variables in the analysis.
3. The pollution haven hypothesis posits that, when large industrialised nations seek to set up factories or offices abroad, they will often look for the cheapest option in terms of resources and labour that offers the land and material access they require. However, this often comes at the cost of environmentally sound practices (Levinson and Taylor, 2008).

REFERENCES

Airports Commission (2013) *Interim Report*. HMSO, London, UK.

Airports Commission (2015) *Final Report*. HMSO, London, UK.

Anger-Kraavi A and Köhler J (2013) Aviation and the EU Emissions Trading System. In *Sustainable Aviation Futures* (Budd L, Griggs S and Howarth D (eds)). Emerald Group Publishing, Bingley, UK, pp. 109–130.

Banatvala J and Rao M (2013) Aviation and public health. *BMJ Editorial* **346**: 1–2.

Bentley D (2014) Unravelling the UK airport capacity conundrum: a review of the main submissions made to the Airports Commission. *Journal of Airport Management* **8(1)**: 14–22.

Berster P, Gelhausen M and Wilken D (2015) Is increasing aircraft size common practice of airlines at congested airports? *Journal of Air Transport Management* **46**: 40–48.

Bows-Larkin A and Anderson K (2013) Carbon budgets for aviation or gamble with our future. In *Sustainable Aviation Futures* (Budd L, Griggs S and Howarth D (eds)). Emerald Group Publishing, Bingley, UK, pp. 65–84.

Budd L and Budd T (2013) Environmental technology and the future of flight. In *Sustainable Aviation Futures* (Budd L, Griggs S and Howarth D (eds)). Emerald Group Publishing, Bingley, UK, pp. 87–107.

Budd L, Griggs S and Howarth D (2013) Sustainable aviation futures: crises, contested realities and prospects for change. In *Sustainable Aviation Futures* (Budd L, Griggs S and Howarth D (eds)). Emerald Group Publishing, Bingley, UK, pp. 3–35.

Connelly J (2013) Coalition, aviation and the descent to 'politics as usual'. In *Sustainable Aviation Futures* (Budd L, Griggs S and Howarth D (eds)). Emerald Group Publishing, Bingley, UK, pp. 219–238.

de Neufville R (2013) Prospects for transport hub airports around London, Appendix 4 of Appendices submitted to the Airports Commission by Gatwick Airport Ltd, pp. 157–193.

Department for Transport (2011) *South East Airports Taskforce: Report*. https://assets.publishing.service.gov.uk/government/uploads/system/uploads/attachment_data/file/4354/south-east-airports-taskforce-report.pdf (accessed 13 August 2018).

Department for Transport (2013) *Aviation Policy Framework*. Cmnd 8584, HMSO, London, UK.
Department for Transport (2017a) *Appraisal of Sustainability: Draft Airports National Policy Statement*. https://assets.publishing.service.gov.uk/government/uploads/system/uploads/attachment_data/file/658789/aos-revised-draft-airports-nps-main-report.pdf (accessed 13 August 2018).
Department for Transport (2017b) *Draft Airports National Policy Statement: New Runway Capacity and Infrastructure at Airports in the South East of England*. https://assets.publishing.service.gov.uk/government/uploads/system/uploads/attachment_data/file/588764/draft-airports-nps-web-version.pdf (accessed 13 August 2018).
Department for Transport (2017c) *Revised Draft Airports National Policy Statement: New Runway Capacity and Infrastructure at Airports in the South East of England*. https://assets.publishing.service.gov.uk/government/uploads/system/uploads/attachment_data/file/654123/revised-draft-airports-nps-web-version.pdf (accessed 13 August 2018).
Department for Transport (2018) *Airports National Policy Statement: New Runway Capacity and Infrastructure at Airports in the South East of England*. https://assets.publishing.service.gov.uk/government/uploads/system/uploads/attachment_data/file/714106/airports-nps-new-runway-capacity-and-infrastructure-at-airports-in-the-south-east-of-england-web-version.pdf (accessed 13 August 2018).
Forsyth P (2014) Using CBA and CGE in investment and policy evaluation: a synthesis, draft. www.pc.gov.au/__data/assets/pdf_file/0018/135180/subdr117-infrastructure-attachment1.pdf (accessed 14 August 2018).
Gillen D and Starkie D (2016) EU slot policy at congested hubs and incentives to add capacity. *Journal of Transport Economics and Policy* **50(2)**: 151–163.
Graham W, Hall C and Morales V (2014) The potential of future aircraft technology for noise and pollutant emissions reduction. *Transport Policy* **34**: 36–51.
Griggs S and Howarth D (2013a) *The Politics of Airport Expansion in the United Kingdom: Hegemony, Policy and the Rhetoric of 'Sustainable Aviation'*. Manchester University Press, Manchester, UK.
Griggs S and Howarth D (2017) Discourse, policy and the environment: hegemony, statements and the analysis of UK airport expansion. *Journal of Environmental Policy & Planning*, January 2017 (online): 1–15.
Hayden A (2014) Stopping Heathrow Airport expansion (for now): lessons from a victory for the politics of sufficiency. *Journal of Environmental Policy & Planning*: **16 (4)**: 539–558.
HC Deb 15 June 2010, vol. 511, col. 48WS.
HC Deb 24 October 2013, vol. 569, col. 507.
HC Deb 25 October 2016, vol. 616, col. 162.
HC Deb 24 January 2018, vol. 635, col. 187WH.
HC Deb 7 June 2018, vol. 642, col. 197WH.
HC Deb 25 June 2018, vol. 643, col. 649.
HL Deb 15 March 2018, vol. 789, col. 1792.
HMG (Her Majesty's Government) (2010) *The Coalition: Our Programme for Government*. Cabinet Office, London, UK.
HMG (Her Majesty's Government) (2012) Civil Aviation Act 2012. Chapter 19. HMSO, London, UK.
House of Commons Transport Committee (2013) *Aviation Strategy, First Report of Session 2013–14*. https://publications.parliament.uk/pa/cm201314/cmselect/cmtran/78/78i.pdf (accessed 13 August 2018).

House of Commons Transport Committee (2018) *Airports National Policy Statement, Third Report of Session 2017–19*. https://publications.parliament.uk/pa/cm201719/cmselect/cmtrans/548/548.pdf (accessed 13 August 2018).

Irvine D, Budd LCS and Pitfield DE (2015) A Monte-Carlo approach to estimating the effects of selected airport capacity options in London. *Journal of Air Transport Management* **42**: 1–9.

Janic M (2015) A multi-criteria evaluation of solutions and alternatives for matching capacity to demand in an airport system: the case of London. *Transportation Planning and Technology* **38(7)**: 709–737.

Levinson A and Taylor M (2008) Unmasking the pollution haven effect. *International Economic Review* **49(1)**: 223–254.

May T (2016) Letter from Theresa May to all ministerial colleagues, 18 October 2016. www.airportwatch.org.uk/2016/10/runway-decision-by-cabinet-due-25th-october-no-commons-vote-and-nps-consultation-for-new-runway-all-next-year (accessed 4 January 2017).

O'Doherty D (2015) Missing connexions: the politics of airport expansion in the United Kingdom. *Organization* **22(3)**: 418–431.

Ryley T (2014) Environmental externalities of air transport. In *The Geographies of Air Transport* (Budd L and Goetz A (eds)). Ashgate Publishing, Farnham, UK, and Burlington, VT, USA, pp. 73–80.

Schabas M (2017) *The Railway Metropolis: How Planners, Politicians and Developers Shaped Modern London*. ICE Publishing, London, UK.

Sherwood P (2009) *Heathrow: 2000 Years of History*. The History Press, Stroud, UK.

Starkie D (2012) European airports and airlines: evolving relationships and the regulatory implications. *Journal of Air Transport Management* **21**: 40–49.

Wickham C (2009) David Cameron: 'No third runway – no ifs, no buts'. Bucks Free Press. www.bucksfreepress.co.uk/news/4694685.David_Cameron___No_third_runway_-_no_ifs__no_buts_ (accessed 13 August 2018).

Zhang Y (2014) The puzzle of aircraft size and traffic growth. *Journal of Transport Economics and Policy* **48(3)**: 465–482.

Chapter 10
Themes

10.1. Bringing forward the common issues

This chapter reviews the themes identified in Chapters 6 to 9 as they relate to the evolution of airports policy for London throughout the 40-year period considered in detail in this book. The chapter starts with forecasts, comparing them with actuals and discussing the terms 'predict and provide' and 'management of demand'. Regional issues can be considered as a subset of forecasting, as the scope for diversion was underpinned by the analysis of data used in forecasting. The next section follows on by discussing to what extent analysis featured compared with political judgement in each key decision. The pendulum swings between attempts at setting a long-term strategy and short- and medium-term policies are considered in the next section. Over the 40 years there has been a general increase in the amount of consultation and involvement, but this has varied in style and quality. One of the most crucial issues in terms of local community involvement has been the number of promises made to limit development, which have then been broken. Many local concerns and proposed limits have been because of environmental impacts, some of which have been continuous issues throughout, while others have arisen or faded depending on location and circumstances. The final section notes the periods when there has been some degree of certainty, compared with those where there was a policy vacuum.

10.2. The forecast is always wrong

Forecasting air-transport demand could easily be the subject of a whole book, or a university course, or even a whole discipline, so this brief section is only a summary of a huge issue as it has affected the evolution of airports policy. Forecasting has been the subject of some memorable quotes, including from Lao Tzu, a sixth-century BC Chinese poet, who said, 'Those who have knowledge, don't predict. Those who predict, don't have knowledge' or from the Nobel laureate in Physics, Niels Bohr, who said, 'Prediction is very difficult, especially if it's about the future' (University of Exeter, 1998). There are also some specific quotes about forecasting in air transport, such as 'Rapid growth makes forecasting difficult' (Sealy, 1967); 'It is difficult to forecast with recurrent shocks' (Bentley, 2014); 'Forecasts are unreliable' (Humphreys, 1994); 'Forecasts are often wrong' (Farrington, 1984); and even 'The forecast is always wrong' (de Neufville and Odoni, 2003). My own favourite quote about forecasts is from Stan Maiden, who was BAA's head of research, who said that forecasting air cargo was 'like trying to push fog through a keyhole with a fork'.

One of the most frequent criticisms of air-transport forecasts is that they are 'predict and provide' or self-fulfilling prophecies. If an 'unconstrained' forecast is made and then facilities provided to meet that demand, then this is undoubtedly the case. The argument is that unconstrained demand takes no account of the external costs of meeting the demand, such as environmental impacts, and that, as a matter of policy, demand should be constrained. For a number of years, it has been accepted UK government policy not to meet demand for all road traffic. Historically, demand for rail travel has been constrained by price, particularly at peak times but, since the mid 1990s, the rail industry and the government, which regulates and funds it, has sought to meet most growth, although this is now creating challenges of overcrowding and the demand for more capacity. In air transport, on a number of occasions, as was shown in the preceding chapters, it has been the case that the provision of capacity has been less than unconstrained demand, although the amount of constraint as a matter of policy has been limited. In practice, airports and airlines have been able to meet more demand than expected by adapting their infrastructure, equipment, processes and services.

One of the key factors in deciding the need for new airport terminals or runways is the capacity of the existing infrastructure, and there has been a consistent trend of increases in the estimates of capacity, in particular when the facility becomes fully used. There are two elements to this – increases in hourly rates and changes in peak-to-off-peak ratios.

The hourly capacity of an airport terminal is measured as the number of passengers that can be accommodated by the facilities at acceptable service standards, such as times to process through check-in and security, or within the space available, for example in departure lounges. The overall capacity is determined by the most constraining facility and airports and airlines have modified these as required. This might be by providing more, such as an additional baggage reclaim unit, or it might be by a change of process, such as the introduction of off-site or self-service check-in to reduce demand on conventional check-in desks. Over the years, many airport terminals have proved themselves capable of handling many more passengers than previously thought.

For runways, the hourly capacity is determined by the number of aircraft that can be safely landed or can take off, allowing for such factors as time to clear the runway, wind shear and overshoot arrangements. Changes in technology (e.g. better radar) and infrastructure (e.g. additional runway turn-offs) have enabled some increases in the hourly rate, but Stan Abrahams, who was responsible for forecasting for the Civil Aviation Authority (CAA) in its early years, told me that estimates of future capacity were often conservative because the controllers are reluctant to be committed to improvements until they can be demonstrated to be safe. For example, the Roskill Commission Research Team estimated that the capacity of Heathrow's two runways would be 82 movements per hour, whereas by 2006 it was 89.

The second element of the capacity estimate is the peak-to-off-peak ratio. This includes the profile of demand through the day, the week and between summer and winter. At Heathrow, the traditional peak hour would be on a Monday morning, when the early long-haul arrivals would coincide with the first wave of outbound European departures. Stan Abrahams told me that in 1980 the peak-to-annual ratio for aircraft movements at Heathrow (the number of aircraft movements in the peak hour divided by the number in a year) was 0.000238 and by 2006 it was 0.000186, giving a 22 per cent increase in the annual capacity. Airlines have added services at times previously thought to be uneconomic, either during the day, on different days or in the off-peak seasons.

The combination of these two factors – increasing hourly rates and changes to the peak-to-off-peak ratio – means that the capacities of airports have grown, irrespective of new facilities. Thus Heathrow's two-runway capacity was estimated to be around 300 000 aircraft movements per year in 1980, and is currently considered to be capable of accommodating around 500 000 (the permitted number is 480 000). Terminal capacity has increased, primarily because new terminals have been built, but the capacity of individual terminals has also increased. For example, Gatwick North Terminal was opened with a capacity of 9 million passengers a year, but with a number of redevelopments and extensions now handles more than 20 million per year. There are other elements to total airport capacity which have from time to time been relevant, for example, road access to Heathrow in the mid 1970s before the extension of the Piccadilly line, or aircraft stands which were considered a constraint at the Heathrow Terminal 5 Inquiry. However, these have been overcome by the provision of additional facilities and therefore the critical capacities have usually been those of terminals and runways.

Forecasts are made by a number of organisations, each with different perspectives, which affect their approach. The government, in the form of the Department for Transport (DfT) and its predecessors, has published forecasts for many years and has developed and refined models with strange acronyms such as NAPDM (National Air Passenger Demand Model) and NAPAM (National Air Passenger Allocation Model). These are often seen as the 'official' forecasts, but Stan Maiden, formerly BAA's head of research, suggested to me that the DfT has not always been well resourced to operate the models and may therefore have published results which demonstrated a lack of understanding of how the air-transport business worked. An example of this was the 2013 forecasts, which were initially used by the Airports Commission, which showed a number of regional airports declining or never growing, contrary to then current, and subsequent, trends. However, government forecasts for total UK demand are better than for individual airports, which is fortunate as one of the key purposes of the government forecasts is to predict future carbon dioxide (CO_2) levels, which is dependent on total demand.

The CAA also prepared forecasts, primarily (at least in its early days) to assist in airspace and runway capacity planning. As Stan Abrahams confirmed, the CAA was influenced by its air traffic control background and there was therefore a tendency to overpredict aircraft movements. Stan Maiden claims that BAA's airport passenger forecasts were prepared with the best-resourced understanding of passengers, based on years of data gathered through surveys and analysis. BAA concentrated on the passengers as the main driver of demand, leaving aircraft movements as a secondary forecast dependent on airline decisions. Airlines prepare forecasts but their planning horizons are shorter. Aircraft manufacturers also produce global and regional forecasts for the purposes of preparing their product range. The conclusion is therefore that government is best at forecasting total passenger demand and CO_2, the CAA is best for aircraft movements, and BAA (as was) best for individual airport passenger numbers. Using different forecasts for different purposes might be acceptable, but they would not necessarily be consistent. Nobody claims to be good at cargo forecasts, hence Stan Maiden's quote about fog, keyholes and forks.

It is instructive to look at how forecasts have compared with actuals. Figure 10.1 shows various government forecasts made since 1970 compared with the actual passenger numbers through Heathrow, Gatwick, Stansted and Luton. Most, but not all, of the forecasts have been higher than the actuals, with the 1971 Roskill Commission report (see Chapter 3) and 2003 White Paper (see Chapter 8) being examples of particular overestimates. On the other hand, the 1993 RUCATSE forecast (see Chapter 7) was considerably below the actual until the mid 2000s. The most recent actual numbers for 2017 are slightly above the high 2013 Airports Commission forecast (see Chapter 9). It is possible to explain each and every difference, but perhaps more significant is to note the general trend of overestimation of forecast demand, although the counter to this is that, with long-term infrastructure, it is always possible to slow down its provision, but rarely can it be sped up.

As we saw in Chapter 6, forecasts made by the Roskill Commission were significant overestimates as they were made on the basis of growth up to the 1960s and did not foresee the dramatic increases in oil prices and the consequent economic downturn in the mid 1970s. Although there is some dispute about the way it was forecast, the introduction of larger aircraft in the 1970s may also have had an effect on the need for more runway, as compared with terminal, capacity. In any event, the lessening of the need for runway capacity meant that the focus would be on expanding terminals where there was spare runway capacity. Forecasts prepared in the later 1970s and 1980s were closer to the actuals, with some underpredicting the outcome. These were

Figure 10.1 Various forecasts of air passengers at Heathrow, Gatwick, Stansted and Luton compared with actuals
(Data from CAA, graph compiled by author)

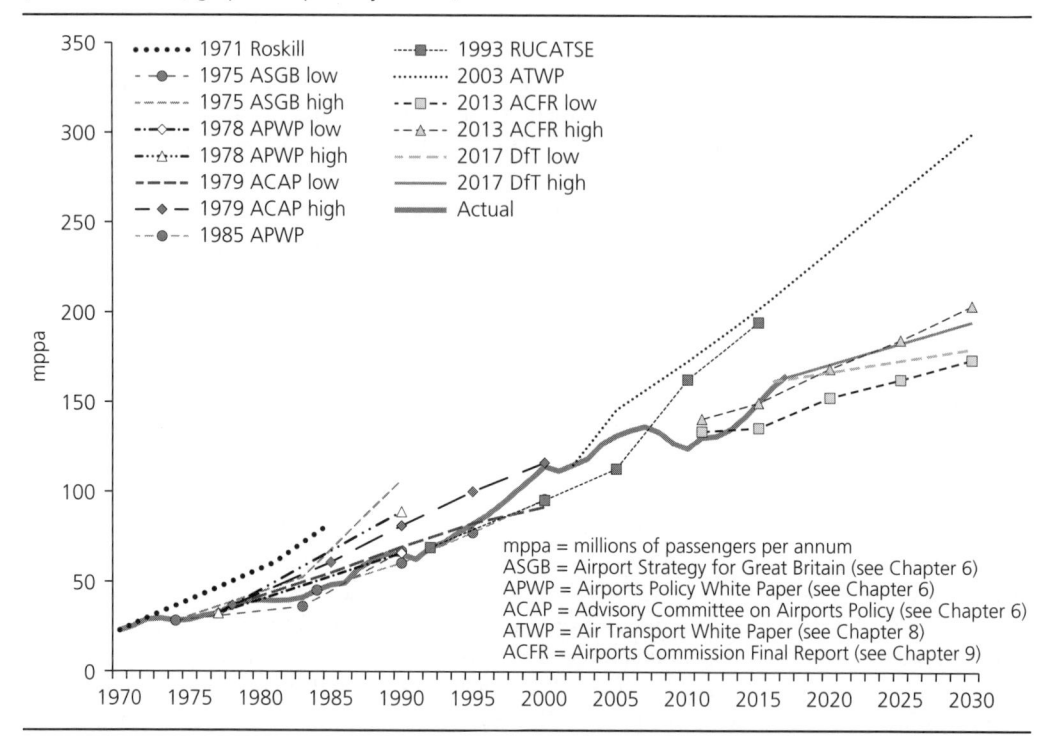

the basis of the Heathrow Terminal 4, Gatwick North Terminal and Stansted inquiries and were generally in line with the actual outcome up to about 2000.

The key forecast of the 1990s was in RUCATSE and also turned out as an underprediction for the ten years from 1995, but in the longer term it had predicted an upturn whereas the actual reflected the downturn in the economy in 2008. In any event, this forecast was not used during this period of policy vacuum. However, the question of aircraft size re-emerged as the main forecasting issue in the 1990s at the Heathrow Terminal 5 Inquiry, where there were disputes about whether the five-terminal and two-runway capacities would be in balance, or whether Terminal 5 would lead to a need for a third runway.

The 2003 White Paper was the first to claim that the unconstrained forecast would not be met by the proposed capacity increases, thereby seeking to address the accusation that the policy was 'predict and provide'. This forecast was also the first to take account of the cost of carbon. However, as we noted earlier, the capacity provided by the policy would have been only about 10 per cent less than unconstrained demand and this did not stop the criticisms that the policy was pro-growth and would contribute to climate change. Glaister et al. (2006) note that the White Paper said that building capacity to meet demand would not be sustainable, but also suggest that 'its statistical support... rather struggles to demonstrate that the capacity being provided so far ahead is needed but does not represent "predict and provide"' (p. 145). The authors also note that government's wider transport policy is not to provide ever more capacity on roads, railways and ports, as well as airports. While this has certainly been the case for roads, it is interesting to note that railways continue to plan (although do not always succeed in providing) to meet peak-hour demand. However, the 2003 White Paper forecasts were downgraded in the 2006 Progress Report and, after the 2008 economic downturn, became hopelessly unrealistic.

The forecasts by the Airports Commission used a scenario approach and looked at two alternative carbon-limitation methods. There has been less criticism, although the issue of aircraft size remains as a key determinant of the date by which additional runway capacity is required. As at the end of 2017, the actual outturn is just above the Commission's high forecast. As with government forecasts, there has been criticism of the individual airport forecasts, in particular from Gatwick Airport, which has noted that actual levels of traffic have significantly exceeded the forecasts. At the time of writing in 2018, the government has just issued new forecasts which show higher levels of growth based on actual trends since the last forecasts were published in 2013. Individual airports have produced their own forecasts to support their proposals.

10.3. Why does the regional issue keep appearing?

In this section, the word regional is used as shorthand for 'outside the South East'. The regional debate is partly related to the question of forecasts, but is also wider. It has long been a concern of governments that there is an imbalance in a number of economic factors between different regions, including employment, earnings, business activity and house prices. Passengers with origins and destinations outside the South East often have to use a South East airport because there is no service from nearer to home. This was apparent from the mid 1970s onwards when the Airport Strategy for Great Britain consultation gave equal consideration to the regional issue and the South East. Charter flights, and more recently low-cost carriers (LCCs), have served the regional market by providing a wide range of flights, but the long-haul and business markets have had a much greater focus on the South East, and at Heathrow in particular. While there are complexities and historical reasons for this, the basic cause is that airlines find that their revenue per flight is much more for a Heathrow service than for any other airport.

The regional issue reached its zenith during the 1981–1983 Airports Inquiries, when the North of England Regional Consortium (NOERC) fought a strong campaign and sought to oppose expansion at Stansted. It is somewhat ironic that the Manchester Airport Group, which remains majority owned by the local authorities in the Manchester area and which was the main driving force behind NOERC, eventually bought Stansted Airport. Manchester Airport did not oppose Heathrow Terminal 5 and it was rather busy during the 1990s with its own proposals for a second runway. The regions in general were supportive of the policies in the 2003 White Paper, not surprisingly since they proposed expansion at a number of airports.

More recently, the regional issue has split into a number of different arguments. Some regions, perhaps best exemplified by the West Midlands and Birmingham Airport, continue to criticise the fact that passengers with regional origins and destinations have to use Heathrow for many long-haul and business flights. Others, such as Manchester and Newcastle, and in Scotland, while developing some long-haul services, have also sought guarantees that domestic flights can continue, in particular to Heathrow. This line has also been adopted by a number of regions and airports that do not currently have flights to London, such as the South West and Liverpool, who see the prospect of flights to Heathrow as potentially very valuable. In the Airports Commission debate about the relative merits of Heathrow and Gatwick, Edinburgh Airport supported Gatwick's case, while Glasgow supported Heathrow, although this may not be unconnected with their ownership (Edinburgh is owned by the same group as Gatwick, and Glasgow has common ownership with one of the owners of Heathrow).

Regional issues are often a key matter raised in debates and other parliamentary activity. This is not surprising, given that the House of Commons consists of MPs representing their constituencies. In such debates, constituency issues often dominate, and there are two distinct arguments:

from those promoting their local airport and those who oppose development because of the adverse impact on their constituents. Government arguments, either in Parliament or in policy publications, seek to promote the national interest, but often fail to persuade MPs that this should overcome their constituency interests. One example of this is the argument about demand from regional airports. Many MPs from the regions, and indeed the communities they represent, do not understand why there are not more flights from their local airport to a wider range of destinations, and passengers with origins and destinations therefore have to travel via a London or even a non-UK airport. Apart from Heathrow slots, there are no supply-side limits and no administrative or licensing restrictions on additional flights from regional airports. The government, and the aviation industry, has not succeeded in explaining the reasons for this imbalance, and therefore the arguments continue.

Although the regional diversion argument has been rejected at virtually every inquiry and study, it is clear that many airports outside the South East have succeeded in growing, often at a much faster rate than South East airports. The share of total UK demand met by non-London airports has grown from around 25 per cent in the mid 1970s to around 40 per cent today and this has meant significant absolute growth in passenger numbers. Much of this is due to the success of LCCs in meeting, and to an extent generating, demand for leisure and VFR (Visiting Friends and Relatives) journeys. LCCs were not apparent in the UK until the 1990s and Stan Maiden accepts that the biggest failure of the forecasting community was that this growth was not foreseen.

10.4. What is the best way to combine analysis and judgement?

The pendulum has swung back and forth between the technocratic application of analysis and the exercise of judgement. Analysis was to the fore in the Roskill Commission and most recently in the Airports Commission, whereas judgement seemed to be more significant in the 1970s, 1980s and 2000s.

The Roskill Commission is incorrectly remembered as making its recommendation solely on the basis of cost–benefit analysis, which sought to value some environmental effects, including noise and historic buildings, but where the dominant factor was access time. It is notable that other major transport projects at the time, such as the London Underground Victoria line, and subsequent rail and road improvements, were also selected on the basis of benefit/cost ratios, where travel-time improvements dominated the analysis. However, although the Roskill Commission used this analysis to assist, it also considered other evidence before making its recommendations. Notwithstanding, the analysis was put to one side by the government decision to proceed with the Maplin project, based on Colin Buchanan's minority recommendation, which, as noted in Chapter 3, had no quantification. An interesting but probably pointless question would be 'Would the Roskill Commission's majority recommendation of a new airport at Cublington also have been cancelled?' Given that the analysis on which the Cublington recommendation was based meant it would have been more robust economically, there is an argument that it might have gone ahead. However, the shocks of the 1970s were so great that this marginal economic benefit would probably not have been sufficient to save it.

The 1975–1976 Airport Strategy for Great Britain consultation, the 1978 White Paper, the Advisory Committee on Airports Policy (ACAP), the Study Group on South East Airports (SGSEA) and the decisions announced in December 1979 included a good deal of analysis but owed much more to judgement. Typical of this was the ACAP and SGSEA exercises, which quantified effects in the most appropriate units (for example, the number of people affected by particular noise levels, the costs of construction, or the journey times for access), then left the judgement of the relative merits of the options to politicians. There was also a significant input in terms of qualitative material, not least at the public inquiries into Heathrow Terminal 4,

Gatwick North Terminal and Stansted, where local people were able to describe their experiences and concerns. The outcomes of these inquiries were to approve the proposals and undoubtedly many of the opponents felt that their evidence was ignored, although inspectors were certainly influenced to an extent, for example in setting limits on the number of aircraft movements at Heathrow, and in rejecting proposals for a second runway at Stansted. The fact that these limits were later overturned shows that the weakness of the system is not that the decisions were faulty but that they do not have longevity.

The balance of quantitative and qualitative evidence at public inquiries can be seen in the Heathrow Terminal 5 Inquiry. Although, at 525 days, this was the longest airport public inquiry, the reason for its length cannot clearly be related to the amount of quantitative analysis. Undoubtedly some topics, such as aircraft noise, air quality and road traffic, involved large studies, often using modelling of future situations according to assumptions. Many experts were involved in giving evidence, which was challenged, although there was also a lot of agreement. But the agreement often ended when it came to judging the effects of a particular quantification. The prime example of this is aircraft noise. While there were some differences in the numbers put forward by the parties, the main difference was that the opponents of expansion did not accept that the number of people affected could be measured by the 57 dB L_{Aeq16h} contour (see Chapter 5). Instead, they suggested that a range of measures should be considered, and that 54 dB was the appropriate level for the L_{Aeq16h} contour. To demonstrate this, witnesses described how they felt about the effect of aircraft noise. The inspector concluded that Terminal 5 would cause 'substantial harm' in noise terms, but that the noise impact should not be so great as to rule it out entirely and a number of noise-related conditions should be imposed.

The role of scientific analysis increased significantly as climate change rose up the agenda in the late 1990s and 2000s. The Kyoto Protocol had been agreed in 1997, at around the time that the government was embarking on the preparation of a new aviation strategy. There were many international, government and academic studies of climate change and the contribution to it by aviation. One of the key papers which comprehensively described the history and sought to look to the future was by Lee *et al.* (2009), which refers back to the initial Inter Governmental Panel on Climate Change report on the contribution of aviation. That is a very complex subject requiring much detailed analysis, as is illustrated by a diagram from the paper, reproduced as Figure 10.2. This is actually a very simplified chart but is difficult to follow, in particular from a layman's viewpoint.

Unlike noise, which has a direct effect which individuals experience, climate change effects are less immediate, albeit no less, and probably more, significant. For airports policy, this has meant that climate change has not been so much of an issue at public inquiries, given that the technical evidence is so difficult to present and is not backed up by the qualitative experiences of local residents.

It has also been argued that the climate change effects of individual airport developments should not be considered because most of the emissions occur when the aircraft are en route and that the location of the origin and destination are not relevant. On the other hand, some climate scientists argue that 'until technological and operational solutions can decarbonise air travel at rates well beyond the pace of expansion in the industry, policy measures must place a constraint on growth, for example, through delaying plans for increased airport capacity' (Bows-Larkin and Anderson, 2013: p. 81). The Airports Commission discussed the effect of increasing capacity on climate change in detail and included alternative ways of taking it into account in the forecasting exercise. The Commission's conclusion was based on the advice of the Committee on Climate Change, which was again based on extensive analysis, but it remains a contentious issue because it is dependent on forecasts of future scenarios, not just in the aviation sector.

Figure 10.2 Schema showing the principal emissions from aviation operations and the atmospheric processes that lead to changes in radiative forcing components. Radiative forcing changes lead to climate change, as measured by temperatures and sea levels, for example. Climate change creates impacts on human activities and ecosystems and can lead to societal damages.
(Adapted from Prather *et al.* (1999) and Wuebbles *et al.* (2007). Taken from Lee *et al.* (2009))

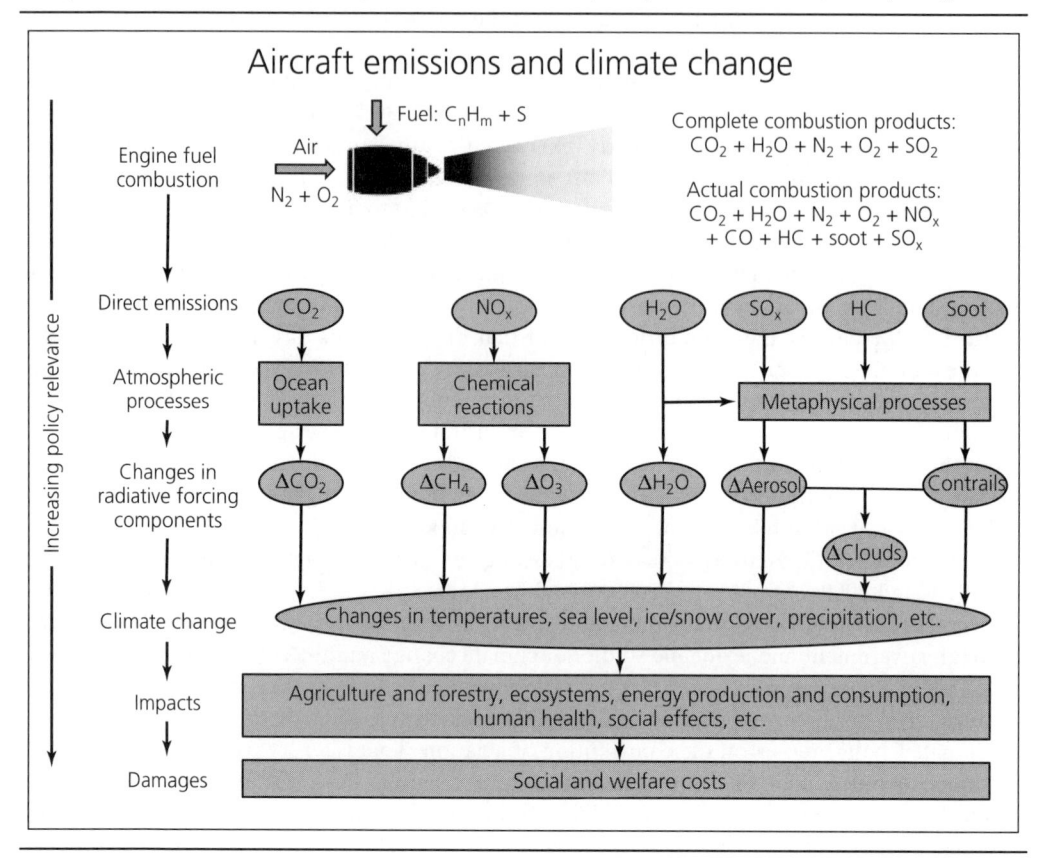

10.5. Should we take incremental steps or have a long-term strategy?

Although it is possible to have a long-term strategy involving incremental steps, it is often the case that the longer-term strategy contains large concentrations of capacity at particular airports. However, some of the studies, events and inquiries can be categorised in this way, with the 1970s and 1980s being the prime example of an incremental approach and the 2003 White Paper being an attempt at a long-term strategy.

The 1970s and 1980s approach of consultation, studies, policies and inquiries – the Airport Strategy for Great Britain (1975–1976), Civil Aviation White Paper (1976), Airports Policy White Paper (1978), Heathrow Terminal 4 Inquiry (1978), ACAP and SGSEA (1978–1979), Gatwick North Terminal Inquiry (1980), Airports Inquiries (1981–1983) – was clearly incremental in dealing with the short term before the longer term and looking at relatively small increments of capacity at each inquiry. Although the three main increments (Heathrow Terminal 4, Gatwick North Terminal and Stansted new terminal) were all approved, there were a number of statements or agreements about limits (Heathrow 275 000 Air Transport Movements (ATMs), Gatwick second runway legal agreement, Stansted no second runway), which, at the time, may have given local communities some comfort. However, as we have seen, these promises were not kept, at least in terms of these further expansions reappearing on the agenda and, in the case of Heathrow, being abandoned by the mid 1980s. Despite this, the policy enabled each of the airports to expand and gave the local communities and other organisations (such as road and rail providers) a basis on which they could plan.

The incremental strategy can also be described as a system approach. As noted in Chapter 2, multi-airport systems have been identified around the world and, with three of the four main London airports owned by the BAA, it was possible to plan, finance and operate them as a system. The 1978 White Paper had classified the London airports (including Luton) as a Category A International Gateway Airport System. This was not universally popular, as some academics and airlines wanted them to compete and not to finance development at one airport from the profits at another, but it was accepted by government, even after privatisation, as the way for the London airports to operate.

Given the policy vacuum of the 1990s, there was certainly no long-term strategy during this decade. The Heathrow Terminal 5 proposal was a large increment which, given the airport's status as the airlines' first choice for many types of service, meant that most demand could be met for many years. It could be argued that Terminal 5 was the last piece of the incremental jigsaw that had started in the 1970s, but on the other hand it was clearly ruled out in those earlier studies and only came back into play when Stansted's second runway was rejected.

The New Labour government from 1997 had a clear desire for long-term planning and, in the event, 13 years in power to implement its policies. The 2003 White Paper was a 30-year strategy and had the longest forecast horizon of any such policy document. Glaister *et al.* (2006) criticised this long-term strategy as it was 'far in advance of the forecasters' technical ability to demonstrate need' (p. 144). Although these forecasts were supposed to have taken account of environmental costs, they were still very optimistic, and resulted in a need for two new runways in the South East, plus additional runways and other developments throughout the UK. The forecasts were undone by the economic downturn of 2008 onwards. Although no one had foreseen this downturn, it was nevertheless highly risky to base a policy on continuous economic growth.

And so in 2010 we revert to a period of incremental, short-term policies. Very short term, in that the South East Airports Taskforce of 2011 looked for immediate improvements but clearly avoided any longer-term thoughts, while the longer-term strategies of the 2003 White Paper had been abandoned. By 2013, the Airports Commission had prepared an Interim Report which also included some short- and medium-term incremental measures, but it was not until October 2016 that the government announced a policy decision to support a third runway at Heathrow. Even this is not a comprehensive policy, but the government's intention is to publish a new White Paper, probably in 2019.

10.6. What is the best way to consult and involve stakeholders?

The relevant Oxford Dictionary (2017) definition of consulting is 'to have discussions with someone, typically before undertaking a course of action'. The Cabinet Office has issued guidelines on the principles of consultation (Cabinet Office, 2016), which suggest that consultations should be informative, targeted, engaged and capable of scrutiny. Over the 40 years considered in this book, consultation has taken a number of forms, ranging from attendance by representatives to widespread opinion polling.

But consultation does not mean seeking agreement. Many consulted parties feel aggrieved at the end of the process if the decision goes against them, especially when the majority of views oppose a development which is then approved. However, consultation is not like an election or a referendum, so there is no requirement to accept the majority view. Of course, the question is, 'a majority of who?' Should it be the majority of residents within a certain radius, in which case is it 5 miles, 10 miles, 20 miles or 100 miles? Should it be those who are adversely affected? Should businesses have a vote, as well as residents? Should foreign passengers have a say? Clearly these are impossible questions to answer and, as in many other forms of public decision-making, we elect our governments to make these decisions on our behalf.

The post-Maplin period began in 1975 with a consultation, the Airport Strategy for Great Britain (see Chapter 6). Even before these documents had been published, the Department of the Environment (DoE) had written to local authorities inviting their views, and the consultation resulted in around 1000 responses, mostly from local authorities and local community groups. Some aviation industry representatives had been involved in the preparation of the documents, although others did respond to the consultation. Responses do seem to have been taken into account, as the DoE reflected many of the local authorities' views in their drafts, with the Department of Trade (DoT) reflecting the aviation industry, which it sponsored. The 1978 White Paper was then published, followed by ACAP and SGSEA and the public inquiries at Heathrow Terminal 4, Gatwick North Terminal and the Airports Inquiries of 1981–1983 (see Chapter 6). ACAP and SGSEA had wide memberships from government departments, local authorities, industry and users but not local community, amenity or environmental groups.

Public inquiries are, of course, opportunities for significant involvement where anyone can present evidence and challenge others. In addition, the pre-inquiry process involves consultation by the applicant and the local authorities and local media are usually able to report on activity. The three inquiries between 1979 and 1983 enabled many parties to present their views. The applicant, BAA, prepared a statement of case alongside the formal applications and published technical reports on a range of issues. Supporting evidence was presented by airlines, business groups and trade unions. However, as noted earlier, sometimes the supporters were not completely aligned and there was always a risk of a case being undermined, as happened when airlines indicated that they supported the proposals, but were not planning to use them themselves. The local authorities led the opposition but of course took a local perspective, such that some local authorities supported schemes elsewhere as an alternative to expansion in their locality. Community groups were able to present their evidence from the unique perspective of living in the locality. Sometimes this is consistent with the views of experts, for example when locals and experts are describing the ecology of a particular area. But one area where obtaining agreement has always been a challenge is noise. Experts deal with noise as an impact experienced by the community as a whole, using averages, whereas individuals react differently and, naturally, experience the effects personally.

One criticism of public involvement is that the applicant usually has significant resources whereas the opponents are much more constrained. Local authorities do not have large funds to pay for consultants and lawyers, and community groups rely mostly on public subscriptions or members devoting their time for free. Against this it can be argued that some groups may not be representative of the population (but what population, as posed above?) and it was also the case that the inspectors at all three inquiries between 1979 and 1983 went out of their way to ensure that individual witnesses were able to present their evidence.

One other area of involvement is through Parliament, where MPs representing their constituents can directly challenge ministers on policy. A crude measure of the interest shown by MPs is the number of times the words 'airport' or 'airport policy' appear in Hansard. This includes references in debates on legislation, policy statements and other parliamentary devices, as well as written questions, in both houses. Figure 10.3 shows the number of such mentions over the years 1975 to 2017 (the data does not include written answers from 2011 onwards). Such mentions will include multiple occasions, for example in a debate about airports. Many of the mentions are

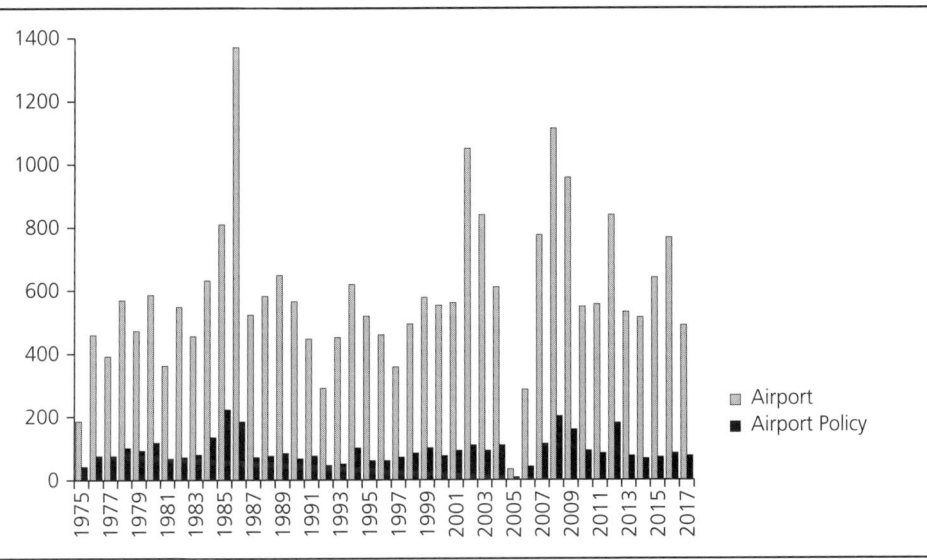

Figure 10.3 Number of mentions of 'airport' and 'airport policy' in Parliament, 1975 to 2017 (Compiled by the author from Hansard data; data does not include written answers from 2011 onwards)

nothing to do with airports policy for London and the South East but, nevertheless, the peaks do seem to coincide with major policy events. Mentions fluctuated in the 1970s, with the 1978 White Paper and ACAP and SGSEA. A high point in 1980 is partly related to the policy statement of December 1979, which was debated in early 1980. The number of mentions then rises steadily through the early 1980s to a peak in 1985 and 1986, when the White Paper announcing the outcome of the 1981–1983 Airports Inquiries was published, and the Airports Bill passed through Parliament. These peaks have not been exceeded since. Activity then reduced, although by the end of the 1980s there were a number of debates about runway capacity. There were some low points in the 1990s, the period of policy vacuum, but also some peaks coinciding with the start and end of the Heathrow Terminal 5 Inquiry. There were particular peaks in 2002 and 2003 associated with the White Paper, and then a very quiet period when, remarkably, the word 'airport' was not recorded in Hansard between 16 March 2005 and 6 June 2006. At this time, planning for new runways at Stansted and Heathrow was under way, but perhaps there was little for MPs to get to grips with. However, parliamentary activity soon ramped up in 2007 after the publication of the 2006 Progress Report and the planning application for Stansted's Generation 1 expansion, increased again in 2008 and was also high in 2009, when the government approved a third runway at Heathrow. Data from 2011 onwards does not include written answers so probably understates the level of activity. However, there was a peak in 2012 associated with the Aviation Policy Framework (APF) and the setting up of the Airports Commission. At the time of writing, the number of mentions in 2018, when the government published the final National Policy Statement (NPS), which was then debated in Parliament, is already well ahead of 2017.

In the early 1990s, the RUCATSE study did not have any public involvement, its members being government departments, local authority and industry representatives and community groups. There was a consultation after the report was published and some parliamentary activity but, as noted in Chapter 7, the Heathrow Terminal 5 proposal was by then heading to a public inquiry.

As with previous inquiries, Heathrow Terminal 5 enabled widespread involvement and, given the size of the proposal and the large population potentially affected, many groups and individuals took this opportunity to present and challenge evidence. As with previous inquiries, there were many other types of involvement, including public meetings, opinion polls, letters to residents and media briefings, organised by the various parties.

The consultations of the early 2000s marked a new attempt at much wider involvement and resulted in over half a million people being involved. Although the vast majority of these were through a questionnaire, the number of individuals and organisations submitting detailed responses was also very high, and these were analysed in detail before the White Paper was published. Apart from noting the number of responses, the White Paper makes a few references to the consultation, noting, for example, that

- noise was a key environmental impact in the public mind
- there was little support for cash as an alternative to sound insulation
- there were concerns about urbanisation as a result of airport expansion, both nationally and in particular at Stansted
- there were concerns about the safety risks of bird strikes in the Thames Estuary
- adding two new runways at Stansted found little support
- there was a need for more studies on air quality at Heathrow
- concerns were expressed about pressure on the labour market from an expanding Heathrow.

There were further consultations in the 2000s, for example when BAA began the process of obtaining approval for a second runway at Stansted, and when the government made progress on the Project for the Sustainable Development of Heathrow. There was no formal consultation about the change of policy in 2010 when these projects were cancelled, except that a general election could be considered as the ultimate in public involvement, with a government voted out of office for its policies and its record, and a new government elected because of its manifesto promises.

The South East Airports Taskforce had a limited membership, but the 2013 Aviation Policy Framework, which replaced the 2003 White Paper, was preceded by a scoping document in 2011 and a draft in 2012 (see Chapter 9). A full report of the responses to the draft was published alongside the APF, analysing the 491 submissions. The largest single category of respondents was members of the public (181), followed by local government (89), business associations (45) and local community groups (37). This is not a particularly large response and, as by then the longer-term issues had been referred to the Airports Commission, many of the draft policies were not controversial. There was, however, significant disagreement with the proposal to retain 57 dB L_{Aeq16h} as the key measure of noise annoyance, and with the proposed compensation schemes, environmental regulations and guidance on master plans. The final version of the APF included some minor changes based on these responses and the Airports Commission went much further, particularly on noise.

The Airports Commission arranged its consultation and involvement in different ways from previous exercises. There were some public meetings, but they were limited in time and scope, for example not requiring the presentation and challenging of evidence. There were a number of calls for evidence and consultations on particular issues, but perhaps the greatest difference from previous exercises was the amount of material published online. Undoubtedly previous inquiries had resulted in masses of documents, reports, transcripts etc., but realistically, this was available only to participants at the inquiries. The Airports Commission published all of its material online, thus making it available to everyone. Some 72 000 responses were received on the three shortlisted options, 90 per cent of which were from campaigns or were coordinated by a group, 9 per cent from individuals and 1 per cent from organisations (SYSTRA, 2015). Of the campaign responses, the vast majority came from the Back Heathrow campaign, with relatively few from opposition groups at either Heathrow or Gatwick. There were some responses from coordinated groups opposing expansion, but still relatively few compared with the Back Heathrow campaign. It is not clear how much notice the Airports Commission took of these campaign responses, as they are not referred to in the Final Report (Airports Commission, 2015).

After the government decision of October 2016 to accept the recommendation for a third runway at Heathrow, the next step in the process was the publication of a draft NPS in early 2017. An NPS is part of the process set out in the Planning Act 2008 (as amended by the Localism Act 2011) and, under the Act, is issued in draft for consultation. The consultation lasted until May 2017. A revised draft NPS was published in October 2017, with a further consultation period. The draft NPS was then subject to parliamentary scrutiny, approved by Parliament in 2018 and was 'designated'. The next step is for the promoter, in this case Heathrow Airport, to submit a draft Development Consent Order (DCO) and the Act also requires that this is consulted on and considered at inquiry, with specified timescales. Heathrow Airport issued an initial consultation in January 2018 and has promised further consultations as the plans are developed. There are therefore a number of opportunities for stakeholder involvement for this process.

In addition to taking forward the Heathrow third runway proposals, the government is also preparing a new, longer-term, UK-wide aviation strategy. The first consultation on this began in August 2017 (Department for Transport, 2017) and ran until October, and the intention is to publish a Green (consultation) Paper later in 2018. It is possible that this will lead to a new White Paper to replace the 2013 Airports Policy Framework, which represents current policy.

10.7. Should promises be made and how can they be kept?

Throughout the period considered, and before, there have been attempts to set limits to the expansion of particular airports. Most of these promises have been broken. Not surprisingly, the issue of broken promises has been one of the most contentious elements of the evolution of airports policy.

The first set of limits considered in this book are those set in the 1978 White Paper (see Chapter 6). For Heathrow, this supported a fourth terminal but ruled out a fifth, even in the longer term. The wording used was that 'Heathrow's ultimate development should not go beyond that of a four-terminal airport' (Department of Trade, 1978: p. 27). The reasons for this limit were noted as surface access and noise. ACAP and SGSEA, which then considered longer-term options, did not include further expansion at Heathrow. The policy was confirmed by the decision announced in December 1979 on the Terminal 4 application, which added the 275 000 ATM limit as a further control on expansion. Local authorities and communities, although they had opposed Terminal 4, were at least content that a limit had been set. Initially BAA accepted this limit and worked towards expansion at Gatwick and Stansted to accommodate longer-term growth. But British Airways (BA) always opposed limits on Heathrow expansion and was able to bring the issue back on the agenda by allying with opponents to Stansted expansion and supporting the Terminal 5 application at the Airports Inquiries of 1981–1983. Inspector Graham Eyre's logic for overturning government policy was that the evidence showed that noise would be much less of an impact than previously thought and that studies of a main-line rail link would indicate whether the surface access challenge could be met. He was also critical of the 275 000 ATM limit, noting that it was already close to being exceeded. While it is, of course, right that an inspector should be led by the evidence, it is more surprising that the government was prepared to overturn its own policy, which had been set only a few years earlier. In the lead-up to the publication of the 1985 White Paper, Secretary of State for Transport Nicholas Ridley was clearly concerned about this, but was persuaded that the logic of the Terminal 4 inspector had been overtaken by events. It can only be speculation, but the persuaders must have included BA, which, under Lord King, was turning from a loss-making, state-owned organisation to a profitable private-sector company. The policy set out in the 1985 White Paper noted that the application for Terminal 5 had not been approved, and some hailed this as a victory, including Toby Jessel, the MP for Twickenham, saying that many people would be 'immensely grateful and relieved at the decision not to build a fifth terminal and to turn down the current planning application' (HC Deb 5 June 1985). However, the reality was that, although it took many more years to implement, this was the point when the promise was broken.

The broken promise of Heathrow Terminal 5 was one of the key issues at the 1995–1999 inquiry and the number of days occupied by the discussion of policy was noted in Chapter 7. BA had the merit of being consistent in its case as it had always supported the proposal, but BAA's situation was not comfortable and relied on two key arguments. First, the planning regime required a demonstration that there were no real alternatives to the proposal being put forward, and this had meant that BAA had to oppose the Terminal 5 application at the 1981–1983 Airports Inquiries, when it was trying to secure approval for a new terminal at Stansted. Secondly, the situation had changed, given the outcome of the studies into the acquisition of the Perry Oaks site and a main-line rail link, with the latter completed and operational by the time that the Terminal 5 Inquiry finished.

Similar arguments applied to the next promise, not to build a third runway at Heathrow. Again BA was consistent in not wanting this to be ruled out, but BAA sought to show that a fifth terminal would not require a third runway. BAA went further and asked for the third runway to be ruled out, judging that this would be a condition of approval. In the event, the inspector gave this request little weight because, by the time he was writing his report, the government had embarked on the major review of policy which was to lead to the 2003 White Paper. It was therefore not necessary for BAA to request that the third runway be ruled out and the fact that they did so, and later supported the proposal and even said that the request had been a mistake, took the community distrust of BAA's pledges to a much higher level.

It was the David Cameron-led coalition government that cancelled the third runway in 2010, with an infamous 'no ifs, no buts' tag (Wickham, 2009). Cameron had been replaced as prime minister by Theresa May by the time the government decided in 2016 that the third runway should be supported. Much has been made of the difference between the proposed third runway that was cancelled in 2010 and the current proposal in terms of location and operation, but this cuts no ice with the objectors.

The situation was different at Gatwick, where there was spare runway capacity and policy support for a second terminal. The 1978 White Paper had referred to the ultimate development being with two terminals and ACAP and SGSEA had not considered any further expansion. Although it upset British Caledonian Airways (BCal), and the government made it clear that it was not a party to it, BAA's legal agreement with West Sussex County Council (WSCC) not to build a second runway for 40 years provided significant comfort and certainty to those concerned about the airport's expansion. Over the 40 years, a second runway has been considered (in RUCATSE, in the 2003 White Paper and as one of the shortlisted options of the Airports Commission) but the fact is that the agreement has not been broken.

Stansted has a long history of being considered for development and it has been difficult to provide certainty. The 1979 decision was to bring forward plans for a two-runway airport, but the 1985 White Paper ruled out the second runway element. However, a second runway reappeared in RUCATSE and was the first (in timescale) proposal for new runways in the 2003 White Paper. It was then cancelled in 2010, but reappeared as an option in the Airports Commission's work, although it did not make the shortlist. There have been limits on the number of ATMs at Stansted, which have been changed with parliamentary approval. Although these provide a potential method of limiting growth, in reality they are only a process for involving Parliament in agreeing their increase and, as such, are not in the same league as the other pledges noted here.

While this section has concentrated on the major promises and commitments, most of which were broken, there have been many conditions and limits that have been adhered to. In particular, conditions attached to planning permissions have the force of law behind them and have to be met. Each of the approvals have had a list of conditions, Section 106 agreements and obligations, ranging from detailed design elements to soundproofing schemes for local residents. It is, of course, possible for such conditions to be changed, by the same planning application process through which they were imposed or, of course, by legislation, but the vast majority of the conditions have been adhered to.

A conclusion that can be drawn is that promises by government, even if stated as government policy in a White Paper, cannot be considered as cast-iron guarantees, and history shows that many have been overturned. This is not uncommon in many policies, and no government can be bound by policies of its predecessors. The one agreement that has survived is the 40-year BAA/WSCC agreement not to build a second runway at Gatwick. Although some may argue that it is only accidental that it has not been broken, it can also be concluded that the difficulty of breaking it, and the compensation that would be involved, made it much more durable than a government policy.

10.8. Has consideration of environmental impacts changed?

Chapter 5 was devoted to environmental issues, so this section seeks only to summarise the ways in which this topic influenced the evolution of airports policy, primarily in terms of changes of emphasis.

Aircraft noise has been a problem ever since the first airfields were established, but it became a particular concern in the 1960s because of the rapid growth in activity and the introduction of jet aircraft. The decision-makers of the 1970s understood the challenge, but believed that the issue would reduce significantly with the second and later generations of jet engines. Undoubtedly, the noise from individual aircraft has declined dramatically, but the effect of much larger numbers of aircraft (which is taken account of in the average noise measures) was not understood. The way noise is measured has changed over the years, first with the replacement of the NNI by the L_{Aeq} measure (see Chapter 5 for an explanation). However, the latter, although it has a robust statistical and acoustic basis, is now considered insufficient to explain the social impact of aircraft noise, so more recent analyses have used a number of metrics.

Noise has had different effects at each inquiry. Proposals for terminal expansion mean more passengers and therefore more flights, but flight paths are not usually changed, so the impact is on the same areas. The general position is that the growth in the number of aircraft movements has been balanced by the reduction in the noise of individual aircraft, at least in term of the L_{Aeq} measure. However, that is not the case with a new runway, where people previously unaffected will begin to experience noise, which may be balanced by a reduction in the effect on people currently affected. There are also differences between airports. Heathrow's flight paths over large areas of London mean that the numbers of people affected are 10 or 20 times more than at other airports. However, ambient noise in urban areas means that aircraft noise may have less of an impact compared with rural locations. The ambient noise level is also different between night and day, such that night noise may have a worse impact in urban areas than in less populated parts. Current noise limits permit more night movements at Gatwick and Stansted than Heathrow.

While it has been difficult to relate noise measurements to individual people's experience, it is possible to impose enforceable controls using the measures. Individual aircraft can be certificated on the basis of standard noise measurements, and this has been achieved on an international basis through the International Civil Aviation Organisation (ICAO) (usually referred to in terms of the chapters of an annex to the Convention on International Civil Aviation). It is also possible to impose conditions on the amount of noise made at an airport and to require regular reports. Mitigation can be provided by grants for sound insulation. At each inquiry, study, consultation or other event, a package of such measures has resulted.

Relating noise back to the question of limits discussed in section 10.7 and also referring back to the section in Chapter 7 on average loads, it is interesting to speculate on what might have happened to the noise climate at Heathrow if the 275 000 ATM limit had been retained. Currently, the average number of passengers per aircraft is around 160. Although many large aircraft operate at Heathrow, the largest numbers of aircraft movements are by the A320 and B737 aircraft types, which have a capacity of 150–200. If the 275 000 ATM limit had been retained, this would have meant an average load of around 270 passengers per aircraft. This would have meant far fewer small aircraft, and a much greater use of the larger types, such as the A380, B747, A330 and B777. Larger aircraft are more noisy than smaller types of the same era, so the limit would not have resulted in a proportionate reduction in noise (although given the criticism that the L_{Aeq} measure does not adequately reflect the impact of numbers, this may well have been acceptable to some).

10.9. Can we avoid policy vacuums?

The first word of the subtitle of this book is 'indecision' and the most obvious periods to which this might apply were the early 1990s, the early 2010s and 2015–16, although there have also been periods when options were being studied and, until a decision was made, there was a period of uncertainty. Uncertainty is the key, as the industry and local communities are equally interested in knowing what the policy is, so they can plan their future accordingly. A distinction should be drawn between indecision and a decision not to do something. While the proponents of a scheme may claim that a decision to refuse a proposal is indecision, the objectors will clearly claim this as a victory. However, as noted above, many such decisions did not stand the test of time.

The second half of the 1970s, following the Maplin Review, involved a consultation, White Paper and further studies before decisions were announced in December 1979. However, this is one of the periods when the apparent absence of a long-term strategy was being addressed during a period when there was no immediate pressure for one. The 1980s then saw the completion of a number of terminal projects, giving certainty to all.

However, pressure built again in the 1990s as aircraft numbers grew. The RUCATSE study sought to identify the options but was inconclusive and was overtaken by the Terminal 5 Inquiry when, as noted in Chapter 7, the absence of policy was a key factor, and the cause of much grief, not only about the terminal proposal, but also about the next steps and the longer term. Fortunately for the inspector, he was able to put the longer-term issue to one side as, by the time he made his recommendation, the government had embarked on a quest for a long-term policy, which became the 2003 White Paper.

It is ironic that the certainty of a long-term policy set out in the 2003 White Paper did not survive more than seven years. Opposition groups worked hard to overturn these policies, supported by a growing concern about both local air quality and climate change impacts, but events within the industry also contributed to the change. The sale of BAA to Ferrovial, the opening of Terminal 5, operational challenges related to snow and security and the Competition Commission's review of BAA all led to reputational damage that undermined the plans. The cancellation of the new runways in 2010 was a clear decision not to expand and, at the time with passenger and aircraft numbers declining, there was not an immediate problem. But, as with the economy in general, growth returned to the aviation industry and the reputation was restored, for example as Terminal 5's facilities began to be appreciated, and with the smooth opening of the new Terminal 2. Gatwick and Stansted, under new ownership, also began to establish separate reputations.

Setting up the Airports Commission in 2012 was criticised by some as 'kicking the problem into the long grass', particularly as the timetable set required the final report to be submitted after the 2015 general election. However, it could also be considered similar to the late 1970s, when it was known that options were being considered for a long-term policy. Nevertheless, there was a period of indecision from late 2015 to the decision in October 2016, initially caused by government concerns about the robustness of some of the environmental evidence, but later caught up in the EU Referendum and subsequent change of prime minister and Cabinet.

Finally, while clear, long-term decisions are obviously best for all concerned, there can be a debate about which is worse – indecision or counter-decision. Indecision is bad enough, but counter-decision is probably worse as it destroys credibility in the process, wastes resources and probably has the greatest impact on individuals in affected local communities. Cancelling Maplin in 1974 and the new runways in 2010 and breaking the promises not to expand Heathrow beyond four terminals are probably the worst examples of counter-decisions over the last 40 years.

REFERENCES

Airports Commission (2015) *Final Report*. HMSO, London, UK.
Bentley D (2014) Unravelling the UK airport capacity conundrum: a review of the main submissions made to the Airports Commission. *Journal of Airport Management* **8(1)**: 14–22.
Bows-Larkin A and Anderson K (2013) Carbon budgets for aviation or gamble with our future. In *Sustainable Aviation Futures* (Budd L, Griggs S and Howarth D (eds)). Emerald Group Publishing, Bingley, UK, pp. 65–84.
Cabinet Office (2016) *Consultation Principles 2016*. www.gov.uk/government/uploads/system/uploads/attachment_data/file/492132/20160111_Consultation_principles_final.pdf (accessed 9 January 2017).
de Neufville R and Odoni A (2003) *Airport Systems Planning, Design and Management*, 2nd edition. McGraw-Hill, London, UK and New York, USA.
Department for Transport (2017) *Beyond the Horizon – The Future of UK Aviation: A Call for Evidence on a New Aviation Strategy*. https://assets.publishing.service.gov.uk/government/uploads/system/uploads/attachment_data/file/636625/aviation-strategy-call-for-evidence.pdf (accessed 13 August 2018).
Department of Trade (1978) *Airports Policy*. Cmnd 7084, HMSO, London, UK.
Farrington JH (1984) A third London airport: options and decision-making. *Built Environment* **10(3)**: 168–180.
Glaister S, Burnham J, Stevens H and Travers T (2006) *Transport Policy in Britain*, 2nd edition. Palgrave Macmillan, Basingstoke, UK.
HC Deb 5 June 1985, vol. 80, col. 310.
Humphreys I (1994) Review of runway capacity to serve the South East; the RUCATSE report. *Journal of Air Transport Management* **1(3)**: 183–184.

Lee D, Fahey D, Forster P, Newton P, Wit R, Lim L, Owen B and Sausen R (2009) Aviation and global climate change in the 21st century. *Atmospheric Environment* **43(22–23)**: 3520–3537.

Oxford Dictionary (2017) *www.oxforddictionaries.com* (accessed 9 January 2017).

Prather M, Sausen R, Grossman AS, Haywood JM, Rind D, Subbaraya BH (1999) Potential climate change from aviation. In *Aviation and the Global Atmosphere* (Penner JE, Lister DH, Griggs DJ, Dokken DJ and McFarland M (eds)). Intergovernmental Panel on Climate Change, Cambridge University Press, Cambridge, UK.

Sealy KR (1967) The siting and development of British airports. *The Geographical Journal* **133(2/June)**: 148–171.

SYSTRA (2015) *Analysis of the Airports Commission's Consultation Responses*. https://assets.publishing.service.gov.uk/government/uploads/system/uploads/attachment_data/file/438143/analysis-of-the-airports-commission_s-consultation-responses.pdf (accessed 13 August 2018).

University of Exeter (1998) *Famous Forecasting Quotes*. School of Engineering, Computing and Mathematics website. www1.secam.ex.ac.uk/famous-forecasting-quotes.dhtml (accessed 6 June 2017).

Wickham C (2009) David Cameron: 'No third runway – no ifs, no buts'. Bucks Free Press. www.bucksfreepress.co.uk/news/4694685.David_Cameron___No_third_runway_-_no_ifs__no_buts_ (accessed 13 August 2018).

Wuebbles D, Gupta M, Ko M (2007) Evaluating the impacts of aviation on climate change. *Eos Trans. AGU* **88(14)**: 157. doi:10.1029/2007EO140001.

Chapter 11

Is London unique?

11.1. Introduction

Air transport is a global business and airports are subject to international regulations and guidance, but there are still many differences in decision-making due to culture, politics and geography. Several texts have described airport planning in different parts of the world. In this chapter, a few examples are considered from elsewhere in Europe, North America, the Middle East, East and South East Asia and Australia. In the UK outside London and the South East there are many thriving airports which, although subject to the same policy and planning regimes, have had different experiences, and this chapter also considers a few of these.

11.2. Europe: some centralised planning, some devolved

Airports in the EU are affected by EU policy, although decisions on individual airports are made at national level. In a Eurocontrol report entitled *Challenges of Growth 2013* (Eurocontrol, 2013), a most likely scenario suggested that there would be 50 per cent growth in European air travel from 2012 to 2035, with 12 per cent of demand not being accommodated due to capacity constraints at airports. The report says, 'The capacity gap is the equivalent of nine fully used runways, but impossibly spread around the 21 cities that lack airport capacity' (p. 4). Some EU policies, for example favouring airport development in peripheral or developing regions, have had negative results. For example, some Spanish airports have received investments for social and economic reasons yet have remained unused as no airlines wished to use them. As noted in Chapter 2, although airlines are the primary customer of airports, they often have little say in the planning and development of airports (de Neufville and Odoni, 2003).

11.2.1 France

Centralised planning is evident in a number of European countries. France has a history of central direction and uses elite engineers to run airport developments (de Neufville and Odoni, 2003). France's planning system includes the option of a project being declared of public utility, which, in effect, reduces the need to justify it at later stages, which might be seen as similar to the UK process of preparing a National Policy Statement (NPS). At around the same time as Stansted was rejected as a third London airport in 1968 (see Chapter 3), the French began planning a third Paris airport at Roissy, which became Paris Charles de Gaulle (CDG) when it opened in 1974. The location is 16 miles (25 km) north of the city centre and its opening required the scaling back of operations at Le Bourget, about 6 miles (10 km) away, although Le Bourget remains in use for business aviation and the Paris Air Show. At the time, the larger airport was Orly, to the south of the city, and Orly has remained open, initially for domestic flights only, but now with international and domestic services. Sufficient land for six runways at CDG was acquired (four have been built) and additional terminals have been constructed. CDG handled 69.5 million passengers in 2017, making it the second-busiest airport in Europe after Heathrow. CDG, Orly, Le Bourget and a number of other smaller airports in the region are owned and operated by Aeroports de Paris (AdP). AdP is a *société anonyme*, with 50.6 per cent of shares owned by the French state and the remainder by various investors and Schiphol Group. Growth at CDG has not been without controversy, in particular as communities have grown nearby which are affected by aircraft noise. The airport has space to continue growing and there are no current plans for more runways. Rail access is a particular feature at CDG, especially long-distance rail services on the TGV network, some of which are provided as intermodal services with airlines, and this has probably reduced the growth in short-haul flights, particularly domestic.

There have been plans in the past for a fourth Paris airport at Chaulnes, 50 miles (80 km) north of the city, linked by a TGV line, but these are not currently being pursued, although it is possible that they may have to be revived if CDG and Orly run out of capacity in the future. Clearly, the timing of the completion of CDG (1974), just as the Maplin project in the UK was being cancelled, and the amount of land acquired, has meant that Paris has not had to face the decision on a new airport site since then. There has, however, been controversy and opposition to a new airport proposed at Nantes, in western France. The existing airport is close to the city and handled 4.8 million passengers in 2016, but the promoters of the airport said that the existing airport cannot be expanded. Opposition to the proposed new airport has been longstanding, and is mainly related to the taking of land. There have been large demonstrations, involving groups from the whole country, but a referendum in 2016 produced a 55 per cent majority in favour of the new airport. However, in early 2018, the French government decided to abandon the plan (Willsher, 2018).

11.2.2 The Netherlands
Schiphol has been Amsterdam's airport since 1916 and the whole area is land reclaimed from the Haarlemmermeer polder. After World War 2 (WW2) the airport was expanded, requiring the demolition of a small community, and expansion has continued. The Netherlands has a strong and well-developed tradition of spatial planning, and the expansion of Schiphol Airport has been part of the National Policy Document, which focused development on 'mainports' including Schiphol (Healey, 2004). Schiphol is owned by the Dutch Ministry of Finance (69.77 per cent), the municipalities of Amsterdam (20.03 per cent) and Rotterdam (2.2 per cent) and AdP (8 per cent). Schiphol handled 68.5 million passengers in 2017, making it the third-busiest airport in Europe. When considering expansion in 2006, the government set up the 'Alderstafel' or 'Alders Platform', named after its chair, former minister Hans Alders, which facilitated agreements on the medium-term growth of the airport. These agreements include limits on the number of aircraft movements, operational restrictions, sums of money to be made available to local communities (which are relatively large in relation to the number of passengers or persons affected) and other issues. The airport is continuing to expand, with a new terminal, but there are no plans for further runways. The Alderstafel was examined by the UK Airports Commission and undoubtedly influenced their recommendation for a Community Engagement Board associated with a third runway at Heathrow (Airports Commission, 2015: p. 300).

11.2.3 Germany
Germany provides some interesting examples, each of which has unique features. Unlike France and the Netherlands, airport policy is more decentralised, with the Länder (federal states or regions) and cities holding substantial shares in the airports.

Frankfurt is the country's largest airport (see Figure 11.1), handling 64.5 million passengers in 2017, making it Europe's fourth busiest. It is 51.35 per cent publicly owned, with the remaining shares held by various investors. The site was established in the 1930s and converted for civil

Figure 11.1 Frankfurt Airport in 2017 (Google Maps). The third runway has a north–south orientation and the fourth is the shorter east–west runway. Terminal 3 is being built with three piers to the south of the runways on the old USAF Rhein-Main Air Base.

operations after WW2, after US forces rebuilt the two east–west runways and established the Rhein-Main Air Base. Berlin's post-war situation meant that its airports could not be developed, and the federal capital was in the small city of Bonn, so Frankfurt became the country's largest airport somewhat by default, although the city is only the fifth largest in Germany. What is now Terminal 1 opened in 1972, along with a rail station. Plans for a third runway in a north–south orientation were drawn up in 1973, but these provoked massive protests by residents and environmentalists concerned about noise and the loss of trees in Frankfurt City Forest. These protests continued into the 1980s and coincided with a rise of the German environmental movement during that decade. However, the third runway opened in 1984 but protests against it continued. Two police officers were killed in 1987 and this effectively ended the protests. Because of its orientation, the third runway's capacity cannot be fully used and it is used for take-offs only.

Frankfurt's Terminal 2 opened in 1994 next to Terminal 1 and connected to it by a people mover. A second rail station for Intercity-Express (high-speed) trains opened in 1999. Plans for a fourth runway were prepared in the late 1990s but, given the experiences with the third, the airport sought to involve local residents. As with Amsterdam Schiphol, the UK Airports Commission was encouraged by the arrangements at Frankfurt, although the Commission did not recommend these for Heathrow, preferring the Schiphol model (Airports Commission, 2015: p. 302). A fourth east–west runway, shorter than the others, was approved for landings only, and there was to be significant noise mitigation and a night-flight ban. The new runway opened in 2011 but the night ban was initially not implemented because of the impact on freight operations, but it has been re-imposed through the courts. The Airports Commission noted the impact of this night ban on airline schedules, showing that airlines were able to re-schedule passenger flights outside the night-ban hours, although they did not discuss the impact on freight operations (ibid: p. 282). Despite the agreement and the night ban, protests continue at Frankfurt. Every Monday evening there is a demonstration in the terminal, calling for the closure of the runway or a longer night ban and no further expansion (Airport Watch, 2017).

Although no further runways are planned at Frankfurt, the airport is expanding by the provision of a third terminal on the site of the old Rhein-Main Air Base, which closed in 2005.

Munich was served by Riem Airport until 1992, but its location, surrounded by developed areas, meant that it could not expand and there was also a significant noise problem. Planning for a new airport began in 1963 and the decision was made on the site in 1969. However, there were numerous legal challenges and, although construction began in 1980, the new airport did not open until 1992. A village with around 500 inhabitants was demolished. Munich Airport is owned by the Free State of Bavaria (51 per cent), the city of Munich (23 per cent) and the federal government (26 per cent). The new airport was initiated when Franz Joseph Strauss was Minister-President of Bavaria. The airport is formally named after Strauss, who was a private pilot with a particular interest in aviation. During the period when the Munich plans were being prepared, Frankfurt was suffering from capacity shortages and Berlin was still divided, so Lufthansa decided to create a second hub at Munich. In 2017 the airport handled 44.6 million passengers, making it the second busiest in Germany. There are restrictions on aircraft movements at night, but there are exemptions, meaning that the ban is not absolute. Plans for a third runway are now being progressed, but have been the subject of further objections. Around 60 000 objections were made to the first plans in 2007. A city referendum resulted in 54 per cent of voters opposing and 46 per cent supporting the plan and an 80 000-signature petition. There have also been court hearings at various levels, with the federal courts overturning the appeals and giving approval in 2015. However, the project is not yet proceeding as it does not have the support of all three of its shareholders, in particular the city of Munich. While the airport was established and has expanded, there have been many challenges and objections over the years, which are ongoing. On the one hand, the ownership structure may have enabled the airport to be developed through sheer political pressure, but it has undoubtedly taken much longer than originally planned.

Berlin is a particular case for two reasons. Until the fall of the Berlin Wall in 1989, the city was divided in two, and West Berlin was surrounded by East Germany. This had led to the Berlin Airlift of 1948–49. There were two airports in West Berlin, at Templehof and Tegel. Templehof had begun operations in the 1920s, but had limited runway lengths on a small site, and closed in 2008. Tegel was established in time to contribute to the airlift but became a commercial airport in 1960. Flights were permitted only by American, British and French airlines but numbers grew and Tegel became Berlin's main airport in 1975. By 2017, Tegel was handling 20.5 million passengers. Schönefeld was the main airport for East Berlin, and by 2017 it handled 12.9 million passengers. With reunification, Berlin was re-established as the federal capital and it became possible to consider all options for airports. Three sites were considered, all to the south of the city in the State of Brandenberg, all based on existing airfields. The selected site was at Schönefeld, which was closest to the city and had existing road and rail links, but would have the worst noise impact, although better than the existing situation at Tegel, which would be closed. The ownership of the airports was transferred to Flughafen Brandenberg GmbH, which is owned by the States of Berlin and Brandenberg (37 per cent each) and the federal government (26 per cent).

The second reason for Berlin being a particular case is that the development of the new airport has been delayed for several reasons. The first plans were based on a private-sector development but, in 2003, negotiations ended and it was decided to develop the airport under public ownership. Policy approval was given in 2004 by the State of Brandenberg but there were legal challenges until 2006. Construction began that year and some 300 residents were relocated from the site. A new southern runway was built and the northern runway was created from one of the existing runways at Schönefeld. The terminal and rail station were also built and were completed by 2012. However, when commissioning, it was discovered that there were design and construction flaws that meant the airport could not be opened. As of 2018, the projected opening date is 2020. Several managers and politicians have lost their jobs and one was prosecuted for corruption. In the meantime, the existing airports at Tegel and Schönefeld have had to accommodate the growth.

These two issues – the re-unification of Germany and the commissioning problems – have made the Berlin Airport story unique and there do not appear to be any policy lessons that would be applicable elsewhere.

11.2.4 Sweden

The case of Stockholm Arlanda Airport may have some lessons for the UK situation. The site was selected as long ago as 1946 as the existing airport at Bromma could not be expanded. The first runway at Arlanda opened in 1954 but was not used for scheduled services until 1960. Terminals and a second runway were added as traffic grew and airlines moved services from Bromma, although the latter remains open. Approval for the third runway, which opened in 2003, was given on the basis of some strict environmental controls, including its use during peak hours only and a carbon dioxide (CO_2) cap, set in 1990 at 347 200 tonnes. Just under half of the carbon comes from aircraft, around one half from ground transport and the remainder from airport buildings and other activities. Despite passenger numbers and road traffic increasing, the carbon limit has been maintained by reductions in aircraft emissions, but in particular by an extensive carbon-reduction programme for ground access, including new rail links and the significant change to hybrid and electric vehicles at the airport, including taxis.

The Arlanda carbon cap contrasts with UK policy, which is to work towards overall reductions in the use of carbon across all sectors through national carbon budgets (see Chapter 5). The difference is that, whereas the Arlanda carbon cap is specific to the airport and requires the airport and its partners to take action in order to grow, the UK policy is nationwide and therefore requires collective action by all airports and their aviation partners, and also can employ trading between sectors. However, it is clear that Heathrow expansion can be permitted only on the basis of limiting road traffic, in part because of its impact on local air quality (as compared with the global impact of carbon).

11.2.5 Austria

Carbon dioxide emissions are also an issue at Vienna Airport, where a Federal Administrative Court ruled that a third runway would result in carbon emissions exceeding Austria's international commitments to reduce greenhouse gases. The airport appealed the ruling, citing EU regulations which state that airlines, not airports, are responsible for in-flight emissions, and arguing that airlines will simply operate from elsewhere (Allett, 2017). In June 2017, Austria's Constitutional Court annulled the lower court's decision (Anon, 2017a). As noted in Chapter 5, the UK position is that individual airport developments do not count towards carbon targets but, as set out in the Airports Commission's final report, a third runway at Heathrow would be compatible with those targets (Airports Commission, 2015).

11.3. North America: most airports are city or state owned
11.3.1 The USA

In the United States, most decisions on airports are made by states or city governments, airlines are guarantors for bonds and communities are often represented on airport boards. Planning in the USA is usually undertaken by generalists rather than specialists and plans are suggestive rather than directive. Physical airport layouts in the USA reflect airline preferences (for example, in airside layouts) and low use of public transport (de Neufville and Odoni, 2003). More recent concerns about airport development in the USA have arisen as a reaction to growing delays (Morrison and Winston, 2008). There is criticism that developments have not kept pace with growth as a result of the public ownership, financing and management of airports (and air traffic control and security). There is a US national airports plan covering 3300 of the country's 19 000 airports, but federal funding is not aligned with use. Morrison and Winston suggest that congestion pricing and privatisation should be implemented instead of political interest group lobbying and administrative action. Bentley, writing in 2014, noted that as a result of the current system, there had been no new major infrastructure (i.e. new runways) built in the USA since 1995 (when the new Denver Airport opened).

In the years leading up to Denver opening in 1995, new airports were established in the USA at Dallas Fort Worth (see Figure 11.2), Houston and Washington, and many existing airports were redeveloped and expanded, including in Atlanta, Chicago, Los Angeles, New York and San Francisco.

Dallas Fort Worth Airport (DFW) handled 67.1 million passengers in 2017. In the 1920s, both cities had their own airports but there were early proposals for a joint airport, which did not come to fruition until the 1960s, by which time Dallas Love Field had become the main airport for the cities. A commission was set up and recommended a site equidistant from the two cities and voters in the cities approved the plan in a referendum in 1967. DFW occupies over 7000 hectares (nearly 30 square miles) and has seven runways. In order to help DFW become established,

Figure 11.2 Dallas Fort Worth Airport
(Photo NASA (Wikimedia Commons))

restrictions were placed on operations at Love Field (limiting the size of aircraft and the destinations). However, Southwest Airlines, the first of the modern era of low-cost carriers (LCCs), began operating from Love Field in 1978 and eventually the restrictions were removed, and it now handles 15.6 million passengers per year.

Voting on propositions is a well-used US state process, often on a financial proposal. A similar vote in 1988 enabled the new Denver Airport to be built, with 63 per cent supporting and 37 per cent opposing (Anon, 1988). Unlike at Dallas, the old airport at Stapleton was closed. Stapleton was very close (3 miles/5 km) to downtown Denver, on a small site and surrounded by development, making expansion difficult. High-rise development in the city was also interfering with airspace and there were noise lawsuits from neighbours. For these reasons the city began the process of searching for a new site and ended up with the world's largest airport in terms of land area (13 500 hectares/52 square miles). The Stapleton site has been redeveloped for commercial and residential purposes. The main controversies about the new Denver Airport were not related to policy, but were firstly the difficulties of commissioning a new baggage system and secondly some rather bizarre conspiracy theories that the runway layout resembles a swastika.

Chicago has two main airports, O'Hare and Midway. Midway was the first to be established in the 1920s and was the main airport until the 1960s, when new jet aircraft could not operate from the short runways. However, Midway's fortunes revived in the 1980s with LCCs and it handled 22.5 million passengers in 2017. O'Hare started life in WW2 as a manufacturing plant for Douglas Aircraft, being close to a large workforce and good transport links. Although it opened as an airport in 1955, growth was slow until jets were introduced in the 1960s. The initial layout had four runways, which intersected, and a major redevelopment of the runways is under way to provide six parallel and two cross runways. The modernisation plan has involved the acquisition of land and the relocation of 2800 residents. There has been significant opposition, including legal challenges, for example in relation to a historic cemetery with 900 graves. There have also been proposals for reliever airports at Gary in Indiana, Rockford in Illinois, and Milwaukee, in Wisconsin, using rail links with Chicago, but none of these have received sufficient support, in particular from airlines. O'Hare handled 79.8 million passengers in 2017.

Washington's airports developed under federal arrangements, with National Airport opening in 1941, close (3 miles/5 km) to the city centre but outside the Capital District of Colombia. Soon after National's opening, it became clear that it would not be large enough and a site was selected for a new airport 26 miles (42 km) from downtown. Other sites were rejected in part because of objections by residents, but the selected site required the demolition of the largely African American community of Willard. After the new Dulles Airport opened in 1962, restrictions were placed on operations from National but nevertheless Dulles was considered as a white elephant for many years, although passenger numbers eventually overtook those at National. However, in recent years National has overtaken Dulles, with 23.9 million passengers in 2017 compared to Dulles's 22.9 million. One of the controversial issues at Dulles was the design, which includes a terminal designed by Eero Saarinen and airside concourses connected by mobile lounges. The mobile lounges are inflexible and costly to operate and have partly been replaced by a fixed people mover. On the other hand, a positive element of the planning of Dulles is that the main access road is owned by the airport authority, which collects toll revenue which is used to fund improvements. The access road also safeguarded the median strip between the two carriageways for use by rail access, and the city's metro Silver line is now being extended to the airport. In 1987, the two airports were transferred under a 50-year lease from the Federal Aviation Agency to the Metropolitan Washington Airports Authority (MWAA). The MWAA is an agency of the states of Virginia and Maryland and the District of Colombia and provides for more local control over the airports. Washington is also served by Baltimore-Washington Airport, which is owned by the State of Maryland and had 26.4 million passengers in 2017.

New York's airports have been redeveloped over a number of years but a challenge remains to provide capacity in the New York region, which has been addressed in a study by the Regional Plan Association (RPA) (Zupan *et al.*, 2011). New York's airports are operated by the bi-state agency, the Port Authority of New York and New Jersey (PANYNJ). The Port Authority was established in 1921 and operates a number of transportation facilities, and acquired the airports in 1947. Newark Airport was initially the only commercial airport in the region, but LaGuardia Airport began operations in 1939. However, it soon became clear that LaGuardia would not be large enough and work began on what is now JFK International in 1943, the latter opening in 1948. New Jersey's Newark Airport was underutilised for some years after the New York airports opened, but grew rapidly in the 1980s with People Express, an early model LCC, and Virgin Atlantic. At various times there have been restrictions on the types of flights at each of the airports in order to seek a better distribution, but these have largely been removed and airlines are subject only to slot regulations and physical limits such as the runway length at LaGuardia. In 2017 passenger numbers were 29.5 million at LaGuardia, 59.3 million at JFK and 43.4 million at Newark. Being surrounded by urban areas, all three PANYNJ airports have a major noise impact, and safety is also a major concern, with a number of accidents affecting residential communities, the most recent in 2001 when an American Airlines A300 crashed in Queens and killed five people on the ground as well as all 260 passengers and crew.

Policy development for the New York region's airports is complicated by the bi-state nature of the PANYNJ, as well as the split of responsibilities between the city mayors, state governors, other public agencies and airlines. The RPA study identified potential growth and considered a range of options, including airspace improvements, reliever airports, new airports, expanding existing airports, high-speed rail as an alternative, and managing demand. The study concluded that three existing reliever airports could provide limited relief but were too far from the cities to be of real value. A site for a fourth airport had been sought over many years, but the RPA study could not find a suitable large, flat and relatively undeveloped site within 40 miles (64 km) of the city, and only one existing airfield that could be expanded, which was 70 miles (113 km) from the city. An offshore site could be developed but would require the closure of one of the existing main airports and would be exorbitantly costly. High-speed rail would not shift a significant amount of demand, and demand management would be contrary to many policies. The study therefore concluded that the only way forward would be to expand the existing airports and it showed options for achieving this. Subsequently, plans for upgrading and expanding LaGuardia and JFK have been proposed, although none of these address the need for more runway capacity identified in the RPA study. These plans will also have to pass through rigorous environmental assessment and other processes before they are approved.

One conclusion that can be drawn from US experience is that many airports have had large areas of land allocated or zoned for many years and so have been able to expand. The nature of many US cities is low-density development (apart from the central business district) and airports have been able to remain sometimes quite close to the city. It is also clear that the role of local politicians is crucial, with city mayors and state governors often exerting significant influence and making decisions on the basis of promoting the city or state. Common ownership of more than one airport in a region has also enabled new airports to grow by restricting operations at the old airport, although this is not always successful, as airlines often prefer the airport located closer to the city centre. Litigation is a common feature of US life, and there have been significant challenges but few that have achieved more than a delay and perhaps some improvements in mitigation and compensation.

11.3.2 Canada

Canada's airports are leased to private-sector operators and the major airports are expanded in accordance with their province or city ordinances. Montreal Mirabel Airport was developed in the 1970s as a replacement for Dorval Airport but the airlines never established services there, and it now serves only as an aircraft manufacturing and cargo centre. Mirabel is often quoted as the key example of a new airport that did not succeed. The site was selected as a compromise between the proposals of the federal government and the province of Quebec, between whom relations were strained. The site was massive (39 000 hectares/150 square miles) and it is 24 miles (39 km) from the city. When it opened in 1975, international flights were required to operate from there but road access was limited and a rail link was not built. The new airport had been planned on the basis that the existing airport at Dorval would soon be full with the booming economy but, after the 1976 Olympics in Montreal, the regional economy stagnated, in part caused by a law which banned the use of languages other than French. International airlines chose to serve Toronto, where connections to domestic flights were at the same airport. Mirabel never handled more than 3 million passengers a year and closed to commercial air transport in 2004. Some land has been returned to its original owners. Dorval Airport remained open and in 2017 handled 18.2 million passengers. Toronto Airport handled 47.1 million passengers in 2017.

11.3.3 Mexico

The current Mexico City Airport is operating at its capacity and, being surrounded by development, is difficult to expand and also creates significant noise impact. Various redevelopments have taken place over the years and, by 2017, the airport handled 44.7 million passengers. It is owned by the city and operated by a public corporation that also operates 22 other airports in Mexico. In 2002, the government announced that a new airport would be built at Texcoco and San Salvador Atenco, 16 miles (25 km) to the north-east of the city centre. However, there were violent protests from local landowners, including occupations of offices and the taking of hostages, and the project was cancelled (Thompson, 2002). Further redevelopments then took place at the existing airport to accommodate growth but in 2014 the government announced that the new airport would go ahead on more or less the same site as proposed in 2002 and the existing airport would be closed when the new airport opens in 2020. Since 2002 the government has acquired all of the land required and, although there have been small-scale protests, construction contracts were awarded in January 2017 (Anon, 2017b).

11.4. The Middle East and East and South East Asia: limited democracy and rapid growth

Many countries in the Middle East and East and South East Asia have seen significant growth in recent years and a number of airports have been built or expanded rapidly. Political systems and cultures are very different from Europe and North America and therefore comparisons often highlight these differences as the reason for the different pace of development. National government control is evident in planning airports in many of these regions which have expanded, along with their based airlines. The planning processes for these airports are almost entirely government-led, with little public or democratic involvement. Nevertheless, a few examples are worth considering, in China, Japan, Malaysia, Singapore and Dubai.

11.4.1 China

Airports in China have expanded rapidly in recent years. Until 1980, the Chinese civil aviation authority and industry was a department of the Air Force. Airports were controlled by the Civil Aviation Administration of China (CAAC) until the early 1990s and were then transferred to local governments (except for Beijing International), some with shares on the stock markets, and with some overseas investment since 2002. Airlines were restructured in the early 1980s and there was rapid growth of air travel in the 1980s and 1990s, but airport infrastructure did not keep pace. However, the transfer of airports to local control in the 1990s led to investment (for example, congestion at Shanghai Hongqiao led to the construction of the new Pudong Airport).

Hong Kong's airport, in the Special Administrative Region, is efficient, profitable and transparently managed and competes with other airports in China and the region (Bentley, 2014; Zhang and Yuen, 2008). However, it is interesting to recall that the planning and development of the new Hong Kong Airport at Chep Lap Kok took place while Hong Kong was under British rule, although this was not democratic government. The then existing airport at Kai Tak was clearly operating at its capacity and was heavily constrained, so the decision was made to construct a new airport on mostly reclaimed land. The site had been identified as early as 1974, but the decision to proceed was not made until 1989. The handover to China in 1997 was seen as a key target date for completion, although in the event the opening date was in 1998. UK firms, including BAA, played a significant role in the planning, design and construction of the new airport. Environmental studies were undertaken, in particular into the effects on the local water environment, but the major improvement in noise by the closure of Kai Tak was seen as a key benefit. The planning and construction of the airport was undoubtedly undertaken very quickly but it is somewhat ironic to note that the next stage of expansion, with a third runway on additional reclaimed land, is taking longer and has involved more consultation under Chinese rule than under the previous British regime. After three years of study, a new master plan was published in 2011, which was adopted in 2012, and the project is due to be completed by 2023.

11.4.2 Japan

Japan has a democratic government system and, like the UK, is a small, densely populated island nation. As in Hong Kong, reclaimed land has been used for many years for airports and other developments. Haneda Airport was first established in the 1930s on the shore of Tokyo Bay and, under US occupation after WW2, many local residents were moved to enable the runways to be extended, with more land being added for later developments, reclaimed from the sea. After the opening of Narita Airport (see Figure 11.3), Haneda was restricted to domestic flights, but this restriction was eventually removed in 2007. Haneda's closeness to the city centre and the ability to connect with domestic flights had always meant that airlines preferred it to the more distant Narita, a situation with some parallels to airlines' views about Heathrow. Once the restrictions were lifted, expansion of Haneda became necessary and a fourth runway was added on further reclaimed land. The decision to build a new airport at Narita was made partly because of noise issues at Haneda, and was announced in 1966. Local landowners had not been consulted and combined with student activists and left-wing political groups to take direct action, including occupations, blockades and equipment damage. Although it is possible to acquire land compulsorily in Japan, these powers are rarely used and some parts of the airport have had to be built around land that has not been acquired. By 2016 Narita handled 39.1 million passengers, while Haneda reached nearly 85 million in 2017.

The difficulty of land acquisition in Tokyo was part of the reason why the new airport for Osaka was built on an artificial island in Osaka Bay at Kansai. Kansai Airport handled 23.2 million passengers in 2016, while the old airport at Itami handled 14.5 million domestic passengers. Itami, surrounded by development, was the subject of lawsuits in the 1960s and 1970s which led to landmark Japanese environmental laws that included a night ban from 9pm to 7am at Itami. However, in recent years, local communities have argued that Itami should not be closed (and the land sold to reduce the debt on Kansai Airport) and have even agreed that jet

Figure 11.3 Tokyo Narita Airport in 2017: the runway could not be built full length and taxiways had to be built around land that could not be acquired (Google Maps)

movements could be increased (as new aircraft are less noisy), so that the economic benefits can be retained.

11.4.3 Malaysia and Singapore

Malaysia and Singapore have experienced rapid and sustained growth over many years and have both developed world-class airports. In Malaysia, Kuala Lumpur's old airport at Subang could not be expanded, so a new site was selected to the south of the city as part of a grand plan for a multimedia super-corridor, which includes the federal administrative capital at Putrajaya and Cyberjaya, an IT-themed new town.

Singapore's strategic location and position as an island means that trade and travel has always been important. The current airport at Changi is the fourth in a sequence and the site was selected in 1975, where there was an existing air base and scope to expand on reclaimed land. The airport was built quickly, opening in 1981, and has been progressively expanded such that in 2017 it handled 62.2 million passengers and nearly 2 million tonnes of freight.

Kuala Lumpur and Singapore are examples of how airports can form a fundamental part of a national economic strategy, in the case of Malaysia as part of efforts to build a knowledge-based economy, while Singapore's strategy is based on trade.

11.4.4 The Middle East

The Middle East has seen significant growth in aviation in recent years although, historically, some parts have played a significant role, for example in the development of the 'empire' routes between Britain and the Far East. Many modern airports were established in the 1970s and 1980s after oil revenues grew significantly and I was personally involved in consultancy work with BAA in Jordan and Iraq. Many European airport companies, such as Amsterdam Schiphol, Aeroports de Paris and Frankfurt, as well as BAA, provided planning, design and operational advice alongside well-known engineering consultants such as Arup, Halcrow and Mott Macdonald. Some of my colleagues were seconded for several years and became established in the Middle East. Even today, some of the key names in Middle East airport management had an apprenticeship in BAA. Whether they find their political masters in these countries any better or worse than those in the UK is an open question, but I can certainly recall that, in Iraq, there was always a military figure at the back of every meeting, to whom all decisions were referred. We wondered why the terminal design was required to have such a large basement, but we discovered later that these were, of course, bomb shelters.

Dubai is the Middle East's largest airport in terms of passenger numbers, handling 88.2 million in 2017, making it the world's third busiest in terms of total passengers and the busiest for international passengers. Flying boats had called at Dubai since the 1930s, but the current airport site was first used in 1960, with tarmac runways added and extended through the 1960s, 1970s and 1980s. By 1990, the airport was handling more than 4 million passengers a year, but the real growth took place after a 1997 master plan for new terminals and other facilities. The airport is wholly owned by the Dubai government and has grown along with Emirates Airlines (the links between airlines and airports are discussed in Chapter 2). There are claims by some (particularly US) airlines that Emirates is unfairly financially supported by the Dubai government and, at the time of writing, this is unresolved. Emirates has acquired the world's largest fleet of Airbus A380 aircraft, and this may have been in part due to the limited runway capacity at Dubai Airport (average loads are 200 passengers per aircraft movement, compared with 160 at Heathrow). The two runways are not far enough apart to be operated independently, which means their capacity is less than other two-runway airports with wider-spaced runways. Recognising these capacity limits, a second airport has been established at Jebel Ali, some 23 miles (37 km) from the centre of Dubai city, as part of Dubai World Central, a planned residential, commercial and logistics complex. The site covers 14 000 hectares (35 000 acres) and the ultimate capacity is planned to be between 160 and 260 million passengers and 12 million tonnes of cargo per year. Al Maktoum

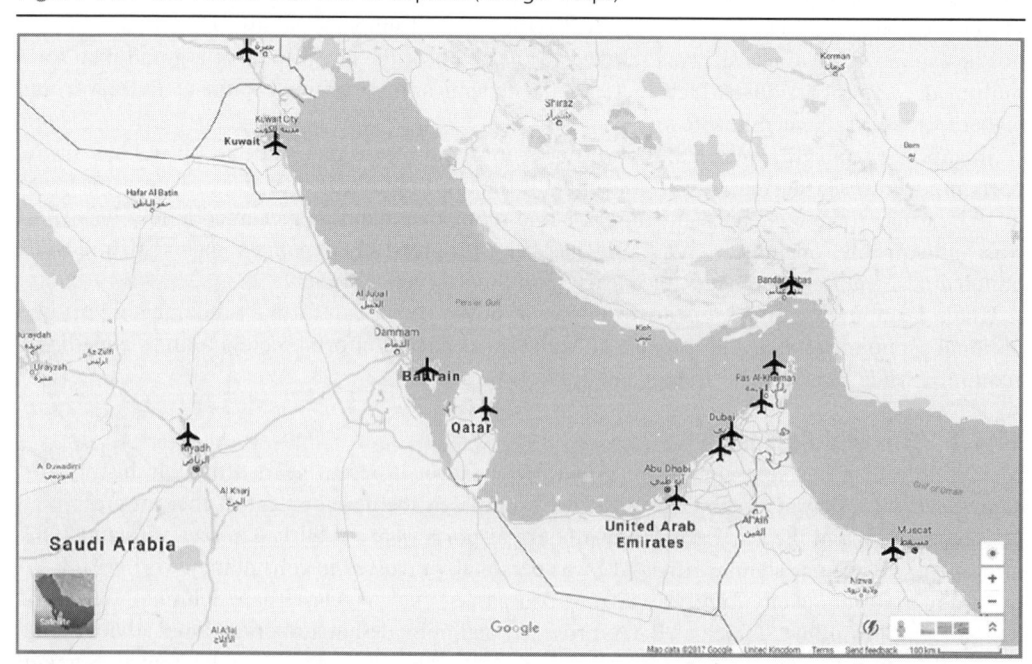

Figure 11.4 The Persian Gulf and its airports (Google Maps)

International Airport opened in 2010 but, as of 2016, still handled only around one million passengers. Undoubtedly further growth will have to take place at the new airport, but it is also likely that the airlines, particularly Emirates, will be unwilling to move while they can continue to grow at the existing site. However, decision-making is opaque, so it is not clear what will happen or when.

The next-largest airport in the region is at Doha, handling 37.3 million passengers in 2016, whose growth is linked to that of Qatar Airways, followed by the airports at Jeddah and Abu Dhabi. One of the issues which arises is the number of airports around the Persian Gulf (see Figure 11.4), and whether they are all likely to continue to grow. It is to be expected that every country will want its own airport, but some are clearly designed to serve more than just their local demand. However, it is apparent that the development of some airports, along with the route development of their based airlines, has resulted in growth way beyond local demand and has contributed to economic growth and diversity away from a dependence on oil revenues.

11.5. Australia: some similarities with London

Studies of the situation in Australia (for example Forsyth, 2008) reveal the influence of politics on airport planning. State governments have significant ownership shares and may force airports to make unprofitable investments to promote the region (the example quoted by Forsyth is Adelaide), which has not been helped by the light-handed approach to regulation. However, the history of Sydney's airports, which may have some parallels with the UK (Bentley, 2014), has been influenced by politics:

> If the history of Kingsford Smith Airport in Sydney shows anything, it shows the tendency of the centralised two-party system to act in the private, rather than the public, interest. The 50-year history also shows that no amount of rational argument about planning, cost/benefit, the environment, the welfare of residents or even the efficiency of Australia's airports carries any real weight in decision making. It has demonstrated the defects of many of our institutions – representative government, the centralised two-party system, the self-serving nature of our bureaucracies and our inability to cope with the forces of deregulation, privatisation, and globalisation.
>
> (Fitzgerald, 1998, quoted in May and Hill, 2006: p. 444)

In 2014, the Australian government announced that approval would be given for a Western Sydney Airport (WSA) to be built at Badgerys Creek, some 27 miles (44 km) from the city centre. The operator of the existing Sydney Kingsford Smith Airport has declined the option of developing the WSA, noting that it would require subsidy for a long time, and so the government is proceeding with funding it. The land was acquired by the government in the late 1980s, although it has been leased for farming. There have been environmental objections, mainly related to flight paths, but the airport will be able to operate 24 hours a day, unlike Kingsford Smith, which has a night curfew.

11.6. The UK outside the South East

It is not the intention of this book to consider the detail of how airports policy in the UK has evolved for airports outside London and the South East. However, many of the studies and policy documents relate to the whole of the UK and it could be relevant to the London and South East situation to compare and contrast some examples from other parts of the UK. In this section, the examples considered are the Scottish Lowlands, the North of England and the English Midlands.

Some of the criticisms of the previous attempts to establish a third London airport in the 1960s and the early 1970s (see Chapter 3) were that they did not sufficiently consider the whole of the country. The 1975 Airports Strategy for Great Britain consultation exercise (Department of Trade, 1975 and 1976) did, with the second document specifically covering the regional airports. After the consultation, the 1978 White Paper (Department of Trade, 1978) proposed a national airports policy in which the airports were categorised (see Table 6.1 in Chapter 6). Outside London, Manchester and Prestwick were designated as Category A (Gateway International), while Birmingham, East Midlands, Leeds Bradford, Newcastle and Cardiff were Category B (Regional) and the rest were Category C (Local) or Category D (General Aviation). Other than Prestwick, Scottish airports were not categorised as they were left to the new Scottish Assembly, and neither were airports in Northern Ireland, probably because of the Troubles. Some of these categorisations, which were intended to guide investment and, to some extent, traffic distribution, did not match the actual levels of growth.

As noted in the earlier chapters, regional issues were apparent in a number of the studies and inquiries, in particular at the Airports Inquiries of 1981–1983 (see Chapter 6) and the RUCATSE study of the early 1990s (see Chapter 7), although this was mainly related to the subject of regional diversion. The next attempt at a national strategy came in the 2003 White Paper (Department for Transport, 2003; see Chapter 8). The major consultation exercise that had led up to the White Paper had included the publication of documents for each region in the *Regional Air Services* series of papers in 2000. I was personally involved in analysing the responses to some of these. By this time, I had left BAA and was an independent consultant working for AviaSolutions, who had been contracted to analyse the responses. As ex-BAA, it was felt inappropriate for me to deal with any regions where there were BAA airports, but I was the lead author for the consultation response reports for Northern Ireland, the South West and Wales. The 2003 White Paper was a 30-year strategy covering the whole country, with a chapter for each region, with sections, or at least a sentence or two, on virtually every airport in the UK. There had been a limited attempt at categorisation in the consultation documents, for example with smaller South East airports being designated as first, second or third tier, but the White Paper policies generally recognised a level of growth at each airport for which policy support could be given. The Aviation Policy Framework, which replaced the 2003 White Paper (Department for Transport, 2013; see Chapter 9) was a national document, but contained case studies of only a few regional airports. The Airports Commission reviewed the regional diversion issue, but did not consider the development of regional airports except where they were proposed as an alternative to new capacity in the South East.

11.6.1 Lowland Scotland

It was noted above that Prestwick was designated as a Gateway International Hub in the 1978 White Paper. This was because historically the airport had been an important refuelling stop for transatlantic flights and had become established as a Scottish gateway. As jet aircraft became more efficient, their range increased and the need for such refuelling stops reduced (others were at Shannon in Ireland and Gander in Canada). However, as Prestwick had a long runway and large terminal, it remained the main airport for Scottish long-haul traffic. Prestwick had been part of BAA's initial portfolio from 1966 but Edinburgh was transferred from the Department of Trade (DoT) to BAA in 1971 and Glasgow from Glasgow City Council to BAA in 1975. International flights were permitted from all three airports, but only Prestwick was permitted to handle transatlantic traffic. One famous incident which resulted from this was that the only time Elvis Presley set foot in the UK was at Prestwick Airport, on a US Army aircraft en route from Germany to the USA. Prestwick's monopoly of transatlantic flights lasted until 1990, although by then the need for refuelling had disappeared. BAA sold Prestwick in 1991 and it has had a variety of owners since then, and its fortunes have varied, at one stage handling 2.4 million passengers. In 2013, the airport was bought by the Scottish government for £1, and it handled 0.7 million passengers in 2017.

The present Glasgow Airport dates from 1966, when the site at Abbotsinch took over from the previous airport at Renfrew, which subsequently closed. After the BAA takeover in 1975, traffic grew steadily until the recession of 2008, and in 2017 it handled 9.9 million passengers. Transatlantic operators moved from Prestwick once the restrictions had been removed, although the number of destinations is limited. The 2003 White Paper recommended that land to the north of the airport should be reserved for a second, close parallel runway in the longer term. Interestingly, it notes that the land is unlikely to be developed for other purposes because of its ecological designations, but does not comment on the impact of a new runway on the ecology. A master plan published in 2011 retained the option of a second runway, although it noted that there was no current case for it, but the land would be acquired if it became available (Glasgow Airport, 2011). In 2014, Glasgow Airport was sold, together with Southampton and Aberdeen airports, by BAA to a consortium of Ferrovial (also part owner of Heathrow) and Macquarie Group for £1 billion.

Edinburgh Airport needed a new runway and terminal when BAA took over in 1971, and approval was granted in 1973 after a public inquiry, although there were significant objections from some local communities. Traffic also grew steadily at Edinburgh, with a slight downturn in 2008–2010, and by 2017 was at 13.4 million passengers. The 2003 White Paper supported the option of a second parallel runway at Edinburgh by 2020. Although this would have had some environmental challenges in terms of its impact on the River Almond, it would help to reduce the noise impact at Cramond, the community most affected by the new runway in the 1970s. BAA duly brought forward a master plan for a two-runway airport in 2005 but the plan was not progressed. Edinburgh Airport was sold to Global Infrastructure Partners, the owners of London Gatwick, in 2012, for £800 million. The 2016 master plan still shows land that might be required for a second runway, but the date is now considered to be beyond 2040 (Edinburgh Airport, 2016). Nevertheless, the fact that the land is safeguarded may well prove to be very appropriate if the airport does seek approval to proceed sometime in the next 20 years. However, as discussed in Chapter 9, it is notable that this did not sway the decision not to support a second runway at Gatwick (where land had been safeguarded) rather than a third runway at Heathrow (where it had not).

As there are three airports serving Lowland Scotland, plans for a single large airport to serve the two major cities have surfaced from time to time, for example at the Edinburgh Airport Inquiry of 1972. The proposal arose again in the 2002 consultations but the majority of respondents opposed it and the 2003 White Paper did not support it.

There may be some lessons from Scotland for South East England. One of the differences is that there was a surplus of capacity, albeit in the wrong place (at Prestwick). A second difference is that demand has not yet reached a level where any of the airports are operating at their full capacity, so the decisions on their expansion are a long way ahead. However, one of the lessons that could be applied is that, despite this long timescale, safeguarding and land acquisition are taking place, which could make the eventual implementation of additional runways somewhat easier.

11.6.2 North of England

In the North of England, there are two issues that have been particular features of the way airports policy has developed: the number of airports and the role of Manchester. The 2003 White Paper discussed ten airports in the region and in the 2011 Census the population was 14.9 million, with the main urban centres in Manchester and Merseyside, Leeds and Sheffield, and Newcastle. Some of the airports are close to each other and their catchment areas overlap, and there are also overlaps with Scottish airports to the north and Midlands airports to the south. It could therefore be argued that there are too many airports in the region, and it is clear that some have been able to grow while others have not. Manchester dominated the north-west for many years and made competition from nearby airports difficult. Blackpool Airport sought to compete with some LCCs and charter flights but, in 2014, it closed for commercial operations, although it remains open for general aviation. Liverpool Airport had a new runway in 1966 as the old runways were too short, and a new terminal adjacent to the new runway in 1986. The airport was sold by the local-authority owners in 1990 and is now owned by the Peel Group, which also owns other transport infrastructure and property across the North. Passenger numbers at Liverpool grew strongly between 1997 and 2007, in particular with LCCs, which did not expand at Manchester at this time, and have remained stable since then.

Yorkshire and Humberside has also seen competition between airports, with winners and losers. Leeds Bradford, in public ownership until 2007, handled 4.1 million passengers in 2017, having grown steadily, if not spectacularly, in the previous 20 years. A new airport opened in 2005 at Doncaster, developed on an old RAF airfield by the Peel Group, and grew rapidly to more than 1 million passengers, but then declined and only exceeded that figure again in 2016. Doncaster Airport has had several brand identities, but is now known as Doncaster Sheffield Airport, the latter city being larger and probably more well known, even though it is more distant (the airport is 18 miles/29 km from Sheffield compared with 3 miles/5 km from Doncaster). A new airport was opened in Sheffield in 1997 but, because of the limited site, it had only a short runway, although this was thought to be suitable for similar aircraft as operate at London City Airport. However, it never managed to attract many passengers and closed in 2008. Humberside Airport was owned by the local authorities until bought by the Manchester Airports Group in 1999, with the local authorities retaining a minority share. However, Manchester sold its shares in the airport in 2012 to the Eastern Group, which also operates Eastern Airlines. Although Humberside at one time handled more than half a million passengers, by 2016 it was down to 0.2 million.

Newcastle is more distant from its competitors and, as with other airports in the region, grew quickly in the 1990s and early 2000s, and in 2017 handled 5.3 million passengers. It is majority owned by seven local authorities, with a minority share owned by an Australian-based investor. One of Newcastle's current concerns is a possible loss of traffic to Edinburgh, given the Scottish government's plans to reduce Air Passenger Duty (APD). While aviation policy remains a reserved matter (meaning that decisions are made at a national level by the UK government), certain taxes, including APD, are devolved to Scotland. Teesside Airport has minority local authority ownership, with the majority owned by the Peel Group. It has declined rapidly in recent years, from 0.9 million to 0.1 million passengers, although attempts were made to rebrand it by calling it Durham Tees Valley Airport, and it now concentrates on non-commercial air-transport activities and some land has been earmarked for non-aviation development. Carlisle Airport serves a sparsely populated area and competes with Prestwick and Glasgow airports, but has also tried rebranding as Carlisle Lake District Airport. It is also the location of the headquarters of its owner, the Stobart Group, which also owns London Southend Airport and an airline.

The changing ownership and rebranding of a number of airports in the North of England shows that competition has resulted in different outcomes, with Liverpool, Manchester, Leeds Bradford, Newcastle and probably Doncaster Sheffield doing well, while Blackpool, Sheffield City, Humberside, Durham Tees Valley and Carlisle have all had difficulties.

Manchester Airport is in a different league from the other airports in the North of England and handled 27.8 million passengers in 2017. It serves the whole of the North of England for a number of long-haul destinations, and also competes strongly in the leisure and short-haul markets. Manchester Airport is majority owned by ten local authorities, with the minority owned by Australian investors. In turn, the Manchester Airports Group (MAG) owns London Stansted, Bournemouth and Humberside Airports.

Manchester Airport led the North of England Regional Consortium (NOERC) at the 1981–1983 Airports Inquiries, which opposed the development of Stansted on the basis that demand should be diverted to the regions (see Chapter 6). As was discussed in Chapter 10, the regional theme was a feature of many of the studies and inquiries and, although many policies have sought to encourage the development of regional airports, it has never been policy to constrain the London airports as an attempt at diversion. However, by the time of the Terminal 5 Inquiry of 1995–1999, Manchester Airport had dropped its opposition and, as noted above, eventually became the owner of Stansted and now seeks to promote its growth.

Manchester Airport's particular claim to fame in terms of airports policy is that it gained approval for and built a second runway. The second runway is a close parallel design and was considered at a public inquiry in 1994–1995 and the issues included land acquisition, the green belt designation, ecology and noise. Economic arguments were made in favour of the new runway. There was significant opposition from a number of local groups and, after permission was granted in 1997, direct action took place on the site, although the protestors were eventually cleared (Butcher, 2010).

11.6.3 The Midlands

To an extent, the English Midlands also has an excess of airport capacity, and it is also squeezed between the South East's airports and Manchester. The two main airports are Birmingham and East Midlands, with smaller airports at Coventry and Wolverhampton. Coventry was at one stage hoping to attract significant traffic, but it has now settled for particular specialist roles for mail, freight and business aviation. Because of its central location, East Midlands has also established itself as a major air-freight hub for DHL, UPS and TNT, as well as providing leisure passenger flights. By 2017 it was handling 4.9 million passengers and 300 000 tonnes of freight, making it the UK's second-busiest freight airport, after Heathrow.

Birmingham Airport is the region's largest, handling 13 million passengers in 2017. It is now well established with a range of business, leisure, long- and short-haul flights. Seven local authorities own 49 per cent, the Ontario Teachers Pension Fund has 48.25 per cent, and the remaining shares are held by employees. The 2003 White Paper supported proposals for an extension to the existing runway to enable long-haul aircraft to operate, and a second runway to the west. The runway extension was approved in 2009 and completed in 2014. There was significant opposition to the second runway, in part due to the land that would need to be acquired, and the plans were not taken forward. However, a second runway in a different location, associated with the completion of the HS2 rail project and plans for a major commercial development to the east of the airport (the Birmingham Gateway), has appeared on plans. Birmingham Airport promoted the idea of a second runway in its proposals to the Airports Commission, which were based on significantly improved connectivity provided by HS2. The Airports Commission did not agree and also noted the relatively high noise impacts, so the proposal was not taken forward, although the Commission did suggest that it should remain an option for the longer term (Airports Commission, 2013).

The 2003 White Paper also considered a new airport option, to replace both Birmingham and East Midlands. Although this would have reduced the noise impact at the existing airports, there were other environmental and social impacts and the White Paper did not support the proposal.

11.6.4 Regional conclusions

Overall, the examples from the rest of the UK outside London and the South East show that there is generally enough capacity, at least in terms of runways, and therefore the very controversial proposals for acquiring land for new runways are few and far between. It may also be the case that some local ownership of these airports has meant a better alignment of interests, and the need to 'rebalance' the UK's economic geography has meant that there is often good local support for the economic benefits. However, one factor tends to hang over the development of regional airports policy, and that is the willingness of airlines to serve the airports. This was partly covered in Chapter 2, where it was noted that airports succeed where the airlines that serve them succeed. British Airways' attitude to regional airports has been the subject of some criticism over the years, but the fact is that, like any other commercial airline, they have no obligation to run a route that is loss-making. BA and its predecessor BEA once had an extensive domestic network, with hubs at many UK airports, but these have been cut back such that BA now concentrates on feeding its Heathrow hub from eight regional airports, as well as providing for point-to-point demand at both Heathrow and London City. The gaps have been partly filled by other airlines with lower cost structures, and also by links with European hubs (particularly Amsterdam) to meet the demand for long-haul routes. Some cities that have lost their Heathrow link have been very supportive of a third Heathrow runway because it comes with a promise that these links can be restored. Where the regions have done well is in serving the local demand for short-haul flights, with charters and LCCs providing an extensive range of European destinations. For some regional airports, the holy grail is a long-haul service, and some have achieved this on a limited basis with transatlantic flights, but more recently the Middle East carriers have provided an alternative way of flying to the east via their hubs. One element of government policy that can assist is the subsidisation of routes. This is possible under EU law if the destination is in a peripheral region, or if there is some particular economic reason, but the circumstances are limited.

It can therefore be concluded that, in overall terms, there is unlikely to be a need for major policy decisions outside London and the South East (for example, for a new runway) for many years. In the meantime, the local policies of land safeguarding and acquisition would seem to be the best way to keep options open. That is not to say there will not be many controversial local issues to deal with, such as new flight paths, terminal and other capacity expansions and improving sustainability, many of which will require policy support. However, there seems to be little appetite, or need, for a prescriptive national policy, rather one that enables local economic and environmental issues to be considered in a national framework, which can then lead to rational decisions.

11.7. Conclusion – do others do it better?

The main question to ask is 'Do any countries do airports policy better than the UK?' Some of London's competitors in the rest of Europe, such as Amsterdam and Paris, seem to have planned ahead better, so that there is spare capacity, and less environmental impact. The Frankfurt and Munich examples show that airports policy has not been easy in Germany, and the current difficulties with the new Berlin airport have added another twist. North American airports have been developed where there has been land available, but more difficulties have arisen in the older cities, like New York. Local politics influences the way in which US airports develop, although often ownership by the city or state ensures that the economic benefits are given greater weight. The Western concept of democracy does not operate in all countries in the Middle East and East and South East Asia, which means that, where a country's economy is growing, it has been possible to expand airport capacity very quickly. The long sagas of Montreal Mirabel in Canada and the Western Sydney Airport in Australia show that some countries' experiences are worse than the UK. The non-London UK examples are difficult to compare with London, other than to note that, perhaps as in the USA, local ownership ensures that economic considerations are given higher weight in any decisions.

REFERENCES

Airport Watch (2017) The 200th Frankfurt airport Monday Demo (Montagsdemo) against the noise will be on 30th January. Airport Watch website, 7 January 2017. www.airportwatch.org.uk/2017/01/the-200th-frankfurt-airport-monday-demo-montagsdemo-against-the-noise-will-be-on-30th-january (accessed 1 September 2017).

Airports Commission (2013) *Interim Report*. HMSO, London, UK.

Airports Commission (2015) *Final Report*. HMSO, London, UK.

Allett T (2017) Battle against the ban. *Airports International* **50(4)**: 6–8.

Anon (1988) Denver Airport plan is passed. *New York Times*, 18 May 1988. www.nytimes.com/1988/05/18/us/denver-airport-plan-is-passed.html (accessed 1 September 2017).

Anon (2017a) Austrian court overturns Vienna Airport extension ban. Airwise website, 29 June 2017. http://news.airwise.com/story/austrian-court-overturns-vienna-airport-extension-ban (accessed 1 September 2017).

Anon (2017b) Construction contract awarded for the future Mexico City Airport. *Airports International*, 11 January 2017. www.airportsinternational.com/2017/01/construction-contract-awarded-for-the-future-mexico-city-airport/18387 (accessed 1 September 2017).

Bentley D (2014) Unravelling the UK airport capacity conundrum: a review of the main submissions made to the Airports Commission. *Journal of Airport Management*: **8(1)**: 14–22.

Butcher L (2010) *Aviation: Manchester's second runway, 1993–2001*. SN/BT/101, House of Commons Library, London, UK.

de Neufville R and Odoni A (2003) *Airport Systems Planning, Design and Management*, 2nd edition. McGraw-Hill, London, UK and New York, USA.

Department for Transport (2003) *The Future of Air Transport*. Cmnd 6046, HMSO, London, UK.

Department for Transport (2013) *Aviation Policy Framework*. HMSO, London, UK.

Department of Trade (1975) *Airport Strategy for Great Britain: Part 1 The London Area*. HMSO, London, UK.

Department of Trade (1976) *Airport Strategy for Great Britain: Part 2 The Regional Airports*. HMSO, London, UK.

Department of Trade (1978) *Airports Policy*. Cmnd 7084, HMSO, London, UK.

Edinburgh Airport (2016) *Masterplan 2016–2040*. https://s3-eu-west-1.amazonaws.com/edinburghairport/files/2016/11/Edinburgh_Airport_Masterplan_15112016.pdf (accessed 13 August 2018).

Eurocontrol (2013) *Challenges of Growth 2013*. www.eurocontrol.int/sites/default/files/content/documents/official-documents/reports/201307-challenges-of-growth-summary-report.pdf (accessed 13 August 2018).

Fitzgerald P (1999) Sydney Airport's third runway: a case study of flawed EIS processes. *Urban Policy and Research* **17(2)**: 123–130.

Forsyth P (2008) Airport policy in Australia and New Zealand: privatization, light-handed regulation, and performance. In *Aviation Infrastructure Performance: A Study in*

Comparative Political Economy (Winston C and Rus G de (eds)). Brookings Institution Press, Washington, DC, USA, pp. 65–99.

Glasgow Airport (2011) *Our Vision: Glasgow Airport Draft Master Plan 2011*. www.glasgowairport.com/media/1686/master-plan.pdf (accessed 13 August 2018).

Healey P (2004) The treatment of space and place in the new strategic spatial planning in Europe. *International Journal of Urban and Regional Research* **28(1)**: 45–67.

May M and Hill S (2006) Questioning airport expansion – a case study of Canberra International Airport. *Journal of Transport Geography* **14**: 437–450.

Morrison S and Winston C (2008) Delayed! US aviation infrastructure policy at a crossroads. In *Aviation Infrastructure Performance: A Study in Comparative Political Economy* (Winston C and Rus G de (eds)). Brookings Institution Press, Washington, DC, USA, pp. 7–35.

Thompson G (2002) Mexico drops planned airport after protests from peasants. *New York Times*, 3 August 2002. www.nytimes.com/2002/08/03/world/mexico-drops-planned-airport-after-protests-from-peasants.html (accessed 1 September 2016).

Willsher K (2018) France abandons plan for €580m airport and orders squatters off site. *The Guardian*, 17 January 2018. www.theguardian.com/world/2018/jan/17/france-abandons-plan-for-580m-airport-in-west-of-country (accessed 14 February 2018).

Zhang A and Yuen A (2008) Airport policy and performance in mainland China and Hong Kong. In *Aviation Infrastructure Performance: A Study in Comparative Political Economy* (Winston C and Rus G de (eds)). Brookings Institution Press, Washington, DC, USA, pp. 159–192.

Zupan J, Barone R and Lee M (2011) Upgrading to world class: the future of the New York Region's airports. Regional Plan Association, New York, USA.

Le Blond, P
ISBN 978-0-7277-6365-5
https://doi.org/10.1680/ilap.63655.161
ICE Publishing: All rights reserved

Chapter 12
The future

12.1. What could happen in the next 40 years?

In a book about the past, it is probably foolish to try to predict the future, especially having noted how difficult it is to forecast it (see Niels Bohr's quote in Chapter 10). I will instead suggest a number of scenarios, and leave it to the reader to consider which of these, if any, are more or less likely. A period of 40 years is sufficiently far into the future that short-term fluctuations can be ignored. Indeed, I would be less confident about the next five years than about the long term over decades. I will consider the following scenarios

- no new runways
- Heathrow third runway
- Gatwick second runway
- Heathrow third runway and Gatwick second runway
- Gatwick second runway and Stansted second runway
- other scenarios.

12.1.1 No new runways

In this scenario, the third runway at Heathrow does not get built, for whatever reason, and no other new runways are built in the South East of England before the middle of the century. Of course the reasons for not building it are important. If it is because the growth in demand has flattened out, then planners may begin to consider this as a long-term trend. If it is because it has failed to gain permission or that policy has changed, there will be continual pressure on slots at Heathrow. In any event it will have little impact in the short term, as the new runway would not have been available before the mid 2020s. However, the industry will begin to plan for a two-runway Heathrow and a one-runway Gatwick and this is likely to result in a number of changes.

The first and most obvious effect of limiting Heathrow to two runways (and Gatwick to one runway) would be a growth of aircraft size. We have seen how this factor has changed in the past and how the simple arithmetic leads to the current average load of about 160 passengers per aircraft movement (80 million passengers a year divided by 500 000 aircraft movements). If average loads were 200 passengers, 500 000 aircraft movements would deliver 100 million passengers. An average load of 200 passengers (a modest 0.6 per cent annual growth rate over 40 years), at 80 per cent load factor, is an average aircraft size of 250. This is significantly larger than the current typical short-haul aircraft, the Airbus A320 and Boeing 737, but could be a target for the next generation of short-haul types, which could be in service within 40 years. In the medium term, it is possible that versions of larger types, such as the Airbus A350 and Boeing 787, carrying up to 300 passengers, could be developed for short-haul operations. It is certainly possible within current types to see the replacement of the A319 (130 seats) with the A320 (160 seats) and the A321 (200 seats). For long-haul aircraft, the A380 (500 seats) is extensively used at Heathrow, but there are still many routes where the Boeing 777 (350 seats) is the norm, and also many new routes using smaller types (e.g. the Boeing 787).

As well as using larger aircraft, airlines may consider altering frequencies. For long-haul flights, some routes operate at relatively high frequency (e.g. British Airways Heathrow–New York JFK is eight per day). It is possible that airlines might consolidate such flights, particularly with code-sharing partners. It is also possible that airlines will drop (or not start) marginal routes that operate at low frequencies. Similarly for short haul, high-frequency routes can be consolidated and low-frequency routes dropped. Perhaps most at risk would be the domestic flights that have been proposed if the third runway is delivered, and some of the lower-frequency routes now operated (e.g. Inverness, Leeds–Bradford), in particular as they tend to be operated by smaller aircraft.

Airlines have a short-term ability to flex their transfer product and, at Heathrow, this would be most so for British Airways. If BA wishes to fill otherwise empty seats on flights, it can lower the prices on connecting services to attract transfer passengers. In a scenario where flights are filled with demand from point-to-point passengers, it is possible to reduce the proportion of transfer passengers from the current level of around 30 per cent.

The inevitable effect of demand for runway slots exceeding capacity would be that the price increases. Slots are currently traded for upwards of £10 million per daily pair, and it would be very tempting for an airline to sell if they are being used for a marginal route. The impact on fares is also inevitable if demand exceeds capacity, and the airlines will be able to achieve higher yields. This would affect the UK economy in terms of tourism and trade, making the UK a more expensive place to visit and to do business in.

For Heathrow Airport, this scenario would also have a number of impacts. No new runway infrastructure would be built, but undoubtedly the airport would wish to invest to improve the efficiency and resilience of the existing runways. More larger aircraft stands would be needed, and this could be a challenge within the existing limited site. The terminals would need to be expanded, but this would appear possible with the schemes now planned. Some improvements to surface access would also be needed, particularly if the number of terminating passengers grows disproportionately as the percentage of transfer passengers falls. Again the current schemes would be more than adequate, but financial contributions from the airport would have to be lower, so perhaps the more marginal schemes, such as the southern rail link, would be more challenging to implement.

What impact would this scenario have on the local community surrounding Heathrow? The communities of Longford and Harmondsworth, which would have been demolished for a third runway, would be retained. In terms of noise, the impacts would be mixed. In total average noise terms, there is unlikely to be much difference, as larger aircraft are noisier than smaller types, but there would be fewer of them. In terms of individuals, there would be no flight paths associated with a new runway that would overfly people not currently affected, although there would be changes to routes, as are currently being implemented, in any event. It is almost certainly the case that this scenario would not enable a night ban to be implemented, as airlines would seek to use late and early flights as much as possible, given the shortage of slots. As noted above, an increase in the proportion of terminating passengers would have a disproportionate effect on road traffic, but employee-related traffic would be less than with a third runway, and overall traffic volumes would be less. In turn, this would make the achievement of legal limits for air quality less challenging.

What would the effect of having no additional runway capacity at Heathrow, or anywhere in the South East, have on other airports? Gatwick is already close to its capacity, so the ability to accommodate any more flights or passengers is limited. There could be a small impact on aircraft size, as described for Heathrow, but not in terms of frequencies as Gatwick's routes are not generally high frequency. The price of slots at Gatwick is also significantly less than at Heathrow. Luton has relatively limited scope to expand and is unlikely to be able to accommodate much of the excess demand. Stansted does have the capacity to accommodate more flights and, with additional terminal capacity, passenger numbers could continue to grow and some airlines may take the opportunity to establish new types of routes there. This would put pressure on the already creaking surface-access arrangements but could enhance the business case for improved rail infrastructure and services. The smaller London airports would also see growth, particularly London City, although the amount of capacity available there and at Southend is small in comparison with the shortfall.

Some airports outside the South East have proposed this scenario, and may achieve higher rates of growth in it. Birmingham Airport, with an HS2 station nearby, could attract some demand from north of London and Bristol Airport could attract some from the west of England. Other airports will lose frequency or even services to Heathrow.

Overall, this scenario will see growth significantly constrained by the lack of capacity, meaning a loss of business from the UK. Airlines and airports will adapt, but the price of air travel will rise. Some environmental impacts will be reduced, but less than proportionately to the reduction in aircraft movements. If demand continues to grow and the price of air travel rises, there will undoubtedly be attempts to redraft policy and there will be much debate about the degree of 'predict and provide' versus 'demand management'. Past experience says that this scenario is unlikely to come about through a definitive policy decision not to build new runways, rather as a result of the inability to implement policy decisions. This would then have the effect of not giving certainty and would leave the aviation industry and local communities around airports without a clear picture of the future.

12.1.2 Heathrow third runway

This is current (as of 2018) government policy and Parliament has approved the National Policy Statement, but the proposal has yet to be approved at a local inquiry. Even then, it is for Heathrow Airport to decide if it wants to implement the proposal, and its owners will have to decide if the investment will provide a return.

Nevertheless, this scenario assumes that these steps are completed, and the runway is built. The effect of this has been fully described in the work of the Airports Commission, and so is only summarised here so that comparisons can be made with the other scenarios.

While the new runway capacity may be released in stages (perhaps to meet environmental limits), it is likely that airlines will seek to fill the new capacity very quickly after it becomes available. Some of this might be for new routes and some for increased frequencies, but the immediate impact is likely to be a slowing down or even a reversal of the trend of increasing aircraft size. At least initially, BA, and maybe other airlines, will allocate more capacity to transfers. One intriguing possibility in this scenario is whether low-cost carriers (LCCs) would seek to establish services at Heathrow. A limited number of flights by LCCs already operate from Heathrow (Veuling, Eurowings) and some of the legacy airlines are morphing their short-haul services towards the low-cost model. EasyJet indicated at one stage that it would want to base 14 aircraft at Heathrow. The increase in the supply of slots should mean a fall in their value and fares should be held down, although there will need to be a careful balance with any additional costs that result from the investment. In turn, the impact on trade and tourism should be positive.

The infrastructure plans for a third runway have been well publicised, involving new terminals and airside concourses in addition to the runway and its associated taxiways, and a wide range of supporting facilities. The surface-access arrangements, including new rail links, have also been well described. The eventual infrastructure may be different from the current proposals, in particular as the airlines have expressed concern about the costs and, in any event, the requirements are likely to change over 40 years.

Similarly, the impacts on the community are fully described (although much disputed). Several hundred homes in Harmondsworth and Longford will be taken and their residents will have to move. Overall noise levels will be less than at present, but there will be significantly more aircraft movements and people not currently affected will be newly overflown. There will be a night ban, and a number of other mitigation and compensation packages. Achieving legal air-quality limits will be a challenge, as it will be in many UK cities. Despite the improved public transport, it will also be a challenge to limit road traffic, in order to keep within air-quality limits and avoid levels of congestion that would make the airport unworkable (as was nearly the case in the mid 1970s). These challenges could constrain the growth of Heathrow but are also likely to incentivise the introduction of radical new technologies and operating practices.

What will happen elsewhere? It is possible that an expanded Heathrow, especially if served by LCCs (or legacy airlines using the low-cost model), could absorb much of the growth over the decade or two after the new runway opens. Until then, growth at the other airports could be strong, but there would then be an immediate impact on their numbers. In the longer term, towards the end of the 40 years, it is likely that all South East airports would be operating close to their capacities. In the rest of the UK, regional airports would continue their growth, much as they have in the past decade, and several would gain new routes to Heathrow.

Overall, this scenario will see growth enabled, albeit not completely unconstrained, and the economic benefits should be significant. There will be changes in the environmental impact with some gains and some worsening, and it will be challenging to achieve the legal limits and targets. Certainty would be achieved for two or three decades, although undoubtedly the situation from around 2040 will require further policy decision-making.

This scenario is based on the recommended third runway option rather than the alternative extended northern runway option. The latter would have some of the characteristics of the third runway, although its proponents suggested that it would have many of the benefits but fewer of the disadvantages (such as the loss of residential property).

12.1.3 Gatwick second runway

For this scenario to happen, the third runway at Heathrow would not have been implemented, as in the first scenario considered. Note that a further scenario considers both the Heathrow third runway and the Gatwick second runway.

Although Gatwick Airport says it is ready to implement its second runway proposals, it is likely there would have to be further analysis before it became government policy. The Airports Commission concluded that it would be feasible but, given that its final report unanimously recommended Heathrow, it is unlikely that a failure to implement this recommendation would then mean that policy simply reverted to Gatwick. Before a new National Policy Statement could be drafted, it is likely that an independent group (perhaps a 'mini Airports Commission') would need to be established to review the evidence. Nevertheless, the process could lead to a policy supporting a Gatwick second runway, which could then be implemented with the following impacts.

The provision of a second runway at Gatwick could transform the airport and enable it to operate different types of services, in particular to business destinations. History shows us that airlines will be slow to take up the opportunities, but LCCs, both short and long haul, may be quicker and establish this wider range of services to capital cities. Most airlines currently at Heathrow will probably seek to remain there, and some of the impacts described in the first scenario, in terms of aircraft size, route frequency and transfer traffic, may well occur. But the difference will be that airlines will have the opportunity to establish new services at Gatwick and some will choose to do so.

Building the infrastructure at Gatwick would be relatively uncomplicated. The land is safeguarded and acquisition, although it would uproot some homes and businesses, would be straightforward. The biggest challenge at Gatwick is undoubtedly the need to improve rail access. The issue here is that the growth of non-airport passengers on the Brighton Main Line has resulted in the downgrading of the airport rail services and the inability to meet airport growth. Schemes to increase capacity on the Brighton Main Line exist, but are expensive, and require government action, so this element would be outside the airport's control.

The community impacts of a second runway at Gatwick have been documented in the Airports Commission's reports. Overall noise levels would increase, but the numbers are significantly less than those affected at Heathrow. There would be no real difficultly in achieving local air-quality limits. Undoubtedly, local communities and their representatives would put up a strong case against a second runway, and it would be interesting to see if the 'Tory grandees' (see Chapter 6) are still around and if they have any influence.

As noted above, most airlines would seek to remain at Heathrow. Stansted and Luton might see their growth curtailed. Birmingham Airport supported the Gatwick second runway proposal, perhaps on the basis that it would not compete for north-of-London business, but airlines wanting to serve London are more likely to choose a two-runway Gatwick over a one-runway Birmingham. Other UK airports might be able to retain or establish new domestic flights to Gatwick, but their viability would be less than to Heathrow because of the more limited transfer opportunities.

Overall, a Gatwick second runway would provide only part of a solution, as it would only partly relieve the pressure at Heathrow. Many airlines would be reluctant to move from Heathrow, but it could create opportunities for others. Environmental impacts would be less than at Heathrow, but not insignificant. It would provide certainty for a few years, but would probably lead to a need to reopen the policy questions later.

12.1.4 Heathrow third runway and Gatwick second runway

This scenario assumes that Heathrow's third runway is built and that demand at Gatwick continues to grow such that its owners believe there is a business case for a second runway. It would require a further government policy but, assuming this does not take place until after the Heathrow third runway is in operation, it would not be out of line with the Airports Commission's recommendations for the longer term (from 2040 onwards). Perhaps the most intriguing aspect of this scenario would be the reactions of airlines. Given a choice, history tells us that most airlines would prefer Heathrow but, if they are well established at Gatwick, would EasyJet and Norwegian prefer to grow there?

The infrastructure and impacts for this scenario would be as described above, except that the build-up would be slower, at least from the time that both new runways are in operation.

12.1.5 Gatwick second runway and Stansted second runway

This scenario follows from the Gatwick second runway described in section 12.1.3, and therefore assumes that a third Heathrow runway is ruled out forever, an assumption which history tells us is unlikely. As noted above, the initial impact of a Gatwick second runway would be to curtail growth at Stansted but, if South East demand continued to grow and there was nowhere else to accommodate it, a second runway at Stansted could be viable.

The infrastructure and impacts of a second runway at Gatwick have already been described, but little detailed attention has been given to a second runway at Stansted since BAA's G2 project of the 2000s. The current owners, Manchester Airports Group, made a submission to the Airports Commission with a range of options, including a closely spaced second runway, a wide-spaced runway, and a four-runway layout. Others, including Boris Johnson when he was the Mayor of London, also proposed a major expansion of Stansted, but these proposals were not examined in detail by the Commission. This scenario does not envisage a four-runway hub (which would replace Heathrow) and, indeed, if Heathrow and Gatwick both have two runways, a four-runway Stansted would simply not be viable. The options for close- or wide-spaced runways have their pros and cons (close spacing has less capacity but less land take) and the environmental impacts would be less than at Gatwick. However, as with Gatwick, the key challenge would be to provide sufficient surface access infrastructure and services. Unlike at Gatwick, this would be straightforward to provide by the four-tracking of the Lea Valley Line, the provision of a second rail tunnel beneath the airport, provision of an additional lane on the M11, and various other improvements.

12.1.6 Other scenarios

Undoubtedly there are other possible scenarios that could be envisaged, but I venture to suggest that they are less likely, or would contain elements of those described above. There are those who argue that air transport has reached a tipping point and that, with oil production declining and the effects of climate change becoming severe, air transport should and will decline. If this is apparent in the near future, then no new runways will be built and other growth plans will be curtailed.

None of the scenarios above includes the creation of a new major hub airport, either at Stansted or the Thames Estuary. Some argue for this, with the consequent closure of Heathrow, but history is not on their side. Perhaps if Maplin had not been cancelled in 1974, and Heathrow and Gatwick had been constrained within their then current boundaries and Stansted not developed, we might today have a major hub airport in the Thames Estuary with the necessary support infrastructure. But, whatever its merits, it is now too late, even taking a long-term view.

12.2. Learning from the past: how can we repeat successes and avoid mistakes?

Success means different things to different groups. To the air-transport industry and most of the business sector, success means having sufficient airport capacity to meet demand at a reasonable price. Most of the rest of the UK would probably agree, with the added proviso that the global impacts of aviation should not make life worse for future generations, for example with a concern about the impact on climate change. Local communities will have mixed views, in particular affected by the amount of disturbance, be that from noise, air quality, traffic congestion or other impacts, but balanced by the economic benefit of employment. The definition of mistakes, or failure, can probably achieve a wider degree of agreement, as nobody wants to see decisions overturned, policies reversed or promises broken.

No UK government is bound by the policies of its predecessors and herein lies the challenge. Our democracy is designed to ensure that the will of the country prevails and there have been two particular occasions, in 1974 and 2010, when a change of government brought about a significant change in airports policy. The new governments of 1974 and 2010 would of course argue that they were right to reverse the policy as the previous policy was wrong or had been overtaken by events. But were these decisions in the long-term interest of the country? A Thames Estuary hub airport has been considered from time to time but consistently rejected, so it could be argued that the 1974 cancellation was the right decision. The 2010 decision is more open to doubt, as the same government soon began a process which led to the reinstatement (albeit with some changes) of the proposal to build a third runway at Heathrow.

But not every change of government led to a change of airports policy. In 1979, the otherwise radical new Conservative government continued with the strategy that had evolved under a Labour administration. The radical change brought by the Conservative government was privatisation, but I contend that this had little impact on the development strategy, at least until the break-up of BAA in the late 2000s. In 1997, the New Labour government inherited a policy vacuum, but was then able to develop a long-term strategy, although it became too ambitious and failed to recognise fully increasing concerns about climate change. Policies also change without a change of government, as demonstrated by the 1985 decision not to proceed with a second runway at Stansted and to overturn the four-terminal limit at Heathrow. So, if we can't rely on governments to provide long-term consistency, what can we do? In my view there are two actions that can be taken: legal agreements and safeguarding land.

The legal agreement which is best known in airports policy is the 40-year deal struck between BAA and West Sussex County Council in 1979. Any legal agreement should be read in full, so a summary is incomplete, but in essence the deal was that BAA would not build a second runway, although it would be permitted to convert a taxiway to be used as an emergency runway, in return for the council not arguing that a second terminal (for which planning permission was being sought at that time) would lead to a second runway. Not everyone thought the agreement was a good thing, but it gave confidence to the local authorities, and perhaps to the wider local community. Roy Vandermeer, the inspector at the Heathrow Terminal 5 Inquiry, recognised that a legal agreement was the only effective and conclusive means of protecting against an additional runway (see Chapter 7). It did not stop a second runway being considered in a number of studies (RUCATSE in 1993, the 2003 White Paper and the Airports Commission), but none of these resulted in it being recommended. How influential the agreement was in these studies is difficult to judge, but Russell Sunderland's interpretation of the phrase 'have regard to' gives a clear steer (Sunderland was the civil servant who led the RUCATSE study; see Chapter 7). Although not the only factor, my view is that the confidence the agreement instilled also led to a good working relationship between Gatwick Airport and the local authorities, which facilitated the growth of the airport.

There are other types of legal agreement: for example, 'Section 106 agreements' (named after a section in the 1990 Planning Act) are often used to describe some detailed obligations agreed in return for planning permission. Lease agreements may relate to a particular piece of land (for example, the land at Southend and Biggin Hill airports is owned by the local authority and leased to the operator).

I am no lawyer, but it seems to me that the advantage of a legal agreement is that it requires both parties to agree and that, if they do not, it is settled in court, potentially with compensation payable to the aggrieved party. This seems to be a more straightforward and clear process than relying on politicians who are invariably swayed by the issues of the day. Would a legal agreement not to build a fourth runway at Heathrow work? The airport would, of course, have to be given something in return, and this could be an agreement to cooperate in making the impact of the third runway acceptable (whatever that may mean). Government would not be bound by such an agreement, of course, but undoubtedly would 'have regard to' it in any future policy studies.

Safeguarding land for future development is a well-established planning process that does not positively require that such land is used for the development, but prevents incompatible development and, probably more importantly, shows the local community that it is possible that it will be used in the longer term. The 2003 White Paper proposed that land at Heathrow, Gatwick and Stansted should be safeguarded, but only at Gatwick did the local authority implement this element of the policy. This safeguarding remains to this day, despite the 2010 policy of the coalition government. At Heathrow and Stansted, probably because the local authorities there were fundamentally opposed, the land was not safeguarded. Local planning processes, under which safeguarding can take place, are deliberately designed to take a long time, so that their policies endure, and it is somewhat ironic that the slowness of the process resulted in land at Heathrow not being safeguarded, although this is now evolving government policy, while land at Gatwick is safeguarded, although evolving government policy does not call for this. Objectors will, of course, oppose any such safeguarding, but a long-term view would suggest that the Gatwick safeguarding should remain and that land at Stansted should also be safeguarded. It is probably too late for Heathrow as, if the Development Consent Order (DCO) leads to the approval for a third runway, the scheme will have been implemented. Note that land for second runways at Glasgow and Edinburgh airports has been identified and may well be safeguarded in the local plans.

Beyond these two specific measures, what else can be done to avoid mistakes and achieve success? Incrementalism seems to have been successful as a strategy for providing for growth when and where it arises, but has limits when the increments are so large as to be very significant in terms of impacts, such as with a very large terminal or a new runway. Incrementalism is also unsatisfactory to local communities who want to know where it will all end. In my view, incrementalism, combined with a long-term view about the ultimate level of development in a defined timescale enshrined in a legal agreement, together with the safeguarding of land, is the right approach.

Finally, there is the issue of compensation. It is sometimes claimed that other countries are better at compensating those who are affected, although this is probably not true in less democratic states. Nevertheless, early, proactive and generous compensation may well ease the burden for those directly impacted. Compensation will not meet the needs of those who claim an unquantifiable loss, or those who believe that the growth of air transport is incompatible with our carbon targets, but it will help some. BAA's experience in acquiring land at Stansted in the early 1980s showed what could be done.

It is unlikely that any future airports policy will be satisfactory to all, but in my view, long-term certainty is a key objective. Government sometimes seeks this long-term view, but is rarely able to achieve consensus and, to be fair, circumstances change. But a robust interpretation of the phrase 'have regard to', which requires anyone wanting to change policy to have a pretty good reason for doing so, should be applied.

Chapter 13
Conclusions

13.1. Have the book's objectives been achieved?

The objectives of this book have been to describe how policy for the expansion of London's airports has evolved over the last 40 years or so and to see if there are positive or negative lessons to be learned to help in the future evolution of policy. Positive or negative could depend on your perspective, whether you are likely to benefit or be impacted by expansion, but it is clear that one element that seems to be sought by all sides is certainty. So the research tries to focus on the reasons for certainty when it occurred, and on why certainty was interrupted by uncertainty.

13.2. A reminder of the book's structure

The first few chapters of the book provide the background and context for the main research. Some of the issues covered make excellent research themes in their own right, and have been covered by other authors. But it is important to provide this context as it helps to explain the starting point for the main research, and many of the constraints which continue to be relevant, a prime example of which is the initial setting of Air Services Agreements between countries, which started at the end of World War 2.

What I have called the main research covers the period from the mid 1970s to the present day (at the time of writing, mid 2018). The mid 1970s was chosen for several reasons, not least because it was the start of my personal involvement in these issues, but it also marked one of those major decision points which have occurred occasionally. From that date, the studies, consultations, inquiries and decisions are described in some detail in a conventional timeline style, with attempts to provide context by noting other events of their time. For convenience, this part of the book is divided into four chapters, each scanning a decade or more, but which in some respects approximate to four different approaches to the evolution of policy. Nevertheless, a number of common themes are identified in each period and these are summarised at the end of each of these chapters.

The themes are brought together in Chapter 10, and it is noticeable that, despite different approaches of different governments and different circumstances, some themes do keep recurring, which makes the lack of continuity and uncertainty particularly frustrating. But this does enable some conclusions to be drawn.

After bringing these themes together, the book takes a brief look beyond London, to see if there are any common features with other parts of the world, and indeed other parts of the UK. There are some common themes, but it is probably fair to conclude that there are more unique aspects, not just for London, but for every part of the world.

Chapter 12 is an attempt to look into the future. It does not try to predict, but only provides 'what if' scenarios. However, if those in charge of policy can see some of the scenarios evolving, it is to be hoped that they can take some lessons from the past as to how to deal with them.

13.3. What methodologies were used in the research?
The methodology was described in Chapter 1, and in summary was to seek information from a variety of sources, including published documents, archived files, parliamentary records and personal interviews. These are complementary in that they each provide a different perspective of the same event and, occasionally, although rarely, different records.

13.4. A few final words
As at the date of publication, there is still no clear long-term airports policy for London. Perhaps there never will be, so the search for long-term certainty is pointless. However, although controversy remains, the current round of studies, consultations, inquiries and commissions is nearing the end of its process. A National Policy Statement has now been approved by Parliament supporting the provision of a third runway at Heathrow. Further steps are then required before the airport can be permitted to start building, including a local inquiry and, undoubtedly, legal challenges. There is then a question as to whether the airport will decide to proceed with the investment. But, for the time being, that is the path we are on.

Arguments about the pros and cons of expansion at Heathrow will therefore continue for several years, with issues such as acquiring homes, new flight paths, air-quality limits and road traffic continuing to be debated. Many claims and counter-claims will be made by opponents and supporters and they will seek to persuade decision-makers, including planning inspectors, judges and politicians, of the merits of their arguments. Any of the decision points could result in the proposals being delayed or abandoned but, if this does not happen, a decision to proceed could occur by the early 2020s. There would then be a period of construction, with the new runway opening some time in the later part of the decade.

And, after that, what then? History shows that, after a major new increment of airport capacity is provided, the pressure for the next step eases. Undoubtedly there will be other issues in aviation, and transport more generally, which will guide the agenda, for example autonomous and connected electric-powered vehicles. But at some stage, probably 10 to 15 years from now, we will be going through the whole process again. The question is, will we have learnt lessons from the past?

Further reading
Heathrow
Sherwood (2009) provides a history of the Heathrow area from prehistoric times, in particular describing the area before the airport came, and the story of how the airport was established in World War 2. Gallop (2005) is the story of Heathrow from the point of view of the people involved. Alan Gallop was a press man and was able to tell the stories of the crew of the first civil flights from the airport, the personalities and even the prehistoric residents who left behind their archaeological evidence. Woodley (2010) is a history of the airport's first 25 years until 1970. Anderson (2014) describes the airport from 1946 until more recently.

Gatwick
King (1986) looks at Gatwick's history from the 1930s, and Woodley (2014) looks at the airport's first 50 years.

Stansted
Sanders (2016) is a history of Stansted Mountfitchet from prehistoric times and includes some reflections on Stansted Airport.

In addition to these, Donne (1991) is the story of BAA, which commissioned the book, and covers all BAA's airports, including Stansted.

REFERENCES FOR FURTHER READING

Anderson I (2014) *Heathrow: From Tents to Terminal 5*. Amberley Publishing, Stroud, UK.

Donne M (1991) *Above Us The Skies: The story of BAA*. Good Books, Whitley, UK.

Gallop A (2005) *Time Flies: The Heathrow story*. The History Press, Stroud, UK.

King J (1986) *Gatwick: The Evolution of an Airport*. Sussex Industrial Archaeological Society, Sussex, UK.

Sanders P (2016) *On the Beaten Track: A History of Stansted Mountfitchet*. Stansted Mountfitchet Local History Society, Stansted Mountfitchet, UK.

Sherwood P (2009) *Heathrow: 2000 Years of History*. The History Press, Stroud, UK.

Woodley C (2010) *Heathrow Airport: The first 25 years*. The History Press, Stroud, UK.

Woodley C (2014) *Gatwick: The First 50 Years*. The History Press, Stroud, UK.

Index

(Airbus) 40, 50, 75, 138, 161
A350 (Airbus) 7, 42, 106, 161
A380 (Airbus) 44, 81, 89, 98, 138, 152, 161
Abercrombie's *Greater London Plan* (1944) 18
Abrahams, Stan 49, 88, 124, 125
Advisory Committee on Airports Policy (ACAP) 8, 53, 56, 57, 58, 59, 60, 61, 66, 70, 79, 128, 130, 132, 133, 135, 136
agricultural land 45, 58, 61–62
Air Passenger Duty 95, 118, 156
air quality and pollution 39, 44–45
 1991–1997 83
 1997–2010 87, 92, 94, 98
 2010 onwards 115, 117
 future 164
Air Services Agreements (ASAs) 6, 78
air transport history (to 1974) 3–15
Airbuses
 A320 40, 50, 75, 138, 161
 A350 7, 42, 106, 161
 A380 44, 81, 89, 98, 138, 152, 161
aircraft
 long-haul *see* long-haul operations
 movement
  forecasts 49, 63, 76, 77, 125
  limit at Heathrow 63, 65–66, 70, 86, 129
 short-haul, future perspectives 161, 162
 size 7, 49, 76, 77, 116, 126
  future and forecasts 88, 161–162, 163, 164
 technology 6–7
 see also engines
airlines 6
 1930s–1974 3, 7–8, 12
 1974–1991 50, 57, 62, 67
 1991–1997 75
 1997–2010 88
 2010 onwards 106, 117
 airport dependency on 7–9
 Asia and Middle East 150, 152, 153
 Europe 141, 142, 143–144, 144, 145

future perspectives 162, 163, 164, 165
 low cost *see* low-cost carriers
 North America 145–146, 148, 149
Airport Strategy for Great Britain 51, 127, 128, 130, 132
Airport Watch 93, 98, 108, 144
Airports Act (1986) 11, 66
Airports Bill 66, 133
Airports Commission 34, 36, 42, 108, 109, 110–117, 117, 118, 119, 127, 128, 129, 131, 133, 134–135, 137, 139, 143, 147, 154, 163, 164, 165, 166, 167
 Final Report 109, 115, 116–117, 139, 145, 164
 forecasts 110, 115, 125, 127
 Interim Report 110, 112, 116, 131
Airports Inquiries (1981–1983) 26, 32, 60, 61, 66, 80, 127, 133, 136, 154, 157
Airports Policy White Paper 130
Al Maktoum 152–153
Alderstafel (Alders Platform) 142
Ambrose, Geoff 21–22, 54, 55, 57, 58, 62, 65
analysis (reports/commissions/inquiries) 128–129
archaeology 45
Areas of Outstanding Natural Beauty (AONB) 28, 56
Arlanda 145
Ashpole, Hugh 55
Asia, South East 149–151
Australia 153
Austria 145
Aviation Policy Framework (APF 2011) 107, 108, 109, 133, 134

BA *see* British Airways
BAA (British Airports Authority) 1, 9–12, 19, 21
 1966–1974 9–12
 1974–1991 51, 53, 54, 55–56, 56, 57, 58, 60, 62, 62–63, 65, 66, 67–68, 69, 70
 1991–1997 77, 79, 81, 82
 1997–2010 92, 94, 95, 96, 100

173

BAA (British Airports Authority) (*continued*)
  2010 onwards 105, 109
  author and 80, 154
  Mulkern (John) as managing director 55, 56, 65
  themes related to evolution of policy 123, 125, 131, 132, 134, 135, 136
  West Sussex County Council (WSCC) and 55, 70, 92, 95, 136, 167
Back Heathrow 118, 135
Bancroft, Sir Ian 52
BEA (British European Airways) 5, 7–8, 50, 52, 53
Berlin 143, 144–145
Biggin Hill airport 97, 167
Birmingham 157, 163, 165
  second runway 97, 157
Blueprint for a Green Economy 99
BOAC (British Overseas Airways Corporation) 5, 7–8, 50, 52, 53
Boeings
  737 39, 50, 75, 138, 161
  747 40, 49, 53, 75, 76, 138
  777 94, 138, 162
  787 7, 42, 87, 106, 161, 162
Bristol Airport 78, 163
British Airports Authority *see* BAA
British Airways (BA) 50, 53, 94, 135
  British Midland Airways acquired by 157
  London City to New York 7
  regional airports and attitude of 158
  Tom Carter (formerly of BA) 52, 53, 57, 60, 65, 66, 79, 81, 110
  transfer passengers 162
British Caledonian (BCal) 8, 50, 138
British European Airways (BEA) 5, 7–8, 50, 52, 53
British Midland Airways 60
  acquired by BA 116
British Overseas Airways Corporation (BOAC) 5, 7–8, 50, 52, 53
British South American Airways (BSAA) 7–8
Bromma 145
BSAA (British South American Airways) 7–8
Buchanan, Colin 21, 60, 128
business aviation 97

Callaghan, James 51, 53, 55
Cameron, David 34, 99, 115, 117, 129, 136
Canada 149
carbon (carbon dioxide/CO_2) emissions 45, 108–109, 130, 145
  reduction/limitation 98, 99, 108–109, 127
  Sweden and Austria 145
Carlisle Airport 156

Carter, Tom 52, 53, 57, 60, 65, 66, 79, 81, 110
centralised planning, Europe 141–145
Changi 151
Channel Tunnel 30, 35
Charles de Gaulle (CDG) Airport 141–142
Chaulnes 142
Chep Lap Kok 150
Chicago 147
city-owned airports in USA 145–148
civil aviation, history 3, 4
Civil Aviation Act (1980) 60
Civil Aviation Act (2012) 106
Civil Aviation Authority (CAA) 8, 11, 51, 52, 88, 125
  1991–1997 76, 77, 84
  forecasts 125
civil service after Maplin cancellation 51, 52, 70
ClearSkies 93
Cliffe 89
Climate Camp 118
climate change (and global warming) 39, 44, 44–45, 7536, 87, 88–89, 90, 100, 107, 108–109, 118, 129, 130, 166
combustion products 44, 130
commitments *see* promises and commitments
compensation 168
Competition Commission 11, 12, 94, 95, 139
Computable General Equilibrium (CGE) 110
Concorde 35, 50, 83, 87
connecting flights *see* transfer passengers
Conservative Party 49, 66, 98–99, 99, 100, 117
  in government 9, 34, 51, 58, 66, 69, 83, 105–119, 167
  Cameron (David) 34, 99, 115, 117, 129, 136
  coalition with Liberal Democrats (2010–15) 34, 98–99, 100, 105–106
  decisions and further steps following Airports Commission 117–118
  Heath (Edward) as leader of 21, 49
  Thatcher (Margaret) as leader 51, 58, 60, 64, 65, 75, 83
constituencies 55, 78
  geography 32
  regional issues 127–128
consultations 131–135
  national, on long-term strategy 87–90
cost–benefit analysis 25
  Roskill Commission 20, 21, 128
Court Line 8, 50
Coventry/West Midlands 127, 157
Crossrail 82–83, 109
Croydon 17

Cublington 20, 21, 57, 59, 128

Dallas Fort Worth 146–147
Darling, Alistair 27, 90, 92, 93
Davies, Sir Howard 110–111, 115, 116, 117
decision-making 34–36
  incremental *see* incremental decision-making
  rational 34–35, 36
demand (air transport)
  forecasting *see* forecasts
  future perspectives 162, 163
  historical perspectives 4–5
democracy in SE Asia/Middle East, limited 149–151
denationalisation *see* privatisation
Denver Airport 146, 147
Department of the Environment, Transport and the Regions (DETR) 80, 83
  Future of Aviation (2000) 88, 89, 90
Department of Trade (DoT) 27, 41, 53, 56, 58, 132, 135, 154
Department of Transport (Department for transport; DfT; DTp) 27, 29, 64, 65, 77, 78, 93, 97, 108, 117, 125
Development Consent Order (DCO) 29, 117, 118, 135, 168
devolved planning, Europe 141–145
Doganis, Rigas (Professor) 62
Doha 153
Doncaster Sheffield Airport 156
Dorval Airport 149
drainage 46
Dubai 152–153
Dulles Airport 147
Durham Tees Valley Airport 156

East Midlands Airport 157
EasyJet 9, 75, 87, 97, 117, 163, 165
ecological impact 45, 62, 79, 82, 155
economic dimensions of climate change (Stern report) 87, 98
economic growth in SE Asia/Middle East 149–151
economic recessions (financial crises)
  1990s 75
  2008 onwards 87, 94, 95, 96, 97, 105, 106, 155
economies, local 26–27
Edinburgh 127, 135
  second runway 97, 135, 155
Egan, John 75, 76, 81
elections (general) 32, 35
  1974 49
  1979 51, 58
  1992 31

  1997 83, 87
  2001 87
  2005 87
  2010 34, 87, 96, 99, 100, 105, 109, 134
  2015 34, 105, 115, 139
  2017 32, 106, 117, 119
  consequences of change of government 166–167
Emirates Airlines 152, 153
emissions 40, 43–44, 45, 46, 130
  trading 6, 45, 87, 98, 106, 108
  Vienna Airport 145
engines
  design 6, 7
  emissions *see* emissions
  noise *see* noise
environmental issues 39–48, 137–138
  2010 onwards 106, 107, 108, 112, 115, 116, 117, 118
  aircraft technology 7
  climate change/global warming 39, 44, 44–45, 7536, 87, 88–89, 90, 100, 107, 108–109, 118, 129, 166
Equivalent Continuous A-weighted Level (LA_{eq} 41, 42, 129, 137
Europe (and EU) 5–6, 12, 141–145
  centralised and devolved planning 141–145
  pollutants 44
  referendum on leaving the EU 106, 117, 139
Extended-range Twin engine Operational Performance Standards (ETOPS) 7, 67
Eyre, Graham (Inspector) 60, 63, 64, 79, 135

farming (agricultural) land 45, 58, 61–62
Ferrovial (Group) 10, 11, 95, 100, 155
financial crises *see* economic recessions
First World War (WWI) 3
Flying Matters 93, 118
forecasts 123–127
  Airports Commission 110, 115, 125, 127
  'predict and provide' 89, 90, 97, 99, 123, 126, 163
Foulness *see* Maplin
France 141–142
Frankfurt 142–144
Franz Joseph Strauss Airport 144
Freedom to Fly 93, 98
future 161–168, 169
  long-term strategy *see* long-term strategy
Future Heathrow 93, 98
The Future of Air Transport (2003 White Paper) 43, 44, 87, 90–93, 93, 95, 96–97, 98, 99, 107, 108, 126, 127, 132, 133, 134, 136, 137, 138, 154, 155, 157, 167

175

Future of Aviation (2000) 88, 89, 90

G1 (Generation 1) Project 51, 95, 96, 98, 133
G2 (Generation 2) Project 95, 96, 165–166
Gatwick (Airport) 8, 54–56
  air passenger forecasts 126
  in Airports Commission 111, 112, 115
  Gatwick–Heathrow transfers (Airlink) 55, 55–56
  Heathrow flights moved to 8, 51, 55
  noise 42, 43
  North (new second) Terminal 54–56, 60, 62, 65, 67, 70, 75, 95, 124, 126, 129, 130, 132, 136
  ownership 10
  post-war expansion 19–20
  promises regarding 136
  second runway 19, 43, 52, 53, 55, 57, 58, 77, 78, 79, 88, 89, 90, 92, 95, 105, 109, 111, 112, 115, 117, 136, 164–166, 167
    consequences of having it 164–166
    consequences of no runway 162–163
    Heathrow third runway and 165
    Stansted second runway and 165–166
Gatwick Express 69, 109
general elections *see* elections
General Permitted Development Order (GPDO) 29, 54
Generation 1 (G1) Project 51, 95, 96, 98, 133
Generation 2 (G2) Project 95, 96, 165–166
Germany 142–144
Glasgow Airport 97, 155, 156
global dimensions 5–6, 8, 141–153
Global Infrastructure Partners (GIP) 10, 11, 97, 155
global warming and climate change 16, 39, 44, 44–45, 7536, 87, 88–89, 90, 100, 107, 108–109, 118, 129, 130
Goldsmith, Zac (MP) 32, 33, 99
government *see* Conservative party; elections; Labour Party; politics and policy
GPDO (General Permitted Development Order) 29, 54
Grant, Bernie (MP) 69
Grayling, Chris 117
Greater London Plan, Abercrombie's (1944) 18
green belt 28, 45, 56, 59, 79, 81, 82, 83, 89, 157
Greener by Design 93, 118
Greening, Justine 107, 108
Griffins, Roy 66, 94, 117
Gross Value Added 26
groundside access arrangements 49–50
growth (economic) in SE Asia/Middle East 149–151

Gummer, John 33, 99

Hall, Peter (professor) 19, 54, 59
Hammond, Phillip 106, 107
Haneda 150
Harmondsworth 162, 164
Haselhurst, Sir Alan (MP) 32, 55, 67, 78, 94
health impact 46, 107
Heath, Edward 21, 49
Heathrow 54–56, 163–164
  air passenger forecasts 126
  aircraft movement limit 63, 65–66, 70, 86, 129
  in Airports Commission 110, 111, 112, 115, 116, 117
  flights moved to Gatwick 8, 51, 55
  fourth runway 110, 111, 117, 150, 167
  Gatwick–Heathrow transfers (Airlink) 55, 55–56
  groundside access arrangements 49–50
  historical overview (pre-1974) 4, 6, 7–9, 13, 18, 19–20
  local community 162
  noise 42, 53
    Terminal 5 83, 132, 135
    see also Heathrow Association for the Control of Aircraft Noise
  ownership 10
  surface access 69, 79, 82
  Terminal 1 52, 106, 143
  Terminal 2 (new) 106, 139
  Terminal 3 52, 143
  Terminal 4 (fourth terminal) 1, 20, 52, 54, 55, 60, 62, 63, 65, 67, 69, 70, 79, 80, 126, 130, 135, 136
  Terminal 5 (fifth terminal) 2, 11, 28, 30–31, 53, 57, 58, 63, 65, 66, 67, 68, 70, 75–76, 77, 79–84, 88, 90, 129, 131, 133–134, 139
    broken promise not to build 135–136
    Inquiry 75, 76, 79–84, 126, 129, 136, 157, 167
    noise 83, 132, 135
    opening 94, 99, 139
  third runway 1, 2, 29, 30, 43, 44, 53, 80, 81–82, 83, 89, 90, 91–92, 92, 94, 95, 98, 99, 115, 116, 117, 119, 131, 133, 135, 143, 144, 145, 163–164
    broken promise not to build 136
    consequences of having it 163–164
    consequences of no runway 162–163
    future perspectives 161, 162, 163–164, 165
    Gatwick second runway and 165
    north-south 143
    north-west 111, 114, 115, 116, 117, 118
    northern extended 111, 113, 115, 164

south-west 111
support and opposition groups 119
unwanted/promise not to build/cancellation 105, 117, 136
Heathrow Association for the Control of Aircraft Noise (HACAN) 54, 82, 93, 95, 108, 111, 112, 118, 119
Heathrow Connect 82, 109
Heathrow Express 9–11, 69, 79, 82, 83, 109
High Speed 1 (HS1) 30
High Speed 2 (HS2) 30, 108, 109, 157, 163
Highways Agency 82, 95
historical buildings and sites 45
history (the past)
   learning from 166–168
   pre-1974 3–23
   of urban planning 25
Hoggeston 56, 57
Hong Kong 150
Hoon, Geoff 94, 95
hourly rates/capacity 124
House of Commons *see* elections; Parliament
House of Lords 30, 60, 69, 78, 118
HS1 (High Speed 1) 30
HS2 (High Speed 2) 30, 108, 109, 157, 163
hub airport (Thames Estuary) 111, 166
Huhne, Chris 106–107
Humberside Airport 156

IATA (International Air Transport Association) 5, 6, 57, 62, 118
ICAO (International Civil Aviation Organisation) 5, 40, 45, 107, 108, 138
incremental decision-making 35, 46, 49–73
   long-term strategies vs 130–131
infrastructure, transport, planning 27
inquiries (public) 132–135
   Airports Inquiries (1981–1983) 26, 32, 60, 61, 66, 80, 127, 133, 136, 154, 157
   Heathrow Terminal 5 75, 76, 79–84, 126, 129, 136, 157, 167
International Air Transport Association (IATA) 5, 6, 57, 62, 118
International Civil Aviation Organisation (ICAO) 5, 40, 45, 107, 108, 138
international dimensions 5–6, 8, 141–153
interwar years 3, 17
Isle of Grain 111

Japan 150–151
JFK International 148
Johnson, Boris 27, 107, 166

Kai Tak 150
Kansai 150–151
Kingsford Smith Airport 153
Kuala Lumpur 151
Kyoto Protocol 44, 88–89, 129

Labour Party
   Callaghan (James) 51, 53, 55
   in government 8, 20, 33, 34, 87–100
      New Labour 35, 75, 87–100, 109, 116, 131, 167
   Hoon and 94, 95
   Wilson (Harold) leader of 51, 96
LaGuardia 148
Laker's Skytrain 8, 50
land
   agricultural 45, 58, 61–62
   safeguarding 167–168
Langley 56, 57
Lawson, Nigel 66, 67
Le Bourget 141
legal agreements 167
   BAA and West Sussex County Council 55, 70, 81, 136, 167
Liberal Democrats 32, 33, 109, 118
   coalition with Conservatives (2010–15) 34, 98–99, 100, 105–106
Liverpool Airport 127, 156
local communities 131, 132
   economies 26–27
   future perspectives 162, 164, 165, 166, 167, 168
   Heathrow 162
Localism Act (2011) 29, 117, 135
Lockheed TriStar 40, 49, 50, 53, 76
London Britannia Airport 111
London City Airport 7, 9, 68–69, 97, 163
   ownership 10, 11
London Gateway Airport 111
London Mayors 27, 87, 99, 107, 111, 166
London Underground Piccadilly line 50, 69, 82, 83, 109, 125
long-haul operations 67, 127
   future perspectives 161, 162
   history 3, 8, 9, 154, 157, 158
long-term strategy 87–90, 100, 138–139, 167–168, 170
   incremental decision-making vs 130–131
   kicked into long grass (post-2010) 107–109, 139
   national consultations 87–90
   White Paper (2003) 43, 44, 87, 90–93, 93, 95, 96–97, 98, 99, 107, 108, 126, 127, 132, 133, 134, 136, 137, 138, 154, 155, 157, 167

177

Longford 162, 164
low-cost carriers (LCCs) 75, 87, 95, 96–97, 117, 127, 128, 147, 148, 156, 158
  Heathrow 163, 164
  history 5, 8–9, 12
Luton Airport 9, 51, 52, 53, 64, 75, 92, 96–97, 163
  air passenger forecasts 126
  Court Line 8, 50
  ownership 10, 11
  replacement runway 92

M4 46, 69, 82
M11 62, 91, 166
M23 55
M25 56, 58, 67, 79, 82
M40 75
McDermid, Alastair 62, 68, 115
McDonnell, John 89, 94
McLoughlin, Patrick 27, 108
Maiden, Stan 62, 81, 123, 125, 128
Major, John 79
Malaysia 151
Manchester (airport) 11, 61, 111, 127, 156–157
  second runway 97, 127, 157
Manchester Airports Group 10, 11, 111, 156, 157, 166
Maplin (Airport project-Foulness) 1, 21–22, 51, 56, 57, 59, 60, 116, 128
  cancellation 22, 49, 51, 70, 139, 142, 166
  noise and 50
Masefield, Peter 21–22
May, Theresa 92, 106, 117, 136
Mayors of London 27, 87, 99, 107, 111, 166
Members of Parliament *see* constituencies; MPs
Metrotidal Tunnel and Thames Reach Airport 111
Mexico (and Mexico City) 149
Middle East 151–152
Midlands 157
Midway (Chicago) 147
Mirabel (Montreal) 149
mistakes, avoiding 166–168
Monte-Carlo approach 110
Montreal 149
motorways *see* M4; M11 *etc.*
MPs (Members of Parliament) 19, 32–33, 64, 66, 78, 89, 93, 118, 127–128, 132–133
  see also constituencies
'muddling through' planning policy 34–36
Muirhead, Geoff 111
Mulkern, John 19, 55, 56, 65
multi-airport cities or regions 12, 18, 131
Munich 144

Narita 150
National Airport (Washington) 147
National airports plan in USA 146
National Archives 51, 52, 58, 64, 66, 76, 87
national consultations on long-term strategy 87–90
National Infrastructure Plan 107–108, 108
National Parks 28
National Policy Statement (NPS) 1, 29, 117–118, 133, 135, 141
Nationally Significant Infrastructure Project (NISPs) 29
  Development Consent Order (DCO) for 29, 117, 118, 135, 168
Netherlands 142
New Jersey Newark 148
New York 148
A New Deal for Transport (1998 White Paper) 83, 87, 87–88
Newark 148
Newcastle Airport 156
nitrous oxide emissions (NO$_x$) 43–44, 107
noise 39, 43, 46, 47, 134, 137–138
  1974–1991 50, 51, 53, 54, 57, 58
  1991–1997 83
  1997–2010 89, 92, 93, 98
  2010 onwards 107, 112
  Terminal 5 and 83, 129, 132, 135
Norris, Steven (MP) 31, 32, 33, 34, 78, 99, 115
North America 145–149
North of England airports 15–16
North of England Regional Consortium (NOERC) 61, 62–63, 65, 127, 157
North West Essex and East Hertfordshire Preservation Association (NWEEHPA) 19, 57, 89
Northolt (RAF) 8, 17, 19, 90, 97
Nott, John 1, 57, 58, 59

Office of Fair Trading 11
O'Hare 147
Orly 141, 142
Osaka 150–151
ownership of airports 9–12

Paris 141–142
Parliament (incl. House of Commons) 1, 32, 33, 64, 65, 133, 135, 137, 170
  debates 32–33, 37, 37, 54, 64, 66, 118, 133
  MPs *see* constituencies; MPs
  Transport Committee 33, 67, 79, 90, 95, 116, 118
  see also elections; House of Lords

Index

Payne, Norman 21–22, 58, 65, 67, 68, 75
peak-to-off-peak ratios 124
Perry Oaks sludge works site 28, 52, 54, 64, 67, 68, 69, 79, 80, 136
Phillips, John 67, 76
Piccadilly line 50, 69, 82, 83, 109, 125
Plane Stupid 119
planning (policy) and strategies 25–38
   1920s–1974 17–38
   1974–1991 47–73
   1991–1997 75–85
   1997–2010 87–103
   2010 onwards 105–122
   analysis 128–129
   evolution 25
   long-term *see* long-term strategy
   'muddling through' 34–36
   outside UK 141–143
   politics and 31–33
   regional 26–27, 28, 46, 56, 77, 78, 80
   short-term 106–107, 131
   transport 27
   UK planning system 28–30
   vacuum/indecision 1, 75–85
     avoiding 138–139
Planning Act (2008) 29, 31, 83, 117, 135, 167
policy-planning *see* planning
political parties 33
   in power, timescale (1974 to now) 33
   see also specific parties
politics and policy 31–33
Port Authority of New York and New Jersey (PANYNJ) 148
'predict and provide' forecasts 89, 90, 97, 99, 123, 126, 163
Prescott, John 83, 88, 99
Prestwick Airport 52, 154, 154–155
   history 7, 9
Price, Laurie 55, 57
privatisation and denationalisation 9, 34
   BA 60, 65
   BAA 65, 66, 67, 68, 69, 70, 76, 94, 131
Progress Report (2006) 87, 93, 94, 95, 97, 98, 127, 133
Project for the Sustainable Development of Heathrow (PSDH) 94, 134
promises and commitments made (relating to airport expansion) and keeping or breaking them 135–137
   Conservative manifesto (2010) 106
Prospect Park 81
public inquiries *see* inquiries

Qatar Airways 153
Quality of Life Policy Group, Transport Working Group of 33–34, 99
Quendon Hall 61

RAF Northolt 8, 17, 19, 90, 97
railways and trains 69
   Crossrail 82–83, 109
   Gatwick Express 69, 109
   Heathrow Express 9–11, 69, 79, 82, 83, 109
   High Speed 1 (HS1) 30
   High Speed 2 (HS2) 30, 108, 109, 157, 163
   Stansted rail link/Express 62, 69, 109
rational decision-making 34–35, 36
Read, Lionel 63
recessions *see* economic recessions
Regional Air Services (2002) 88, 89, 92, 154
Regional Air Services Coordination Study (RASCO) 89
regional airports 127–128, 153–158
   BA's attitude to 158
regional planning 26–27, 28, 46, 78, 80
   outside South East 153–158
   South East 27, 28, 56, 59, 77
regulation 9–12
Rhein-Mann Air Base 143, 144
Ridley, Nicolas (MP) 64, 65, 66, 67, 136
Roskill Commission 19, 20–22, 30, 31, 36, 39, 41, 45, 49, 50, 53, 57, 59, 60, 70, 124, 128
   forecasts 125
Ross, Brian 89, 96, 111
Royal Society for the Protection of Birds (RSPB) 89, 118–119
runway(s)
   hourly rates/capacity 124
   length increases 6
   new 163–166
     opposition 118–119, 168
     support 118–119
   option of not building any more 161–162
   slots 116
   supply and demand 162, 163
   see also Birmingham; Edinburgh; Gatwick; Heathrow; Luton; Manchester; Stansted
Runway Capacity to serve the South East (RUCATSE) study 31, 75, 77–79, 83, 84, 138, 167
   forecasts 78, 126
Ryanair 9, 75, 87

safeguarding land 167–168
Sanders, Peter 57, 60, 61, 64, 89, 96, 111

Schiphol 142
Schönefeld 144, 145
scientific analysis 129
Second World War (WWII) 3, 4, 17–18, 19
Secretary of State, role 31
select committees 33, 89
Short Take-Off and Landing (STOL) at the London City 68
short-haul operations, future perspectives 161, 162
short-term policies of 2010 onwards 106–107, 131
Singapore 151
Skytrain 8, 50
Smith, Stan 57
smoke 43–44
social factors and demand 5–6
South East Airports Taskforce (SEATF) 106, 108, 131, 134
South East and Eastern Regional Air Services (SERAS) 88, 89, 90, 93, 99
South East Asia 149–151
South East regional planning 27, 28, 56, 59, 77
Southend Airport 163
  history 97
  ownership 10, 11, 156
Southwest Airlines 8, 147
Stainton, Ross 57
stakeholders, consulting and involving 131–135
Standing Conference on London and South East Regional Planning (SCLSERP) 56, 57, 58
Stansted 19–20, 54–56, 60–68, 165–166
  1974–1991 54–56, 56, 57, 60–68, 70
  1991–1997 75, 76, 77, 78, 82
  1997–2010 87, 88, 89, 90–91, 94, 95, 96, 98, 99, 100
  2010 onwards 105, 106, 109, 110, 111
  in Airports Commission 110, 111
  financial viability 67
  five runways 111
  G1 (Generation 1) Project 51, 95, 96, 98, 133
  G2 (Generation 2) Project 95, 96, 165–166
  new terminal 54–56, 60, 62, 63, 65, 68, 136
  noise contours 42
  ownership 10
  proposal and their abandonment (1968) 19
  rail link/Express 62, 69, 109
  second runway 60, 63, 64–65, 70, 77, 78, 89, 90, 92, 95, 99, 111, 134, 165–166
    consequences of no runway 163
    Gatwick second runway and 165–166
    promises regarding 136–137
  Stop Stansted Expansion (SSE) 89, 96, 98, 111, 118

third and fourth (two or three additional) 89, 91, 166
Starkie, David 66–67, 94, 117
state-owned airports in USA 145–148
Stern report 87, 98
Stewart, John 93, 95, 108, 111, 119
Stockholm 145
STOL (Short Take-Off and Landing) at the London City 68
Stop Stansted Expansion (SSE) 89, 96, 98, 111, 118
Study Group on South East Airports (SGSEA) 8, 36, 56, 57, 58, 59, 60, 61, 66, 70, 128, 130, 132, 133, 135, 136
successes, repeating 166–167
Sunderland, Russell 6, 77, 78, 167
surface access 46, 62, 109, 110
  Heathrow 69, 79, 82
Sustainable Aviation 93, 118
Sweden 145
Sydney 153

technology 6–7
Teeside Airport 156
Tegel 144, 145
Templehof 144
Terlecky, Iryna 64, 65, 66
Texcoco and San Salvador Atenco 149
Thames Estuary 27, 45, 78, 89, 92, 93, 107, 110, 112, 118–119, 134, 166
  hub airport 111, 166
Thatcher, Margaret 51, 58, 60, 64, 65, 75, 83
Tokyo 150
Toms, Mike 66
Town and Country Planning Act (1947) 25, 29, 54
Town and Country Planning Association 61, 62–63, 64, 65, 127, 157
trains *see* railways
transatlantic crossings, historical perspectives 7, 9, 52, 154
transfer passengers (connecting flights) 8, 162
  Gatwick–Heathrow (Airlink) 55, 55–56
transport (in general)
  long-term strategy *see* long-term strategy
  planning 27
Transport and Works Act (1992) 29, 82
Transport Committee (House of Commons) 33, 67, 79, 90, 95, 116, 118
Transport Working Group of the Quality of Life Policy Group 33–34, 99
Treasury 21, 27, 53, 56, 58, 107, 108, 115
TriStar 40, 49, 50, 53, 76

UK planning outside London and South East
  see regional planning
Underground (London) Piccadilly line 50, 69, 82, 83, 109, 125
USA 145–148
Uttlesford District Council 60, 64

Vandermeer, Roy (QC) 80, 167
Vienna 145
Vienna Airport, emissions 145
Villiers, Theresa 106, 108
visual impact 46, 62, 82

Washington 147–148
water and drainage 46
West Midlands/Coventry 127, 157
West Sussex County Council (WSCC) 55, 70, 92, 95, 136, 167
Western Sydney Airport 153
Westminster City Council 82
Westminster Hall debates 33, 93, 118

White Papers
  1953 19
  1967 19
  1978 52, 53–54, 56, 57, 79, 80, 128, 130, 131, 132, 136, 154
  1985 64–67, 68, 69, 70, 80, 136
  1998 83, 87, 87–88
  2003 43, 44, 87, 90–93, 93, 95, 96–97, 98, 99, 107, 108, 126, 127, 132, 133, 134, 136, 137, 138, 154, 155, 157, 167
Willingale 56, 57
Wilson, Harold 51, 96
Wilson Committee (1963) 41
Wing Resistance Association 59
Wolverhampton 157
World War I (First World War) 3
World War II (Second World War) 3, 4, 17–18, 19

Yardley Chase 56, 57, 61
Yorkshire 156